FAMOUS AMERICAN MEN OF SCIENCE

J. Willard Gibbs

Famous American
MEN *of* SCIENCE

BY J. G. CROWTHER

Essay Index Reprint Series

ESSAY INDEX

BOOKS FOR LIBRARIES PRESS
FREEPORT, NEW YORK

STANDARD BOOK NUMBER

8369-0040-5

LIBRARY OF CONGRESS CATALOG CARD NUMBER:

69-18925

Contents

List of Illustrations

Foreword

THE PRESENT AGE IS OFTEN DESCRIBED AS
scientific. Science and technology have a very important part
in modern life. Many persons believe that the economic and
social disasters of today are due to the development of science.
Owing to the application of science, almost any sort of goods
can be made in almost any country in almost any amount. The
old balance of industry within countries, and between countries, has been upset. If the world economic depression is due
even in part to the growth of science and technology, then
science and technology are clearly of enormous social, besides
productive, importance in modern life. The investigation of
the role of science in modern life becomes a social duty.

This book on American Men of Science is a contribution
towards this investigation. It contains an account of the
scientific work and lives of Benjamin Franklin, Joseph Henry,
Josiah Willard Gibbs and Thomas Alva Edison. The relations
between the problems they chose to work upon, and the
social needs of their times, are pointed out. Explanations are
offered of the reasons why Franklin created the modern
theory of frictional electricity, and Henry invented the large
electro-magnet and developed the Smithsonian Institution,
why Gibbs studied the theory of heat and created the theoretical basis of physical chemistry, and why Edison invented the
quadruplex telegraph, modern electrical engineering, and the
gramophone.

All of these things were done in America. Have they any
relation to the characteristics of American life?

The progress of science is not accidental. It is due to the needs of the society in which it occurs, and its direction is affected by the conditions of that society.

It is shown that Franklin's electrical researches were conditioned by two climatic factors. He moved from Boston to Philadelphia. As Bogart has remarked, the cold climate of Boston encouraged the wearing of woolen clothes, whereas linen was more commonly worn in Philadelphia. As a consequence, Philadelphia became a depot for linen rags, and hence the center for the raw material of the paper trade. Franklin made a fortune out of paper and printing, and thereby secured the means to buy scientific apparatus, and the leisure to use it. The dry winter climate of the American Atlantic coast made the insulation of electricity easier. Frictional electric machines worked more satisfactorily, and gave more clear-cut results. The definiteness of the results helped Franklin to obtain a clearer conception of the behavior of electricity.

Franklin's greatest gift was the modernity of his mind. He had the most advanced mind of the eighteenth century. He inspired Joseph Priestley to start research, and, as is not generally known, was a necessary part of the chain of causes which enabled James Watt's steam engine to be introduced in industry. He also had an important influence in the creation of chemical industry. He had a marvelous power of perceiving the significance of men. He manipulated and experimented with men as others with things.

The next outstanding figure in American science was Joseph Henry. He was the inventor of the first practicable electro-magnet and electric telegraph. He probably discovered electro-magnet induction before Faraday, though he was five years younger, and had far less opportunity for research. He unconsciously made experiments with radio-waves in 1842. The latter half of his life was spent on the creation of the Smithsonian Institution. In religion and science Henry had very orthodox views. He believed that scientific discovery was a pure activity without any necessary connection with industry and social affairs. And yet, during the second half of his life, his researches were concerned exclusively with problems of economic interest to agriculture and navigation, such as meteorology and fog-signal acoustics.

The Smithsonian Institution was conceived by James Smithson through a desire for social revenge. He was the illegitimate son of the first Duke of Northumberland, and his mother was of royal descent. He resented being disowned by his father, and left his money to the United States in order to found an institution which would be famous when the names of English noblemen have been forgotten. The spectacle of the gentle and pious Joseph Henry conscientiously realizing Smithson's wishes by the creation of the famous Institution is one of the most remarkable in the history of science. It raises many questions concerning the relations between Puritan philosophy and the rise of science, and the influence of class feelings on the motives of individuals.

The Smithsonian Institution is a monument to the Oedipus complex.

The figure of Josiah Williard Gibbs is equally extraordinary. He died within a few hundred yards of where he was born. He became professor of mathematical physics in Yale College, where his father had previously been a professor of Hebrew and sacred literature. In a short period of five years he published a masterpiece of research which has proved to be the foundation of several new branches of science. One of the results of this work showed how mixtures of chemicals could be handled successfully on an industrial scale. In the Great War, England was in danger of destruction through lack of explosives, until one of her chemists showed how to manufacture the needed quantities of ammonium nitrate by the application of Gibbs' phase rule.

During his lifetime, Gibbs' genius was little recognized in America, and not sufficiently recognized in Europe. The explanations of this phenomenon, in terms of the social and intellectual atmosphere of the United States, are considered.

The final subject is Thomas Alva Edison. The question

whether the title "scientist" should be applied to him is discussed. It is concluded that the separation of pure science, applied science, and invention, prevents a true understanding of the history of science. Faraday, Henry, and Maxwell would have had little influence on the world without Bell, Edison, and Marconi. The study of Edison makes the influence of Faraday's discoveries much clearer. The relation of Edison's personality and psychology to the social types and classes which achieve dominance after the Civil War is analyzed. The connection between his inventions and the social and industrial development of the country is explained, and it is seen that his life's work provides some of the most illuminating evidence known in history of the role of science in human society. His contribution towards the reduction of invention to a rational and business-like activity is considered to be his greatest contribution to civilization. He attempted to remove the ancient elements of magic and mystery from invention, and to incorporate it as part of a rational social system.

In the course of the discussions, general aspects of the relation of science to social organization are considered; in particular, the influence of scientific ideas in framing the American Constitution. As Woodrow Wilson pointed out, the men who made the Constitution adopted the notion of balances of power between the President, Congress and the Supreme Court, from Newtonian mechanics. Thus Newtonian mechanics have helped to produce the present deadlocks in American Constitutional affairs. As is well known, Benjamin Franklin was opposed to the Constitution. He agreed to it only because the Convention would not accept a better. It is argued that he opposed the Constitution because he had the spirit of a modern experimental physicist, and, unlike his lawyer colleagues, was not overawed by the prestige of Newtonian ideas.

In concluding this foreword, I have pleasure in recording a number of indebtednesses and kindnesses.

B. Hessen's essay on *The Social & Economic Roots of the*

Ideas of Isaac Newton first showed me how science might be interpreted as a product of human history, in contradistinction to the traditional view that science exists as a thing in itself, with no necessary connection with other things.

Mr. James B. Conant, the President of Harvard University, invited me to lecture at Harvard on the History of American Science. I am deeply grateful for this honor. My lectures were based on the substance of this book.

The authors mentioned in the bibliographies given at the ends of the chapters have provided essential information. I am particularly indebted to the work of Messrs. Dyer, Martin and Meadowcroft on Edison.

Lord Rutherford has kindly presented a photograph, made specially for this book, of one of the models of the Gibbs Thermodynamics Surface, which are in the Cavendish Laboratory, and were made by Clerk Maxwell with his own hands.

Dr. J. A. V. Butler, of Edinburgh University, has read the chapter on Willard Gibbs, and has helped to remove some of the obscurities from it.

The Yale University Press kindly presented me with proofs of the *Commentary on the Scientific Writings of J. Willard Gibbs*, so that it was not necessary to wait for publication before having the advantage of examining this work.

Mr. H. M. Cashmore, the City Librarian of Birmingham, England, gave valuable information on Dr. William Small.

Acknowledgments are due to the following authorities for permission to reproduce illustrations: The New York Public Library for the Duplessis portrait of Franklin; Messrs. Holton & Truscott Smith and Messrs. R. Dunthorne & Sons for Daumier's cartoon; The United States Government for the Wilson portrait of Franklin; the Editor of *The Scientific Monthly* for the portrait of Henry as a young man, for the three portraits of Gibbs, and his home; to the Smithsonian Institution for the two portraits of Smithson, and the later portrait of Henry; and to Harper & Bros. for the cut of Edison's handwriting, the portraits of Edison as a boy, and in middle age, and his birthplace from *Edison: His Life and Inventions*, by Dyer, Martin and Meadowcroft.

I am glad also to thank my publisher and his staff for the extra labor they have given in the passage of the book through the press.

J. G. CROWTHER

March, 1937

General Bibliography

The Rise of American Civilization. Charles A. Beard and Mary R. Beard. 2 volumes. 1927.

The Education of Henry Adams. Henry Brooks Adams. 1918.

Economic History of the American People. Ernest Ludlow Bogart. 1930.

The Federalist. Hamilton, Madison and Jay. EVERYMAN EDITION. 1934.

The Theory of the Leisure Class. Thorstein Veblen. 1899.

Constitutional Government in the United States. T. Woodrow Wilson. 1908.

Civilization and the Growth of Law. W. A. Robson. 1935.

The Declaration of Independence. Carl Becker. 1933.

Freedom versus Organization: 1814–1914. B. Russell. 1934.

Works of Alexander Hamilton. Edited by H. C. Lodge. 1885.

The Spirit of Laws. Montesquieu, with D'Alembert's analysis.

John Adams: Works. Edited by C. F. Adams. 10 volumes. 1850–1856. *Including a Life* (Volume 1) by C. F. Adams, and the *Defence of the Constitutions of the United States of America* (Volume IV).

An Economic Interpretation of the Constitution of the United States. Charles A. Beard. 1925.

The Writings of Thomas Jefferson. Collected and edited by Paul Leicester Ford. 10 volumes. 1899.

Lincoln. W. E. Barton. 2 volumes. 1925.

Lincoln: The Prairie Years. Carl Sandburg. 2 volumes. 1926.

My Diary North and South. W. H. Russell. 2 volumes. 1863.

The History of the American People. Charles A. Beard and William C. Bagley. 1923.

The American Presidents. Herbert Agar. 1933.

The Life Story of J. Pierpont Morgan. Carl Hovey. 1912.

Prosperity: Myth and Reality in American Economic Life. M. J. Bonn. 1931.

Benjamin Franklin
1706-1790

I
THE SCOPE OF HIS IDEAS

II
LIFE AND RESEARCHES
(1) EARLY LIFE
(2) ELECTRICAL RESEARCHES
(3) LATER LIFE

III
SCIENCE AND THE AMERICAN CONSTITUTION

BIBLIOGRAPHY

I

The Scope of His Ideas

I

THE LIVES OF FEW VERY GREAT MEN ARE AS accessible as Franklin's, and have been as thoroughly studied. The completest familiarity with the features and details of his life has not dulled their wonders.

The early date of his birth is continually arresting. He was born only ninety years after Shakespeare died. The comprehensive fertility of his imagination shows his kinship with the great spirits of the Renaissance. He had their love of personal freedom, and was not a puritan, as he was complacent of the illegitimacy of his son, grandson, and great-grandson. The edge of his defense of Polly Baker proves his freedom from sexual complexes and the repressive conventions of the classes which afterwards dominated the nineteenth century. The young friend of Mandeville was never transformed into a courtier of Mrs. Grundy.

Franklin's unsurpassed discretion in diplomacy proves his unconventional behavior was not due to lack of self-control. His *Autobiography* is a description of one of the most extraordinary examples of the conscious organization of a life. To what sort of material was this organization applied? Exceptional physical and mental vitality, and strong passions. He was a powerful swimmer, and thought of becoming a teacher of swimming in London. He lived eighty-four years, during which his activity was almost unparalleled. He published writings during sixty-eight years. It is difficult to recall any other man who wrote sensibly for such a period. Few men of high talent write sensibly for more than thirty years. His vitality enabled him to live actively for double the normal period. He seemed to have had two lives. His first life, when he was influencing the affairs of Boston through journalism at the age of sixteen, was not quite beyond the echoes of Shakespeare's time; and the voice of his second life, when he was participating in the formation of the American Constitution at the age of eighty-one, carried clearly into contemporary times. He was sufficiently far from the Elizabethans to avoid their indiscipline, and he matured before the puritan capitalists had established the dominance of their conventions. He shed the mark of any particular period, and became, like Shakespeare, partly a member of all generations. This is one explanation of his modernity.

Faÿ has given an illuminating description of the social life in Boston during Franklin's youth. There was a dominating group of rich merchants and a turbulent class including colonial seamen and adventurers. Franklin's brother conducted a radical newspaper which reflected the free spirit of the latter class. Franklin received the first opportunity for expressing his personality through this newspaper. He swiftly discovered that radicalism had no future in Boston, so he escaped to Philadelphia, which was less under the shadow of the nineteenth century. These circumstances saved him from being blighted with the cultural narrowness of the industrialism which grew rapidly after the middle period of his life. Franklin's cultural superiority over his successors is demonstrated by the superiority of his style. He could modulate his instrument to the expression of almost all human interests. He was not driven by spiritual anxiety to use a machine-gun style.

The poise of his style and diplomacy was acquired through exercise of his passions and faculties. His temperament was of the sanguine type, which, according to Pavlov, is the best. He cultivated this fortunate temperament, which was in contrast to that of the diplomatically inept Adams, whose mind was tied up with New England complexes. The famous phrase "Ça ira" is an expression of the sanguine temperament.

His praise of economy and practice of self-discipline are additional evidence of his vitality. They were reactions from the natural extravagance, loose-living, and disorderliness, which he criticizes in himself. The outspoken letters he wrote to women in his youth, and his cultivated and amiable relations with women in later life, proves that his sexual passions had been properly moulded. He proposed to Mme. Helvetius when he was about seventy-five years old, and rationalized his sexual interests by trying to arrange the marriage of his son to Polly Stevenson, his grandson to Mlle. Brillon, and his nephew to Mlle. Schweighauser. All of these attempts were unsuccessful, so he probably had more interest than his young relatives in them. A modern psychologist could not have given him better psychological health than he achieved.

He created his literary style mainly out of Addison's, though he was influenced by Bunyan and Defoe. Addison was one of the chief inventors of the mode of literary expression used by the educated part of the English merchant class, who had recently gained control of England. It was the style of a new governing and leisure class whose power was founded on trade.

Franklin adapted the style of the intellectuals of the new English leisure class of 1710–1720 to the purpose of another social class or classes, the small men of property and craftsmen, the American democratic radicals, whom he had joined in Boston, and whom he never completely deserted, for he protested in their interests against the adoption of the American Constitution. He succeeded because he was an American, as these classes were far more powerful at that time in America than in England. His literary virility and greatness was partly due to his creation of a cultural hybrid between the intellectual modes of expression of two social classes. The superior technique of the English leisure-class style was put to the service of the rising American small men of property. English writers pursuing the same object, such as Defoe, had less immediate success, because the prestige of the merchant-capitalist class was at that time greater in England than in America.

Franklin wrote that Pennsylvania adopted his proposal to

issue paper money because he was a better and more convincing writer than any that could be hired by the rich to oppose it.

He lost reputation during the nineteenth century partly because the capitalist and financial classes, which he had opposed, attained almost complete control of American life. His reputation is rising again in the twentieth century, as the opposition to those classes strengthens.

He was mainly a representative of the small man of property. This is the basis of the view of writers such as Faÿ, who describe him as the first bourgeois to attain full human dignity. He was the first bourgeois to stand before kings, without discarding the social and philosophical attitudes of his class, and acquiring those of aristocracy.

This was a great contribution to social emancipation. But Franklin was not only a bourgeois, a small man of property. He was also a representative of craftsmen, and an experimental scientist. In his epitaph he describes himself as a printer, not as a man of property. As the representative of craftsmen and scientists he spoke for the rising classes of the future, the modern men.

The essence of the bourgeois, or small man of property, and the worker or craftsman, has been depicted in Daumier's famous cartoon. Franklin could have spoken for both of those figures, though probably more for the bourgeois. In his later years he was no longer a small man of property, but his strong intelligence prevented him from automatically acquiring the philosophies of the rich. His speeches in the Constitutional Convention did not represent the views of any single class, and least those of the rich. Franklin is bourgeois according to the intellectual characteristics of that class, as described in the brilliant writings of Thorstein Veblen. The habits of thought of the leisure or governing class "run on the personal relation of dominance, and on the derivative, invidious concepts of honour, worth, merit, character, and the like. The causal sequence which makes up the subject matter of science is not visible from this point of view. Neither does good repute attach to knowledge of facts that are vulgarly useful." Members of the leisure class with sufficient mental ability to investigate the external world are commonly "diverted to fields of speculation or investigation which are reputable and futile." "Such indeed has been the history of priestly and leisure class learning." "But since the relation of mastery and subservience is ceasing to be the dominant and formative factor in the community's life process, other features of the life process and other points of view are forcing themselves upon the scholars."

Franklin's intellectual attitude is the perfect illustration of what is to be expected in a leisure-class scientist "of lower-class or middle-class antecedents—that is to say, those who have inherited the complement of aptitudes proper to the industrious classes, and who owe their place in the leisure class to the possession of qualities which count for more today than they did in times when the leisure class scheme of life took shape."

Veblen explains that the growth of science is intimately related to the concentration of the human intelligence on industrial processes. The attention to the properties of materials and the effects of treatment, develops the notion of cause and effect. The spread of this notion undermines the concepts of animism, divine right, and innate superiority in the upper classes. The various branches of science have "made headway . . . in proportion as each of them has successively escaped from the dominance of the conceptions of personal relation or status, and of the derivative canons of anthropomorphic fitness and honorific worth." Scholasticism and classicism were by-products "of the priestly office and the life of leisure, so modern science may be said to be a by-product of the industrial process."

While Franklin was intruding into science, on behalf of the lower middle class, concepts which appeared vulgar to the intellectuals of a former leisure class, John Adams was intruding equally vulgar upper middle-class ideas into law. He remarks that the ancient nations uniformly believed "the Divinity alone was adequate to the important office of giving laws to men . . . and modern nations, in the consecration of kings, and in several superstitious chimeras of divine right in princes and nobles, are nearly unanimous in preserving remnants of it. Even the venerable magistrates of Amersfort devoutly believed themselves God's viceregents . . . is it that obedience to the laws can be obtained from mankind in no other manner . . . are . . . no considerations of public or private utility . . . sufficient to engage their submission to rules for their own happiness?"

Adams wished to substitute the philosophic rationalism, that had been developed by commerce and industry, for the notions of divinity or dominance, as the authority which should convince or persuade men to accept the laws.

2

The character of Franklin's career was influenced by the American climate in at least two ways. Franklin acquired wealth from the printing and paper trade that developed in Philadelphia. He was carried into a position from which he could achieve fame by the growth of these trades, which was due in a considerable degree to local climatic and social conditions. E. L. Bogart has explained that the populations in Philadelphia and Boston wore linen and wool respectively, because the climate of the one was warm, and of the other relatively cold.

Owing to these habits, linen rags were more plentiful in Philadelphia than in Boston. As at the time paper was made out of linen rags, Philadelphia had an advantage as a center for paper-manufacturing, and the industry naturally grew there.

Philadelphia had attracted many Dutch and German settlers. In the eighteenth century the Dutch had exceptional skill in paper-making. One of their countrymen, Rittenhouse, introduced the manufacture in 1690. Thus the Philadelphia paper trade started with the combined advantages of climate and skill. Franklin and his friends were helped in their scientific experiments by the high standard of manual and technological skill largely due to the Dutch and German settlers.

He writes that Philadelphia mechanics could make very good instruments. He had no difficulty in having apparatus made to his designs. One of Franklin's best friends was a Rittenhouse, who was a capable observational astronomer. Franklin gained part of his fortune from investments in eighteen paper mills consuming linen rags. He refers to the energetic assistance he received from his wife in the collection of linen rags.

Today most paper is made out of wood-pulp and esparto grass. The linen trade in England has declined so much by 1937 that it is no longer possible to collect enough fine linen rags in England for the manufacture of the paper for the Bank of England's famous five and ten pound notes, known as "fivers" and "tenners." The paper for these is made from fine linen rags imported from France, as the linen of English rags is now too coarse for the purpose.

This phenomenon reflects considerable changes in English social life. It shows that fine linen is rarely worn; that the taste of the English middle classes in underclothes is declining (parallel to the decline of its taste in literature, the theater and other branches of culture), and that linen is being replaced by artificial silk. It is also a reflection of the greater warmth of the French climate, which preserves the wearing of linen in France.

If paper had been made from wood and clothes from artificial silk in the eighteenth century, Philadelphia would not have become the center of the paper and printing trades, journalism and libraries, and Franklin would not have been carried to power by their growth. He might not have succeeded in making a fortune and retiring at the age of forty in any other trade, or in any other town, and without leisure he would not have become a world-famous scientist. Without his scientific fame he would not have become America's diplomatic genius at Paris. If there had been no linen rags in Philadelphia, there might have been no famous Franklin, and American independence might have been delayed fifty years.

Franklin was helped to economic independence by the Philadelphia climate. He received equally important help from the climate in his electrical researches. When the wind at Philadelphia blows from the northwest, it comes from the interior of the North American continent, and is often extremely dry. Franklin frequently commented on the dryness of the northwest winds. The dryness, which was increased in winter by severe frost, very much facilitated experiments on electrostatics, owing to the dependence of the electrical insulating properties of materials on freedom from moisture.

It is very much easier to draw sparks by combing the hair in a dry North American winter than in a moist English winter, as many persons know from experience. It is even possible to light the gas by drawing sparks from the fingers. Electrostatic experiments made with materials such as glass and fibers, which attract moisture, are much more difficult in damp climates such as those of England and Western Europe, than in North America. English schoolboys are only too familiar with the physics textbooks' account of experiments in electrostatics, with rods of glass and pieces of wool and silk, which do not work satisfactorily. Owing to the moist climate, elementary experiments in electrostatics are as difficult and confusing to the English student as introductory lectures on the theory of limits in the differential calculus.

Until recently, English students were introduced to the study of electricity by experiments in electrostatics. Generations of them have suffered discouragment by this practice, as electrostatical experiments are not easy or convincing when attempted by inexperienced experimenters in a moist climate. The growth of the general knowledge of electrical science in England has been retarded by this mistake in the method of teaching.

Franklin and his friends could make good apparatus in Philadelphia, owing to the excellence of the craftsmen, and the good insulation provided by the dry climate helped them to get strong sparks and striking effects. The striking, easily repeated experiments assisted them to think out clear-cut theories. Nature put her electrostatical problems more clearly to Franklin than to Western Europeans. This helps to explain why Franklin advanced the theoretical analysis of electro-statical phenomena beyond the stage reached in Europe. The American climate may have had some effect on Franklin in another way. Concerning Hamilton's style, H. C. Lodge has written: "There is nothing vague or misty about Hamilton. Everything is as clear and well-defined as the American landscape on a bright, frosty autumn day." Franklin may also have been inspired by the clarity of the American landscape on such days (which happen to be particularly good for experiments in electrostatics).

If the qualities of the climate are able directly to mould those of the mind, evidence of this might be expected in Franklin, who was interested in the weather, and naturally observant. He deduced the track of the cyclonic storms from the observation that an eclipse of the moon was visible at Boston, though obscured by a storm at Philadelphia. This proved the storm visited Philadelphia first, though the wind blew from the northeast. He estimated that the whole storm moved at about one hundred miles per hour. He gave a remarkable theory of how they probably arose in the Gulf of Mexico, and considered them similar in nature, though vastly greater in scale, to water-spouts and whirlwinds.

Franklin's experiments on the absorption of solar radiation by colored bodies are a beautiful example of his scientific ability and utilization of qualities of the American climate. They depend on an adroit exploitation of the snow and hot sunshine available in a North American winter, but not in an English winter. In one of his pedagogic letters to Miss Mary Stevenson, written in 1761, he explains to her that rivers may not run into the sea, as their water may evaporate before it reaches the river mouth. When a river disappears before reaching the sea "the Ignorant might suppose, as they actually do in such cases, that the River loses itself by running under ground, whereas in truth it has run up into the Air." He discusses the evaporation of water by the sun's rays, and describes experiments on the absorption of heat by bodies of different colors. "But first let me mention an Experiment you may easily make yourself. Walk but a quarter of an Hour in your Garden when the Sun shines, with a part of your Dress white, and a Part black; then apply your hand to them alternately, and you will find a very great difference in their Warmth. The Black will be quite hot to the Touch, the White still cool. Another. Try to fire Paper with a burning Glass. If it is white, you will not easily burn it. But if you bring the Focus to a black Spot, or upon Letters, written or printed, the Paper will immediately be on fire under the Letters.

"Thus Fullers and Dyers find black Cloths, of equal Thickness with white ones, and hung out equally wet, dry in the Sun much sooner than the white, being more readily heated by the Sun's Rays. It is the same before a Fire; the Heat of which sooner penetrates black stockings than white ones, and so is apt sooner to burn a Man's Shins. Also Beer much sooner warms in a black Mug set before the Fire, than in a white one, or in a bright Silver Tankard.

"My Experiment was this. I took a number of little square Pieces of Broad Cloth from a Taylor's Pattern-Card, of various Colours. There were Black, deep Blue, lighter Blue, Green, Purple, Red, Yellow, White, and other Colours, or Shades of Colours. I laid them all out upon the Snow in a bright Sunshiny Morning. In a few Hours (I cannot now be exact as to the Time), the Black, being warm'd most by the Sun, was sunk so low as to be below the Stroke of the Sun's Rays; the dark Blue almost as low, the lighter Blue not quite so much as the dark, the other Colours less as they were lighter; and the quite White remain'd on the Surface of the Snow, not having entered it at all.

"What signifies Philosophy that does not apply to some Use? May we not learn from hence, that black Clothes are not so fit to wear in a hot Sunny Climate or Season, as white ones; because in such Cloaths the body is more heated by the Sun when we walk abroad, and are at the same time heated by the Exercise, which double Heat is apt to bring on putrid dangerous Fevers? That Soldiers and Seamen, who must march and labour in the Sun, should in the East or West Indies have an

Uniform of white? That Summer Hats, for Men or Women, should be white, as repelling that Heat which gives Headaches to many, and to some the fatal Stroke that the French call the *Coup de Soleil?* That the Ladies' Summer Hats, however, should be lined with Black, as not reverberating on their Faces those Rays which are reflected upwards from the Earth or Water? That the putting a white Cap of Paper or Linnen *within* the Crown of a black Hat, as some do, will not keep out the Heat, tho' it would if placed *without?* That Fruit-Walls being black'd may receive so much Heat from the Sun in the Daytime, as to continue warm in some degree thro' the Night, and thereby preserve the Fruit from Frosts, or forward its Growth?—with sundry other particulars of less or greater Importance that will occur from time to time to attentive Minds?"

Franklin's contribution to the study of the absorbent properties of common materials has even today not been completed. The Army authorities in England have been inspecting with much enthusiasm recent experiments on the absorbent properties of clothing and building materials, suitable for uniforms and barracks in tropical countries.

Extensive experiments have been made in America to determine the best colours and compositions for the paints used to cover the tanks for storing petroleum. The evaporation of the oil in tanks is wasteful and dangerous, so it is desirable that as little as possible of the heat in the sun's rays should pass through the walls of the tanks into the oil. Experiments have proved that paints such as aluminum paint are the most effective, and minimize evaporation.

3

The clarity of Franklin's thought owed probably more to social than to climatic influences.

The American provinces were still young pioneer communities in Franklin's time. A powerful class of academic scientists had not yet grown. As late as 1801 Priestley, who was then in America, wrote to Humphry Davy that he was "perfectly insulated" from scientific news and developments, owing to the small and scattered number of scientists in the country. Such conditions have bad and good effects. They prevent many men of ability from discovering their bent through education. But if a man has a mind powerful enough not to have to lean much on academic science, such conditions may protect him from acquiring false traditional ideas. Franklin's mind was of this powerful order, and he benefited by his freedom from preconceived notions acquired in European academies. The isolation which would have killed the scientific work of a lesser man protected him from misleading intellectual fashions. The European academic tradition was non-scientific. The study of science at Oxford and Cambridge was not in a healthy condition. The experimental science of the succeeding centuries was being founded outside universities by self-taught investigators such as Guericke and Priestley, and later, Davy and Faraday.

As J. D. Bernal has remarked, Priestley's researches were largely inspired by Franklin. Indeed, Priestley says so. Priestley had a very powerful mind but it was not so bold or keen as Franklin's. Davy wrote of Franklin with profound respect, and deeply appreciated his combination of expository and investigatory power.

4

The masterfulness of Franklin's mind has not been sufficiently recognized. He controlled the intellectual destinies of many remarkable men. Besides deciding the direction of Priestley's career, he influenced that of William Small.

This Scottish mathematical and medical doctor was born in 1734. He emigrated to America and became professor of natural philosophy in Williamsburg. Thomas Jefferson attended his lectures. Jefferson writes in his autobiography that Small "probably fixed the destinies of my life." Jefferson's confidence in the value of rational enquiry, and his distrust of legalistic political forms, may have been strengthened by Small's instruction in science. American political ideas show many peculiar marks of scientific influences. Small and Jefferson were two of the most important agents through which science has left these marks on American political thought. Small's influence on history did not end by fixing the destinies of Jefferson's life. He appeared in another event of immense historical importance. With Matthew Boulton of Birmingham, England, he assisted James Watt to draw up the patent specification of his steam engine with a separate condenser. This was the most important patent in history, and the largest single contribution to the development of modern industrialism.

According to an article by J. Hill, published in the *Birmingham Weekly Post* in 1899, Small's settlement at Birmingham was due to Franklin. Hill writes that Franklin probably became acquainted with Small at Williamsburg.

Franklin made his third visit to England in 1764, and Small returned from America about the same time. Franklin had become acquainted in 1758 with Boulton, the great Birmingham magnate by whom the modern principles of standardization, mass-production and factory organization, were chiefly founded. In May 1765 Franklin gave Small a very earnest written introduction to Boulton. This letter enabled Small to secure Boulton's friendship, and a practice as a medical doctor in Birmingham. Small was a close friend of another Scot, James Watt.

Boulton's engineering factory at Soho, Birmingham, employed six hundred skilled workmen, at that time a huge number. The machinery was driven by a water-wheel. In dry summers there was not enough water to drive the water-wheel. Boulton conceived the notion of installing a steam pumping-engine that would pump the water, after it had run through the water-wheel, back to the supply channel, so that the same water could be used over and over again for providing the factory with power. This arrangement would have made the power supply independent of the weather. L. T. Hogben has informed the writer that other manufacturers in the adjacent pottery district had the same idea, and Boulton may have got it from them.

Such was the scheme which gave Boulton an interest in steam engines. Small saw that his Glasgow friend Watt, with his improved steam engine, might be able to meet Boulton's demand for more satisfactory sources of power for driving his factory. Small strongly urged Watt to come to Birmingham and settle in the town. Watt first visited the Soho factory in 1767, and in Boulton's absence, was shown over it by Small.

For six years Small worked incessantly to promote a partnership between Boulton and Watt. He succeeded in 1774, and Watt settled in Birmingham.

In the next year, 1775, when Small was also about to join the partnership, he died. This is probably the reason why he is not more famous. No publication by him appears in the catalogue of the library of the British Museum.

Boulton and Erasmus Darwin, the grandfather of Charles Darwin, were present at his death. Darwin wrote to a friend on February 25th, 1775: "I am at this moment return'd from a most melancholy scene, the death of a Friend who was most dear to me Dr. Small of Birmingham, whose strength of reasoning, Quickness of Invention, Learning in the discoveries of other men and integrity of Heart (which is worth them all) had no equal. Mr. Boulton suffers an inconceivable Loss from the Doctor's mechanical as well as medical abilities."

Boulton erected a monument to Small in the grounds of his factory. It was inscribed with the following epitaph, composed by Darwin at Boulton's request:

Ye gay and young, who thoughtless of your doom
   Shun the disgustful mansions of the dead,
Where melancholy broods o'er many a tomb,
   Mouldering beneath the yew's unwholesome shade.

If chance ye enter these sequester'd groves,
   And day's bright sunshine for a while forego,
Oh, leave to Folly's cheek the laughs and loves,
   And give one hour to philosophic woe!

Here, while no titled dust, no sainted bone,
   No lover weeping over beauty's bier,

Benjamin Franklin

(*Portrait by Duplessis*)

"*Franklin could have spoken for both of these figures.*"

PLATE I

No warrior frowning in historic stone,
Extorts your praises, or requests your tear.

Cold Contemplation leans her aching head,
On human woe her steady eye she turns,
Waves her meek hand and sighs for science dead,
For Science, Virtue, and for Small she mourns.

It is not, perhaps, great poetry, but it illustrates the connection, through Small and Franklin, between Jefferson, James Watt, Boulton and Darwin; between the destiny of the United States, the steam engine, modern industrialism, and the theory of evolution.

Franklin's part in the introduction of Small, and hence Watt, to Boulton, which led to the introduction of steam power into industry, and the beginning of the contemporary age, is a characteristic example of the operation of his insight. He could perceive better than any other man of his time which things had significance for the future.

5

Boswell has described the occasion when he drew Johnson's attention to Franklin's definition of man.

Boswell: "I think Dr. Franklin's definition of *Man* is a good one—'A tool-making animal.' "

Johnson: "But many a man never made a tool; and suppose a man without arms, he could not make a tool."

These two opinions summarize the difference between two stages of civilization. Franklin's definition contains the basis of anthropological and social science. Comparative anatomists have shown that the evolution of the brain has been stimulated by the coördination of functions necessary for the successful handling of tools. If man had not invented tools he would not have developed as good a brain. If his brain had been less good, his moral and philosophical achievements would have been less.

Franklin's definition is scientific, as it is made in terms open to all observers. No definition of man which includes references to private qualities unobservable by anyone except himself is scientific. John B. Watson could claim Franklin as a behaviorist.

The recognition of the importance of the tool is the key to sociology. The tool is the parent of the machine. It is the producer of goods, and hence of property. The behavior of human society is conditioned by the system of the distribution of property. Law consists largely of rules by which property is distributed, as historians such as Coulton have remarked. Civilization is produced by tools. Experimental science is conducted with the assistance of tools in the form of instruments. Theoretical science is conducted with pencil, paper and symbols, also forms of tools.

Concepts essential for the interpretation of the nature and history of man are implicit in Franklin's definition. It is a perfect expression of the modern spirit.

Johnson's comment exhibits the reaction of a pre-scientific tradition; of a mind whose training had been restricted to theology, literature and scholasticism. It seems to belong to centuries before the Renaissance, yet Johnson was three years younger than Franklin. The younger man could have thundered comfortably with Augustine; the elder could have been at ease with Pavlov.

6

Franklin showed the usual American interest in genealogy. He had compiled a complete account of his ancestors from the middle of the sixteenth century.

The American interest in genealogy probably started from the pioneers' memories of their home country. Their relatives in Europe were inaccessible. As they could not easily go to see them, they thought about them more. "Absence makes the heart grow fonder."

When the country was first settled, no aristocracy was in existence, because there was no civilized population. The pioneers started to make an aristocracy by the criterion of early arrival of ancestors. The search for ancestors in the *Mayflower* stimulated the study of genealogy. The introduction of negro slavery gave another strong stimulation to genealogical studies. Large numbers of persons wished to prove themselves entirely white.

The wide American interest in genealogy has probably provided an important part of the foundation for the American achievements in the science of genetics. The present leaders of world-research on genetics and heredity are Americans such as T. H. Morgan and H. J. Muller.

Modern studies of human heredity give a slight suggestion of the origin of Franklin's extraordinary ability. Like his father, grandfather, great-grandfather, he was a youngest son. L. T. Hogben * has remarked that the statistics of mental ability and defect in London children show that "relatively bright and defective children tend more often to turn up late in the family group. As regards the scholarship children, the significance of this may reside in the possibility that the most favorable social environment for a child is an environment composed of other children."

Franklin belonged to the fifth generation of a series of persons all possessing an extra chance of being bright, owing to their late position in their respective family groups. The five extra chances may all have combined in his favor. The suggestion is speculative, but perhaps not entirely without significance.

The colonization of America put a series of vast biological problems to the early settlers. They knew how to cultivate the various crops, such as wheat, under European conditions, but they had to learn by experiment how to adapt them to American conditions. They also found a highly developed native agriculture, with native plants such as maize, already in existence. Bogart states that the American Indians had bred plants such as maize, beans and squashes, very far from the

* *Genetic Principles in Medicine and Social Science.*

wild original types, and had given them a wider range in climatic adaptation than any comparable plants of the Old World. Carrier estimates that at least one-third of present American agriculture is based on the agricultural inventions of the native Americans before the European invasions.

The Indian method of cultivating maize was horticultural rather than agricultural. The difference of this technique and plant from those of the Old World was striking. European plants and animals introduced into America grew and behaved differently in the new environment.

These circumstances were another spur to American biology, and help to explain its present excellence.

Franklin was interested in the introduction of new crops and plants. He introduced the rhubarb plant, and continually supplied information about rice, silk-worm mulberry trees, and other plants.

The extension of empire by the colonization of North America did not have the same effect on biology as the extension by the conquest and government of less advanced peoples. In North America the settlers had to solve new problems in practical biology, but in India and elsewhere the conquerors had merely to drive and extend a native system that already existed, and extract from it profits to be spent in Europe. The conquerors of subject races are not directly interested in practical biology because they do not work on the land themselves. The divorce between government and technique is one of the causes of the decline of slave and pseudo-slave states.

7

Two of the most remarkable American scientists have been intimately connected with communications. Franklin was connected with the American postal system for more than half his life, and became deputy postmaster general.

Edison became a telegraphist when he was a youth, and his first important invention was an improvement of an electric telegraph instrument. Both of these men traveled considerably in connection with their postal and telegraphic work. Franklin first became interested in electricity during such a visit to Boston.

His influence with the post was essential to the success of his newspapers and journalism, for the postal connections put him at the center of the arrival of news. The continual receipt of news is stimulating to the inquiring and observant mind; and the psychological and practical characteristics of communication provide fertile material for the scientific imagination.

The development of communications encourages new types of political genius. It enables politicians without oratorical gifts to exert influence through journalism and letter writing. Franklin and Jefferson are notable examples. In earlier ages, when public speaking was the chief mode of communication, they would have had far less political influence because they were poor speakers.

8

Faÿ has shown that Franklin was deeply influenced by the theories of the British Pythagoreans. When he was about sixteen years old he happened to find a book written by Tryon, who belonged to that group. Franklin writes that he was converted by Tryon to vegetarianism. It appears that he adopted the theory of metempsychosis from the same source. He may have met some of the British Pythagoreans during his first visit to London, and have acquired a stronger belief in their tenets through discussion with them. He composed a Pythagorean epitaph in 1728, at the age of twenty-three, shortly after his first return from London, and sixty-two years later he willed that it should be inscribed on his tomb, unchanged.

THE BODY

OF

BENJAMIN FRANKLIN

PRINTER

(LIKE THE COVER OF AN OLD BOOK
ITS CONTENTS TORN OUT
AND STRIPT OF ITS LETTERING AND GILDING)
LIES HERE, FOOD FOR WORMS.
BUT THE WORK SHALL NOT BE LOST
FOR IT WILL (AS HE BELIEVED) APPEAR ONCE MORE
IN A NEW AND MORE ELEGANT EDITION
REVISED AND CORRECTED
BY
THE AUTHOR.

Franklin believed that new and more elegant editions of his personality would be issued for ever. This is a version of the Pythagorean belief that when the body dies the soul finds a new habitation in a new human or animal body. Pythagoreans were vegetarians partly to avoid the risk of eating the present habitation of a soul that previously had inhabited a human body.

The importance attached to number and science by the Pythagoreans probably strengthened Franklin's interest in science.

His acceptance of metempsychosis, or transmigration of souls, familiarized him with the notion of things which passed through endless transformation and yet remained indestructible. It prepared his mind for acceptance of the principles of the conservation of matter, and a crude form of the conservation of energy. His ideas on the conservation in nature are advanced for his day.

Metempsychosis predisposed him to conservation. Study of nature confirmed his belief in conservation, and then in later life he began to quote the conservation of matter in support of the metempsychotic beliefs acquired in his youth.

He deduced the probability of human immortality by analogy from the conservation of matter. He wrote in 1785 that he observed great frugality in God's works. Compound substances are continually reduced to their elements, and their constituents used over and over again, and the same species of animals and plants continually populate the world, so God is without the "trouble of repeated new creations."

"I say that when I see nothing annihilated, and not even a drop of water wasted, I cannot suspect the annihilation of souls, or believe that he will suffer the daily waste of millions of minds ready made that now exist, and put himself to the continual trouble of making new ones. Thus finding myself to exist in the world, I believe I shall, in some shape or other, always exist."

The scientific notions of the conservation of matter and energy are to a large degree products of trading and industrial civilizations. In the processes of exchange and manufacture things are continually transformed, yet the products remain. The higher forms of steam and electric machinery cannot be properly designed without an exact knowledge of the transformations of matter and energy, so the modern principles of the conservation of matter and energy come to be exactly established when the demand for refined engine design has become urgent.

The analogies between the notion of the conservation of matter, which is such a characteristic philosophical product of industrial civilizations, and the metempsychotic ideas of the Pythagoreans suggest that Pythagoras himself had close connections with a trading and industrial civilization. It would be interesting to see what might be deduced concerning the trading and industrial features of the Greek society to which Pythagoras' sect belonged from the metempsychotic features in Pythagoras' philosophy.

As Faÿ remarks, Franklin's views on religion are related to Pythagoreanism and Freemasonry. Parton has suggested that Franklin in his youth acquired a belief in the possibility of subordinate gods who superintended the revolutions of the heavenly bodies from Isaac Newton, through conversations with Pemberton, Newton's disciple, about 1726.

In 1790, a month before he died, he answered a friend's queries concerning his religion.

"It is the first time I have been questioned upon it. But I

cannot take your curiosity amiss, and shall endeavour in a few words to gratify it. Here is my creed. I believe in one God, the creator of the universe. That he governs it by his providence. That he ought to be worshipped. That the most acceptable service we render to him is doing good to his other children. That the soul of man is immortal, and will be treated with justice in another life respecting its conduct in this. These I take to be the fundamental points in all sound religion, and I regard them as you do in whatever sect I meet with them.

"As to Jesus of Nazareth, my opinion of whom you particularly desire, I think his system of morals and his religion, as he left them to us, the best the world ever saw or is like to see; but I apprehend it has received various corrupting changes, and I have, with most of the present dissenters in England, some doubts as to his divinity; though it is a question I do not dogmatize upon, having never studied it, and think it needless to busy myself with it now, when I expect soon an opportunity of knowing the truth with less trouble. I see no harm, however, in its being believed, if that belief has the good consequence, as probably it has, of making his doctrines more respected and more observed; especially as I do not perceive that the Supreme takes it amiss, by distinguishing the unbelievers in his government of the world with any peculiar marks of his displeasure."

He was opposed to direct attacks on religion. He left the draft of a letter to a correspondent who had argued in favor of atheism. He wrote that the author should remember that while he might live a virtuous life without religion, the many weak and ignorant men and women require religion to restrain them into virtuous conduct until it becomes habitual. For this reason, an atheist might be indebted to an early religious education, which it would not be decent to spurn later.

"For among us it is not necessary, as among the Hottentots, that a youth, to be raised into the company of men, should prove his manhood by beating his mother."

9

After Franklin finally returned to America he considered the condition of some of the institutions he had founded. He had started the Philadelphia Academy in 1749 as a high school for youths. He had proposed, partly under the influence of Locke, that the courses of instruction should be based on English literature, with emphasis on the cultivation of good habits of reading and pronunciation. His scheme has interesting resemblances to the course of instruction that Faraday devised for himself. Faraday based his own education on the writing of English, and elocution.

Franklin was annoyed to find in 1789 that his Academy had degenerated into an old-fashioned classical school, in which the dead languages had been made the chief subjects, and the teacher of Latin the rector, at a much higher salary than the teacher of English.

It happened that Kinnersley, the teacher of English, was a talented man, who had given Franklin valuable assistance in his electrical researches, and had toured America and the West Indies, lecturing and demonstrating the new knowledge.

If Kinnersley had been made the rector of the Academy, he might have helped to give an early valuable modern impress to American education. The snobbery and blindness of the upper classes of Philadelphia prevented this, for they wished that their children should be taught Latin, because of its social prestige in Europe. The adoption of Latin in the early American high schools was reactionary and tended to put the new American governing classes under the intellectual influence of Europe, while they were struggling for economic independence. It indicated that they had no fundamental philosophical quarrel with Europe. They did not wish to disown the principles of European society, except in so far as they interfered with their own possession of power in America. This produced a conflict which is seen in men such as John Adams, who regarded the ancient learning of Europe as the natural source of knowledge, and yet fought against Europe economically and politically. In spite of his greatness, Adams never lost a petulance which resembles that of an undergraduate who has revolted against the university whose intellectual authority he accepts.

American Latinism helped to establish the authority and influence of American lawyers, which has contributed to the conflict between the pre-Renaissance spirit of American law with the modern spirit of American technology and science.

10

Swift complained that "a usurping populace is its own dupe, a mere under-worker, and a purchaser in trust for some tyrant, whose state and power they advance to their own ruin . . . in their corrupt notions of divine worship, they are apt to multiply their gods; yet their earthly devotion is seldom paid to above one idol at a time, of their own creation, whose oar they pull with less murmuring, and much more skill, than when they *share the leading*, or even *hold the helm*."

The condition of the world in the second quarter of the twentieth century offers much evidence for Swift's opinion. He had a low estimate of human nature. But he also shared the common opinion of his time, that the condition of men could be improved only by a reorganization of the balance of power between the classes. Franklin was not so pessimistic of humanity, nor did he attach much weight to the conception of history as a complex of interacting class forces. He was an experimentalist, and inclined to believe that much was to be discovered by experiment about human beings and the science of politics. This view was valuable, especially as an indication of the direction in which humanity might gain more political knowledge. He was conscious of the limitations of the theorists of the Madison school, who, like Swift, conceived history as a mechanical circus activated by the forces of conflicting social classes. These theorists were the American heirs of the theorists of the English mercantile classes. They assumed that the chief motive forces of history were known, and that nothing more of primary importance was to be discovered by sociologists. As an experimentalist, Franklin could not accept that. His dislike of this view prevented him from appreciating its analytical value. The notion of history as a balance of social forces will give much insight into the nature of the social or political position at any moment, but in the form in which it was accepted in Franklin's time, it was not suggestive of the new forces and positions that might be expected to appear in society in the future.

Franklin's failure as an analyst of social conditions is shown by his surprise at the French Revolution. He had lived in France for ten years just before the Revolution, with extraordinary opportunities for receiving information about the social tendencies of the people, and completely failed to comprehend the portents.

On November 2nd, 1789, he wrote: "The revolution in France is truly surprising. I sincerely wish it may end in establishing a good constitution for that country. The mischiefs and troubles it suffers in the operation, however, give me great concern."

II

Franklin's weakness and strength as a social philosopher were illustrated by his rejection of the conception of history as a balanced interaction of social forces. He could not be contented with a conception that did not include the possibility of the incursion of new factors into history. He disliked the notion of society as a machine that went round and round for ever, without arriving at any new place. Though his rejection of this conception limited his power of social analysis, his belief in experiment and novelty gave him a freedom in interpretation that had some of the advantages of an evolutionary conception of social history. This enabled him to make contributions towards the escape of humanity from the apparently closed circles of historical change.

If the people are to avoid the tendency noted by Swift of appointing dictators over themselves, they must learn that better possibilities exist. They must acquaint themselves with the possibilities of society and nature, and gain some general idea of the system and tendencies of the forces that govern society. Franklin's particular genius was for the first part of this task. No one was more sensitive to new knowledge, and had greater power of explaining it to the people. He was a philosophic journalist. He put a vast range of human knowledge within the reach of the people. Until the people have knowledge they will not know how to avoid dictators.

Modern civilization was produced by the sub-division of labor, and the rise of the specialist. The limitation of the specialist is one of the greatest dangers to society. He tends to exaggerate the importance of his specialty, and to underrate other knowledge. He is naïve on matters outside his subject, and liable to be misled on these by charlatans. He may be protected from deception only by continued broad education during adult life.

As adults will not go to schools for the whole of their lives they must learn through other agencies. The most important is philosophic journalism, in which the general ideas of new knowledge are explained to uninformed persons of adult intelligence. Franklin was one of the first and greatest of the philosophic journalists, whose existence became necessary through the growth of specialization. At the present time, H. G. Wells is a distinguished member of the same class. Both have optimism and love of novelty, and both are weakest in analysis of historical forces.

Specialization enhances individual naïveté, and hence the danger of the rise of dictatorships. The antidote for specialization is the universalism of the philosophic journalist. Franklin is the grandest example of a social type essential to the advance of modern society.

The ability with which he employed journalism is unequaled. As Adams peevishly observed, he made himself the most famous man of his generation. "His name was familiar to government and people, kings, courtiers, nobility, clergy, and philosophers, as well as plebeians, to such a degree that there was scarcely a peasant or a citizen, a *valet de chambre*, coachman or footman, a lady's chamber-maid or a scullion in a kitchen, who was not familiar with it, and who did not consider him as a friend to human kind." Adams writes that his reputation was more universal than that of Leibnitz, Newton, or Voltaire, and he was free from the hatred that canceled the adoration for Louis XIV, Frederick, and Napoleon.

Adams explains that "He had been educated a printer, and had practised his art in Boston, Philadelphia, and London for many years, where he not only learned the full power of the press to exalt and to spread a man's fame, but acquired the intimacy and the correspondence of many men of that profession, with all their editors and many of their correspondents. This whole tribe became enamoured and proud of Mr. Franklin as a member of their body, and were consequently always ready and eager to publish and embellish any panegyric upon him that they could procure. Throughout his whole life he courted and was courted by the printers, editors, and correspondents of reviews, magazines, journals, and pamphleteers, and those little meddling scribblers that are always buzzing about the press in America, England, France and Holland."

Franklin performed his task as a philosophic journalist, an educator of the adult members of democracies, with prodigious skill, and thereby acquired an equal fame.

With his fame and skill he helped to split a reactionary British Empire, and secure an independent United States of America.

As scientist, journalist and diplomat he exhibited an unparalleled combination of great abilities. Neither America nor England has since produced his equal as a universally developed human being.

II

Life and Researches

I. EARLY LIFE

FRANKLIN HAS WRITTEN A FAMOUS AUTOBI-ography and numerous letters, pamphlets and articles, of which about fifteen thousand are extant. As he discussed a vast range of interests in a simple and fascinating style, his writings provide one of the most expressive accounts of a personality. Few geniuses of his degree have possessed a style intelligible to an almost universal public. General influences, including the readability of his writings and the incidents of his career, made him very famous. Many of his contemporaries did not understand him well, and during the nineteenth century his reputation declined. No man will ever be completely comprehended by himself, his contemporaries, or his successors, but the passage of time brings out some perspectives less visible in his own day. Time abets the collection of facts. In the twentieth century many important new details about Franklin have been collected by scholars such as A. H. Smyth and Bernard Faÿ. These circumstances assist a better comprehension of the significance of Franklin in the history of civilization since the Renaissance.

Benjamin Franklin was born at Boston, Massachusetts, on January 17th, 1706. His father, who had left England in 1682 to escape from religious persecution, had strong sense, health, and sociable habits, and died at the age of eighty-nine years. His second wife bore him ten children, of which Benjamin was the youngest boy, and died at eighty-five years. Franklin was the fifth of five generations of youngest sons. As he was the tenth * son his father wished him to become a priest. He had already shown facility in learning. He had "an exceedingly good memory," but could not remember when he learned to read, so he must have learned very early. He was sent to a grammar school at eight years of age to begin education for the church, but left after one year. His father decided he could not afford the expense of a clerical training, so he sent him to a modern school qualifying pupils for trade and practical careers.

Faÿ suggests the economical spirit which prompted Franklin's father not to spend money on education for a learned profession was the formative psychological influence of Franklin's life. When Franklin was an infant, he bought an attractive whistle for an excessive price. His father, with his economical spirit, laughed at him for being swindled. According to Faÿ, this left a psychological complex which never faded from his mind, and gave a utilitarian shape to his character.

He left the second school at the age of ten. His father had been a dyer in England, but could not make the trade pay in America, and had become a tallow candle maker. Benjamin assisted him in this work, but hated it, so his father tried to discover his aptitudes by taking him to watch mechanics and carpenters at work. Franklin records that "It has ever since been a pleasure to me to see good workmen handle their tools; and it has been useful to me, having learned so much by it as to be able to do little jobs myself in my house when a workman could not readily be got, and to construct little machines for my experiments, while the intention of making the experiment was fresh and warm in my mind." Near the end of his life he refers to his love of hammering and carpentering in the bequest of a box of nails to one of his French philosophic friends.

His father finally decided to make him into a printer because he showed a taste for reading. Franklin records that he read Bunyan, R. Burton, Plutarch, Defoe, Locke, and Cocker's Arithmetic. He was apprenticed to his elder brother, who

* Faÿ states he was the ninth.

printed the second newspaper to appear in America. About 1721 he studied an odd volume of the *Spectator*. He trained himself to write by reading this work, making notes of the various points in the essays, or turning them into verse, putting them away, and then re-writing the essays from the notes or verses. He compared his versions with the originals, and observed where they were inferior, and also, in some small points, he writes, where they were superior.

His brother had learned printing in London. He returned to Boston and started a radical paper, under the influence, according to Faÿ, of temperament, youth, consciousness of knowledge of superior culture from the capital city, and the absence of opening for a conservative paper. He ran the paper by attacking the conservatives. One of these was Cotton Mather, who had enthusiastically introduced the technique of inoculation against small pox within two months of the communication of it to Europe by Lady Wortley Montague. As Faÿ remarks, the Conservatives, such as Mather, were prepared to try things they could not understand, while the Liberals, Whigs and rationalists were not. Franklin now was fifteen years old, and assisted in the attacks. Years afterwards he lost his favorite son through neglecting to have him inoculated, and he regretted his early attacks on what proved to be good science.

He wrote a number of articles, the "Dogood Papers," in imitation of *Spectator* essays, and sent them anonymously to his brother's paper, which he was himself helping to print. They had much success, but his brother became jealous when he discovered their authorship, and began to bully him so he ran away to Philadelphia. Franklin attributed his aversion to arbitrary power to this conflict with his brother. Faÿ suggests he was in turn jealous of his brother's superior knowledge of the world and women, and that this also determined him to acquire equal experience.

He became a vegetarian at the age of sixteen. According to Faÿ, he learned vegetarianism from the works of Tryon, an English Pythagorean. He learned the notion of metempsychosis from the same source. Faÿ explains that the notion of metempsychosis had a profound influence on his thought. It is implicit in his epitaph, quoted on page 37. This was written in 1728, and by his will inscribed on his tomb. He found the vegetarian diet economical. It helped him to save money to buy books, and gave him quiet dinner hours, when he could read and meditate alone in the printing shop, while his colleagues had gone to their heavy dinners. His bookishness did not conflict with his health. He was a powerful swimmer, and sometimes drifted for hours in lakes, towed by the string of a kite.

He found work as a printer in Philadelphia. His enterprise and writing talent were noticed by the governors of Pennsylvania and New York. The first of these, Keith, encouraged him to set up his own business, and suggested he should go to England to choose the types. Keith promised to give him letters of introduction to personages in London. Franklin and his friend Ralph, a writer of lively talent but superficial character, sailed before they discovered that the governor, according to Franklin, was one of those men who try to secure popularity by giving more promises than they can keep. Faÿ writes that Keith was unable to help Franklin owing to more creditable reasons. He was intelligent and radical, and introduced paper money, which greatly helped the community. His advanced policy made him enemies, and the absorption in his struggles against them prevented him from giving more help to Franklin.

When the friends arrived in London, they had to find work as soon as possible, instead of buying equipment for a printing shop in America. Franklin was not yet nineteen years old. He immediately got work at an important printer's named Palmer, and presently had to compose the second edition of Wollaston's "Religion of Nature." He disagreed with some of the reasonings, and wrote and printed a little pamphlet concerning them, entitled "A Dissertation on Liberty and Necessity, Pleasure and Pain." A surgeon named Lyons noticed it, and sought Franklin's acquaintance, and took him to a club of which Mandeville, the author of the *Fable of the Bees,* was the leader. Lyons introduced Franklin to Pemberton, the editor of the third edition of Newton's *Principia,* the printing of which was begun about the end of 1723, and finished in 1726. Franklin very much desired to see Newton, and Pemberton promised him the opportunity, but this never occurred. Newton died in 1727.

Franklin discovered an old lady who was willing to board him for thirty cents, or one shilling and six pence, per week. She enjoyed his company and approved his regular habits. He did not drink while at work, and was given the most urgent, best-paid jobs, because he was never absent or blue on Mondays.

Franklin has left numerous accounts of his ingenious personal economies, and abstemiousness. His creed of self-help acquired for him much of his popular fame. Yet in his old age he wrote "Frugality is an enriching virtue; a virtue I never could acquire myself; but I was once lucky enough to find it in a wife, who therefore became a fortune to me."

While in London he taught two of his friends to swim in two lessons. This came to the notice of some gentlemen during a visit to Chelsea, so Franklin stripped and leaped into the river to demonstrate his abilities. He swam to Blackfriars, a distance of more than three miles, "performing on the way many feats of activity, both upon and under the water." After this performance he was advised to open a swimming school.

His friend Ralph became intimate with a milliner. He owed money to Franklin, and had to leave London to obtain work, and commended the milliner to his protection. Franklin tried to seduce her, but was repulsed. Ralph considered the incident canceled his debts to him.

At the beginning of the eighteenth century the intellectual and social life in London was radical, progressive and vigorous. The triumph of the mercantile classes, represented by the dethronement of James II in 1689, was being spiritually consummated. Franklin lived in this atmosphere while he was of student age, and before his mind had become set. He returned to America with the knowledge and the optimism of the ideology of a new governing class. Freemasonry was one of the new social movements arising out of mercantilist social ideas. It was growing rapidly and spreading to other countries. Franklin was immediately attracted by a movement so expressive of the spirit of the period.

Franklin had strong passions. He records that before he was married in 1730 the "hard-to-be governed passion of youth hurried me frequently into intrigues with low women that fell in my way, which were attended with some expense and great inconvenience, besides a continual risque to my health by a distemper which of all things I dreaded, though by great good luck I escaped it."

A. H. Smyth writes that the Franklin manuscripts in the Library of Congress include letters to young women at home and experienced matrons abroad, which contain passages too bawdry to "be tolerated by the public sentiment of the present age" (1906). He considers Franklin remained to the end of life a proletarian in spirit, the descendant of hard-handed blacksmiths, and possessed of "strong and rank" "animal instincts and passions."

His wife was Deborah Read, to whom he had been betrothed before he went to England. He had deserted her, and had married her afterwards, partly from pity and duty.

Franklin returned to Philadelphia after spending eighteen months in London. At first he was unable to find work except with Keimer, his former employer. After some maneuvers he succeeded in starting a printing business with a partner.

About the same time, he formed the Junto club, for intellectual discussions among his friends. This club persisted for forty years. Its membership was restricted to twelve, and the subjects of discussion included ethical questions such as "Is self-interest the rudder that steers mankind?"; "Does the importation of servants increase or advance the wealth of our country?"; "Whence comes the dew, that stands on the outside of a tankard that has cold water in it in the summer time?"—ethics, political economy, and natural philosophy.

Keimer had been forced to reëmploy Franklin because he had obtained a profitable contract to print paper money for the province of New Jersey, and Franklin was the only person in America who could make copper plates for printing notes. Having seen there were profits for a printer in printing paper money, Franklin discussed the principles of paper money with his Junto friends and wrote a pamphlet entitled: "A Modest Inquiry into the Nature and Necessity of a Paper Currency." Under the influence of Governor Keith and this pamphlet Pennsylvania decided to print paper money and Franklin received the profitable contract. He remarked that the common people were in favor of paper currency and the rich against, but the rich had no adequate exponent of their views.

In the course of the argument concerning the nature of money Franklin writes: "as silver itself is of no certain permanent value, being worth more or less according to its scarcety or plenty, therefore it seems requisite to fix upon something else more proper to be made a *measure of values,* and this I take to be *labor.*"

Wetzel suggests that Franklin learned the notion of the labor theory of value from Sir William Petty's "Essay on Taxes and Contributions." Franklin also gives a definition of natural interest on capital. He assumes that rent is the most secure form of interest, and that interest on capital should be equal to that rate, plus an increase proportional to the difference in risk between the investment of the capital in land and in any project.

On May 19th, 1731, he made some notes on his reading of history.

"That the great affairs of the world, the wars, revolutions, etc. are carried on and effected by parties."

The parties follow their immediate interests, which produces the usual confusion of social affairs. As soon as a party gains its point, its members become intent on their particular interests. Few public men act "from a meer view of the good of their country."

Franklin considered founding a United Party for Virtue, whose membership should be restricted to young and single men. Its principles were to resemble those of the Freemasons. He founded the first subscription library in America in 1730, to assist the reading of his friends in the Junto, and contribute to the general education. The library secured through one of the members of the Junto, an influential patron: Peter Collinson, an eminent Quaker connected with the Penn family, and a distinguished botanist. From 1730 until 1768, when he died at the age of 75, Collinson helped to collect and send books for the library, and accounts of the most recent discoveries in agriculture, arts and science. Franklin writes that Collinson sent an electrical machine and an account of the German experiments on electricity in 1745 (he acknowledged the receipt of the machine in 1747). This stimulated his interest in electrical experiments, and Collinson's friendly reception of his letters describing his results encouraged him to proceed with his researches.

The library was imitated throughout the American colonies, with important results. Mrs. John Adams noted at the beginning of the nineteenth century that the common people of America were, on the average, far better informed than those of England.

He introduced *Poor Richard's Almanac* in 1733. He "filled all the little spaces that occur'd between the remarkable days in the calender with proverbial sentences, chiefly such as inculcated industry and frugality, as the means of procuring wealth, and thereby securing virtue."

At this date, almanacs were of great importance. They contained notices of the chief holydays, market days, and other events of the year. They were essential to farmers, shop-keepers, and craftsmen. Many homes possessed only two books: the Bible and an almanac. Franklin adopted the traditional style of the almanacs, but improved it by his superior understanding and literary expression of the proverbial philosophy of the masses. *Poor Richard's Almanacs* had a wide sale in America, and were translated into many languages. They established

Franklin's fame among the masses, and are his most effective literary works. The success of *Poor Richard* was not due entirely to Franklin's literary skill and psychological insight. His *Poor Richard* rode on a scientific horse, as almanacs are records of time. L. T. Hogben and other writers have commented on the profound influence of the construction of almanacs on the cultivation of science. Early astronomy was created in order to construct almanacs for the control of agriculture and the processes of human society. Franklin's understanding of the importance of the sequences of nature was connected with his aptitude for science. Almanacs gave scope to the scientific besides the literary aptitudes of his mind.

In the same year he made a partnership with one of his printers, to start a printing house in Charleston. He provided one-third of the capital, and took one-third of the profits. He extended this system of holding capital in various businesses, and, according to Phillips Russell, invented the American trust. He attributed much of the success of the scheme to the care with which the deeds of partnership were devised.

He published *Constitutions of the Free Masons* in 1734, and an essay "On the Usefulness of Mathematics" in the *Pennsylvania Gazette*, in 1735. He remarks that no business or commerce can be managed or carried on without numbers, and geometry is essential for mariners, architects, engineers, and geographers.

He became clerk to the General Assembly of Pennsylvania in 1736, and postmaster of Philadelphia in 1737; "tho' the salary was small, it facilitated the correspondence that improv'd my newspaper . . . as well as the advertisements."

He began to turn his thoughts to public affairs, and among other projects founded a fire-brigade, the Union Fire Company.

The preacher Whitefield arrived in America in 1739. Franklin writes: "I had the curiosity to learn how far he could be heard, by retiring backwards down the street towards the river; and I found his voice distinct till I came near Front-street, when some noise in that street obscur'd it. Imagining then a semicircle, of which my distance should be the radius, and that it were fill'd with auditors, to each of whom I allow'd two square feet, I computed that he might well be heard by more than thirty thousand. This reconceil'd me to the newspaper accounts of his having preach'd to twenty-five thousand people in the fields, and to the antient histories of generals haranguing whole armies, of which I had sometimes doubted."

Franklin acquired Whitefield's friendship. Faÿ suggests that this enabled him to secure the preacher's demagogic gifts in aid of his own popularity. His rational mind could not appeal to mob emotions, but Whitefield could appeal to them on his behalf. In some degree he used the preacher as his lieutenant of the mob.

Franklin maintained relations with Whitefield for many years. He discussed with him methods of influencing the people, and other problems concerning the arts of salvation and government. He wished to learn from him the psychology of the herd, and how it should be applied. In a letter to Whitefield, written in 1749, he quotes the view of Confucius, that peoples should be reformed by converting the grandees. When this is done, the masses follow by imitation. "The mode has a wonderful influence on mankind; and there are numbers who, perhaps, fear less the being in hell, than out of the fashion. Our most western reformations began with the ignorant mob; and when numbers of them were gained, interest and party views drew in the wise and great. Where both methods can be used, reformations are likely to be more speedy. O that some method could be found to make them lasting! He who discovers that will, in my opinion, deserve more, ten thousand times, than the inventor of the longitude."

Franklin proposed the foundation of the first American Philosophical Society in 1743. The Philadelphia members were to include a physician, botanist, mathematician, chemist, mechanician, geographer and general natural philosopher, besides a president, treasurer and secretary. He offered himself as secretary. The Society was to promote Useful Knowledge. This is in contrast with the purpose of the Royal Society of

London, which was founded to promote Natural Knowledge. The differences in aim show that the two societies were founded on behalf of different social classes, one a leisure class and the other a tradesman's class.

He published an account of a new sort of fireplace in 1744, which he had invented in 1742. He refused to patent it because "we enjoy great advantages from the inventions of others, we should be glad of an opportunity to serve others by any invention of ours."

As colonization proceeded in the Eastern states, wood-fuel became more expensive. Franklin designed a more economical stove, which created enough draught to ventilate the room adequately, and heated enough air to warm the room evenly by convection, and yet allowed a sight of the fire.

He afterwards elucidated the movements of air in chimneys, and explained that the air flowed up or down according to differences in temperature. In the summer, food could be kept fresh by covering it with a wet rag, and putting it in the chimney, where the air current made the water evaporate, and so cooled the food.

There were many wars in Europe and America in 1745. Exposed ports such as Boston feared attacks, and their populations were active in military preparations for defense and counter-attack. During a visit to Boston in 1746 Franklin acquired the military fervor and returned with it to Philadelphia. Many persons in Pennsylvania were nervous over the inadequate defenses, owing to the influence of the pacifist Quakers in the provincial government. Franklin proposed the formation of a militia, and artfully persuaded the Quakers not to oppose it.

He wrote an enthusiastic letter to his brother at Boston, and suggested the Americans should succeed in their attack on Cape Breton because "five hundred thousand petitions were offered up to the same effect in New England, which, added to the petitions of every family morning and evening, multiplied by the number of days since January 25th make forty-five millions of prayers; which, set against the prayers of a few priests in the garrison, to the Virgin Mary, give a vast balance in your favour."

During his visit to Boston, Franklin happened to meet a Dr. Spence, who had just arrived from Scotland, and had brought some apparatus for making experiments with statical electricity. Franklin was fascinated by the apparatus, though it did not work very well, for Spence did not know how to use it properly.

In 1747 Peter Collinson included an electrostatic machine with one of his parcels of books for the library company. On March 28th, 1747, Franklin acknowledged the gift in a letter to Collinson:

Sir,

Your kind present of an electric tube, with directions for using it, has put several of us on making electrical experiments, in which we have observed some particular phaenomena, that we look upon to be new. I shall therefore communicate them to you in my next, though possibly they may not be new to you, as among the numbers daily employed in those experiments on your side the water, 'tis probable some one or other has hit on the same observations. For my own part, I never was before engaged in any study that so totally engrossed my attention and my time as this has lately done; for what with making experiments when I can be alone, and repeating them to my Friends and Acquaintance, who, from the novelty of the thing, come continually in crouds to see them, I have, during some months past, had little leisure for any thing else

I am, &c.

B. Franklin.

Within a few months Franklin and his friends discovered facts and conceptions which transformed the theory of statical electricity. This was an important contribution to the modernization of the human concepts of nature.

2. ELECTRICAL RESEARCHES

THE distinction of Franklin's contributions to the science of electricity becomes clear when his work is compared with that of his predecessors.

The first record of an electrical phenomenon occurs in the writings of Theophrastus in 300 B. C. He described how amber, when rubbed, attracted light bodies. Later writings state that Thales, who lived in 600 B. C., was familiar with this phenomenon, and deduced from it that amber is animated.

Nearly two thousand years passed before anything more was added to the knowledge of electricity. About 1600, William Gilbert of Colchester in England, a physician to Queen Elizabeth, proved that many other substances besides amber could be electrified. His list included diamond and several other real and imitation precious stones, glass, sulphur, and colored sealing wax. The science of electrostatics developed after the Renaissance partly because expanding trade provided a wider variety of materials for experiments. The materials of the early experiments on electrostatics sound like the stock of a shop; diamonds, wax, silk, wool, linen, etc. Gilbert observed that electrified bodies would attract bits of wood, metal, stone, and drops of water and oil. Thick smoke was noticeably attracted but not thin smoke, air or flames. He found that electrical effects were strongest when the air was dry, and the wind blew from the north or east. Under these conditions electrified bodies would retain their charges for ten minutes. Moist air or southerly winds destroyed the electrification. He found that moisture of any sort, such as that carried in the breath, had the same effect. Sprinkling with brandy also destroyed electrification, but sprinkling with oil did not. He presented a drop of water on a dry substance to an electrified body, and observed that it was distorted into a conical shape. Gilbert asserted that magnetism exhibited attraction and repulsion but that electricity exhibited attraction only, and never repulsion. He supposed that electrical attraction is analogous to cohesion. Two drops of water brought into contact rush together. Similarly, an electrified body is surrounded by an effluvium which brings it into contact with the objects it attracts, and makes them rush together.

These researches, and others on magnetism, were a wonderful advance in experimental science. They were an important inspiration to Galileo, who envied their author's achievements. The study of the electrical properties of the atmosphere and gases has led to several of the most fundamental advances in electrical science. The first student of electricity in modern times did not fail to observe the influence of the weather on electrification. L. Hogben has suggested that Gilbert's interest in magnetism was inspired by the desire of British navigators to find some new method of determining longitude. The Portuguese and Spanish navigators used Moorish astronomical methods for determining longitude which depended on the use of eclipses and occultations. With their aid Christopher Columbus discovered America. They were exact, but not useful to the English because they could not be easily used in cloudy northern latitudes.

The famous inventor of the air-pump, Guericke, was the next important contributor to the science of electricity. He invented the first electrical machine. This consisted of a sphere of sulphur which could be rotated on a shaft through its center. The sphere was charged by rubbing it with the hand as it rotated. He discovered electrical repulsion, that two bodies bearing electricity from the same source repelled each other. He noticed electric sparks for the first time, and heard the associated sounds. He observed an effect due to electric induction, which was not appreciated for nearly a century.

Contemporary with Guericke, Robert Boyle discovered that electrical attractions may occur in vacua. He proved by experiment that attracted objects pull the electrified body as strongly as they are themselves pulled. Newton's law of the equality of action and reaction was not yet established.

Electric discharges were first compared with thunder and lightning by Wall, a friend of Boyle, about 1680. Wall published a description of the experiments which inspired this classical suggestion in the transactions of the Royal Society in 1708. His paper, "On the Luminous Qualities of Amber, & cont.," was communicated to the Society by Sloane. Franklin met Sloane in 1726, during his first visit to London, and sold him a purse made of asbestos. Wall's paper contains three remarkable features. Boyle was interested in phosphorus, but disliked the usual method of preparing it, which consisted of evaporating urine. Wall searched for methods of manufacturing what appeared to be phosphorescence, and found that amber and other substances would apparently phosphoresce when rubbed. Indeed, amber would produce big flashes and cracklings, resembling lightning and thunder. He perceived the importance of the discovery, and forecast the event of a genius who would interpret it. Wall concludes his paper with the hope that his observations will commend him to posterity. Several passages are quoted, in order to illustrate the style of one of Franklin's predecessors, and Wall's own scientific talent, and nobility of mind.

"You may remember my telling you many Years ago of my good Friend Mr. Boyle's communicating to me, about the Year 1680, his way of making the Phosphorus with Urine, at the same time desiring me to use all my Endeavours to find out some other Subject, from whence it might be made in greater quantity, and perhaps he might have made the like Request to many more; for, to use his own Words, he said, he really pitty'd his Chymist, who was forced to evaporate so prodigious a Quantity of Urine, to get a very little of the Phosphorus. Soon after, in order to see some Experiments in Chymistry, I lodg'd for a short time at his Chymist's House, one Mr. Bilgar, then living in Mary le Bone Street near Piccadilly, who indeed was equally, if not more importunate with me than Mr. Boyle, to try if I cou'd find out some other Matter from which more might be made than from Urine, telling me there was so great a demand for it, that it wou'd be of very great advantage to him. It being then a very hot summer, I caused a piece of the dry'd Matter in the Fields, where they empty the Houses of Office, to be digg'd up, in which, when broken in the Dark, a great number of small Particles of Phosphorus appear'd. This Matter I carry'd to Mr. Boyle, who viewed it with great Satisfaction, and Mr. Bilgar, by his Direction, fell to Work thereon, but from it cou'd make very little or no Phosphorus, till another Matter was added to it in Distillation, and then he cou'd therewith make large Quantities, to his great Profit; for while I was at his House, I often saw him make it, and sell it for six Guineas, and six Louis d'Ors an Ounce, whereby he got so much Money, that, I believe, he thought himself above his Business, and quickly left England; so that we lost an Honest and Industrious Chymist, and Mr. Boyle a Faithful and Industrious Servant." . . .

. . . "Now, Sir, my being, as you have heard, well acquainted with the Artificial Phosphorus, was the occasion of my making many Reflections about it, and caus'd me to consider, whether there might not be *in rerum natura* other natural ones, besides those that Mr. Boyle and some others have given an account of.

"You well know, Sir, that Humane Urine and Dung do plentifully abound with an Oleosum and Common Salt, so that I take the Artificial Phosphorus to be nothing else but that Animal Oleosum coagulated with the Mineral Acid of Spirit of Salt, which Coagulum is preserv'd and not dissolv'd in Water, but accended by Air. These Considerations made me conjecture that Amber, which I take to be a Mineral Oleosum coagulated with a Mineral Volatile acid might be a Natural Phosphorus, so I fell to make many Experiments upon it, and at last found, that by gently rubbing a well polished Piece of Amber with my Hand in the dark, which was the Head of my Cane, it produc'd a Light; whereupon I got a pretty large piece of Amber, which I caused to be made long and taper, and drawing it gently thro' my Hand, being very dry it afforded a considerable Light. I then us'd many Kinds of soft Animal Substances, and found none did so well as that of Wool. And now new Phenomena offered themselves; for upon drawing the piece of Amber swiftly thro' the Woollen Cloth, and squeezing it pretty hard with my Hand, a prodigious number of little Cracklings were heard, and every one of those produc'd a little flash of Light; but when the Amber was drawn gently and slightly thro' the Cloath, it produc'd a light but no Crackling; but by holding one's Finger at a little distance from the Amber, a large Crackling is produc'd with a great flash of Light succeeding it, and, what to me is very surprizing, upon its eruption it strikes the Finger very sensibly, wheresoever apply'd, with a push or puff like Wind. The Crackling is full as loud as that of Charcoal on Fire; nay five or six Cracklings, or more, according to the quickness of placing the Finger, have been produc'd from one single Friction, Light always succeeding each of 'em. Now I make no question, but upon using a longer & larger piece of Amber, both the Cracklings & Light would be much greater, because I never yet found any Crackling from the Head of my Cane, altho' 'tis a pretty large one; and it seems, in some degree, to represent Thunder and Lightning; but what to me is more strange than all I have been telling you is, that tho' upon friction with Wool in the daytime, the Cracklings seem to be full as many and as large, yet by all the Tryals I have made, very little Light appears, tho' in the darkest Room; and the best time of making these Experiments, is when the Sun is 18 Degrees below the Horizon; and when the Sun is so, tho' the Moon shines never so bright, the Light is the same as in the darkest Room, which makes me chuse to call it a Noctiluca."

Wall concludes his paper, which was the only one he contributed to the Philosophical Transactions, with these noble words:

"I am not without hopes but that some more elevated and happy Genius may arise, under whose Conduct these hints may be carry'd on to a height not easie to be foreseen by Persons of short Views, whose Conceptions are confined within the narrow limits of what's already known, and whose Self sufficiency sooths 'em with a *Ne plus ultra*.

"Thus, Sir, I please myself with the remote prospect of new Scenes in Nature, which, tho' imperfect at present, may in time by some skilful Hand be finish'd and fitted for a nearer view, tho' before that time shall come, nothing may remain of me besides this Testimony of my good Will to Mankind, and particular respect for you."

Wall imagined he had observed a connection between the sparking of electrified amber and the position of the sun.

Isaac Newton made some electrical experiments about 1675. He discovered that electrified glass attracted light bodies on the side opposite to that which had been rubbed. This showed that electrical attraction might pass through a solid dielectric. He supposed that electrified bodies emitted an elastic fluid which freely penetrated glass, and that the emission was performed by vibrations of the constituent particles of the electrified bodies.

In 1670 Picard had observed an electric glow in vacua over mercury, and before the end of the century Italian experimenters of the "de Cimento" discovered that electrified bodies could be discharged by flames.

The ability of glass to take a high electrification was first observed by Hawkesbee, and described, with many other valuable observations, in his book on *Physico-Mechanical Experiments,* published in 1709. He whirled a hollow glass globe, which was electrified by rubbing with the hand. This machine was the forerunner of the glass electrostatic machines. He examined the various glows produced in the air within the globe, when the pressure of the air was varied. He observed that if the globe was filled with dry sand, its strength of electrification decreased. He found that the electrification of a solid cylinder of glass was slightly less, but more permanent, than that of a hollow cylinder. Thus he compared the properties of various dielectrics. Hawkesbee did not clearly distinguish between insulators and conductors. He supposed he could not electrify a metal because "all the attrition of the several bodies I have used for that purpose, have been too weak to force it from it." He believed that friction forced electricity out of bodies.

The progress of electrical research for the next quarter of a century was slow, probably owing to the failure of Hawkesbee's successors to adopt his electrical machine. Experimenters returned to the rubbing of rods, which did not provide them with powerful supplies of electricity, and hence increased the difficulty of their experiments. The incident is an instructive example of the results of neglecting large-scale experiments, and failing to take advantage of increased power provided by improvement of machinery.

This may have some connection with the arrest of scientific and technical development in the early eighteenth century, owing to the ease with which wealth was procured from India, according to the suggestion of G. N. Clark.

A remarkable series of experiments was made by Stephen Gray and his friend Wheeler about the year 1728. They discovered electricity could be conducted along threads of linen or hemp. They constructed lines of thread over a hundred feet long, supported by silk, and succeeded in detecting electricity that had passed from one end to the other.

"Mr. Wheeler was desirous to try whether we could not carry the Electrick Vertue horizontally. I then told him of the Attempt I had made with that Design, but without Success, telling him the Method and Materials made use of, as mentioned above. He then proposed a Silk Line to support the Line by which the Electrick Vertue was to pass. I told him it might do better upon the Account of its Smallness so that there would be less Vertue carried from the Line of Communication, with which, together with the apt Method Mr. Wheeler contrived, and with the great Pains he took himself, and the Assistance of his Servants, we succeeded far beyond our Expectation."

The silk was made as thin as possible, as Gray and Wheeler assumed that its conducting power depended on its thickness. The silk proved to be too thin to support the weight of the thread, so they tried other materials. They tried brass wire, because that could be both strong and thin. But the electricity would no longer pass down the thread, as it seemed to disappear into the brass wire. As the conduction did not appear to depend on thickness, they returned to the use of thicker silk. They found that hempen lines supported by loops of silk would conduct electricity some eight hundred feet.

Thus Gray and Wheeler discovered the distinction between conductors and non-conductors.

These ingenious experimenters studied the effects of elec-

BENJAMIN FRANKLIN
(from B. Wilson's Portrait painted in 1759.)

PLATE II

tricity conducted on to load-stones, red-hot pokers, chickens and boys. Gray proved that liquids could be electrified by charging soap-bubbles.

"I dissolved Soap in the Thames Water, then I suspended a Tobacco-Pipe by a Hairline, So as that it hung nearly horizontal, with the Mouth of the Bowl downwards: then having dipped it in the Soap-Liquor, and blown a Bubble, the Leaf-Bras laid on a Stand under it, the Tube being rubbed, the Bras was attracted by the Bubble."

Gray was a brilliant experimenter, but had a peculiar temperament. In 1739, after Gray's death, Desagulier wrote that he had not entered on electrical researches because Gray, who had wholly turned his thoughts to electricity, "was of a temper to give it entirely over, if he imagined that any thing was done in opposition to him." Gray felt he had a proprietary right in electrical discoveries.

As experimenters in England were afraid of encroaching on Gray, it is not surprising that the next great advance occurred in France. Dufay discovered "that there are two distinct kinds of electricity, very different from one another; one of which I call vitreous, the other resinous electricity. The first is that of glass, . . . the second is that of amber. . . . The characteristic of these two electricities is, that they repel themselves, and attract each other. . . . From this principle, one may easily deduce the explanation of a great number of other phenomena; and it is probable, that this truth will lead us to the discovery of many other things."

Dufay transmitted electricity over spaces of twelve inches of air, when a lighted candle was placed in the middle of the space.

He observed that when he insulated himself and was charged with electricity, sparks visible in the dark could be taken out of him. The number of sparks was increased if a piece of metal was presented to his charged body.

When Gray found that Dufay was not trespassing on his ground, but advancing knowledge, he resumed research. He concluded that if the charged person and the metal were reversed in position, sparks should come from the metal. He tried the experiment, and found that sparks could be drawn from charged insulated iron pokers, etc. Priestley states that this experiment introduced the notion of metallic conductors.

Gray and his friends noticed that when the experiments were performed in the dark, *cones* or *pencils of light* streamed from the metals. They noted separate threads of light in the cones. Thus the brush discharge was discovered in these experiments.

Gray found that a pointed rod discharged a body with gentle snaps, but a blunt rod discharged with one loud snap. From these experiments in 1734 he concluded: "in time, there may be found out a way to collect a greater quantity of the electric fire . . . which . . . seems to be of the same nature with that of thunder and lightning."

Gray died shortly after this date. The day before he died he described to the secretary of the Royal Society some experiments that convinced him that the solar system was operated by electrical forces.

A small charged iron globe was laid on resin. The experimenter held a small body over the globe by a string several inches long. It was found that the body will of itself begin to move in a circle round the globe, and constantly from west to east. With slightly different dispositions, the orbits will be ellipses of various eccentricities. Wheeler and others tried the experiments repeatedly after Gray's death, and concluded that the movement from west to east was due to the unconscious desire of the experimenter who held the string. Gray had been bemused by the planchette.

A new period of electrical research started in Germany in 1740, with the reintroduction and improvement of the machines of Guericke and Hawkesbee. Winkler used a pad instead of the hand for rubbing the glass globe, Gordon introduced a cylinder instead of the globe, and Boze added a metal conductor insulated with silk threads.

The larger electrical powers of these machines allowed new and striking experiments. Small animals were killed by sparks, colors were bleached, and spirits were fired. Small bells and wheels were operated by discharges.

In 1740 Nollet exhibited a continuous electric discharge in a partial vacuum, and described various purple-colored streamers that appeared in the discharge vessel. Grummert produced brilliant discharges in vacuum tubes and suggested in 1744 that they should be used "in mines and places where common fires and other lights cannot be had."

In the same year Winkler suggested that words could be spelt out in bent vacuum tubes, which could be illuminated in the dark. J. W. Ryde translates his account of the experiment: "Some exalted persons, to whom I had the honour of showing electrical experiments, were very delighted when they saw the initial letters of the most illustrious name of Augustus Rex suddenly shine out brightly in a darkened room and noticed the flood of light which instantaneously filled the glass letters." As Ryde remarks, the modern uses of discharge lamps for illumination and display had been proposed in 1744. In 1752 Watson demonstrated a tube 32 inches long which gave a steady light. This was a positive column tube of the type now used for advertising and flood lighting.

By 1744 a large number of properties of electricity had been discovered, many of which were not utilized until the twentieth century. Electrical studies in the eighteenth century, though an expression of the philosophical attitude of the period which was rapidly becoming commercial, were not yet close enough to industrial and commercial interests to receive much direct impetus from those interests. The natural philosophers who appeared with the Renaissance were influenced by many motives. The deepest were economic and material. They applied in the sphere of intellectual work the attitude which the dominant classes of the Renaissance showed to life. This was a concern with the exploitation of the material world. The rise of the city merchants and craftsmen was accompanied by a turn of the philosophic gaze of humanity from heaven to earth, from the world of magic to the world of materials.

The pre-Renaissance ideas of magic persisted strongly into

the succeeding period. In one form, they persisted as entertainment for the leisure classes. This motive was strong among
the early members of the Royal Society. But a study of the
early Royal Society papers shows utilitarian motives were at
least as strong. It has been noticed that the first comparison
of electric discharges with lightning occurred in a research inspired by utilitarian motives, an attempt to find an easier way
of making phosphorus. It appeared that the manufacture of
phosphorus was so profitable that the maker could quickly retire abroad with a fortune. Motives of utility are generally
much more powerful than motives of entertainment; nevertheless, motives of entertainment may have considerable influence. The increase and distribution of wealth that accompanied the Renaissance increased the size of the leisured classes.
A considerable part of the increased number of persons of
leisure spent their time acquiring education. As the size of the
leisure class increased, the proportion of intellectual members
increased. What were these clever persons without work to do?
They could not become monks, because society was no longer
fundamentally interested in the next world. They had to busy
themselves with this world. They unconsciously adapted in
their entertainment the attitude of mind characteristic of the
dominant trading and manufacturing classes. Playing with
scientific instruments and experiments was a vicarious form of
manufacturing.

By the seventeenth century the entertainments of chivalry
appeared ridiculous to the keenest minds. Substitutes for Boc-
caccio were required. The concentration of population made
hunting and the old entertainments less accessible. There was
a demand for more compact forms of entertainment which
could be given in rooms in cities.

Electrical phenomena were particularly suitable for this
purpose. They gave flashes and cracks, and colored lights in
the dark, and could be produced by neat and clean apparatus.
The electricity seemed to be made out of nothing, and appeared far more magical than the false products manufactured
by the messy process of the alchemists.

E. L. Nichols has compared the public excitement raised by the discovery of the Leiden jar with the modern discoveries of X-rays and radium. He explained that the simplicity of the jar made it more striking, as nearly everyone could make experiments with it if he desired, whereas X-rays and radium cannot be demonstrated without complicated apparatus.

Another motive for the popularity of the Leiden jar was the shortage of amusements. There were no cinemas in the eighteenth century, and doubts of the propriety of public executions were beginning.

Kleist discovered the condenser accidentally. He charged a nail that had been inserted in a medicine glass. He found that he received a sharp shock when he held the glass in one hand, and touched the nail with the other. The strength of the shock was increased when the glass was filled with mercury or alcohol.

The Dutch experimenters accidentally invented the jar in attempts to prevent leakages of charge. They surrounded charged bodies with glass to prevent leakage through the air. Water was placed in a glass bottle and charged by a wire. The experimenters accidentally found, like Kleist, that if the glass was held in one hand and connection with the water was made with the other, a surprising shock was experienced.

The wonders of the shocks from Leiden jars excited wide interest. Priestley describes the "sentiments of the magnanimous Mr. Boze, who with a truly philosophic heroism, worthy of the renowned Empedocles, said he wished he might die by the electric shock, that the account of his death might furnish an article for the memoirs of the French Academy of Sciences. But it is not given to every electrician to die the death of the justly envied Richman." (Riehmann, who was killed in St. Petersburg by electricity he had drawn from thunder clouds.)

Everybody was eager to see and feel the effects of discharges from Leiden jars, and in many European countries numbers of persons earned a livelihood "by going about and showing" them.

The properties of the jar were strenuously investigated by

William Watson and a group of fellows of the Royal Society. Watson and Bevis discovered in 1746 that if the outside of the glass bottle was covered with metal foil the strength of the discharge was increased.

"Upon shewing some Experiments to Dr. Bevis, to prove my Assertion that the Stroke was, *caeteris paribus,* to the Glass, that ingenious Gentleman has very clearly demonstrated it likewise by the following Experiment: He wrapped up two large round-bellied Phials in very thin Lead so close as to touch the Glasses everywhere except there Necks. These were filled with Water, and cork'd, with a small Wire running through each Cork into the Water."

They found that such jars could give "a most terrible shock."

This sketch will give an impression of the large number of important electrical phenomena observed by experimenters up to 1746. The accumulation of facts inspired much theorizing, most of which was very speculative. The best theorizing of the date may be illustrated by a quotation from a paper by the gifted William Watson. Here is his theory of the accumulation of electricity:

"Before I proceed further, I must beg Leave to explain what I call the Accumulation of Electricity. To put a similar Case: As we take it for granted, that there is always a determinate Quantity of Atmosphere surrounding the terraqueous Globe, we conceive, when we see the Mercury in the Barometer very low, that there is a less accumulated Column of this Atmosphere impending over us, than when we see the Mercury high. In like manner when we observe that the electrified Gun-barrel attracts or repels only very light Substances at a very small Distance, or that the Snap and Fire therefrom are scarcely perceptible; we conceive then a much less Quantity of electrical Atmosphere surrounding the Gun-barrel. This Power being more, or less, we call the greater or less Degree of the Accumulation of Electricity. This is only attainable to a certain Point, if you electrify ever so long; after which, unless otherwise directed, the Dissipation thereof is general. The Phial of Water of Muschenbroek seems capable of a greater Degree of Accumulation of Electricity, than any thing we are at present acquainted with: And we see, when, by holding the Wire thereof to the Globe in Motion the Accumulation being complete, that the Surcharge runs off from the Point of the Wire, as a Brush of blue Flame."

This is first-class pre-Franklinian theorizing.

Franklin had first seen electrical experiments in 1746. He happened to receive an electrical machine from Collinson shortly afterwards, and he began experimenting with it. As he was isolated in America he had not seen any of the able European experimenters at work, so he was unable to learn any experimental technique from them. Much of the European literature containing descriptions of electrical experiments was not yet accessible to him.

Franklin had virtually retired from business, so he was able to devote his best attention to experiments with the new machine. He reported to Collinson that he was never before "engaged in any study that so totally engrossed" his attention and time. As Rutherford commented in his Franklin Bicentenary Address: "Franklin rapidly contracted the fever of the scientific discoverer," after at first having been animated, probably, by curiosity.

Within a few months Franklin discovered and rediscovered many facts, and began to theorize from them. With Hopkinson he observed "the wonderful effect of pointed bodies, both in *drawing off* and *throwing off* the electrical fire."

He found that a charged shot could be discharged by sifting fine sand on it, by breathing on it, by smoking it with burning wood, by candle-light from a distance of one foot. He supposed that "every particle of sand, moisture, or smoke, being first attracted and then repelled, carries off with it a portion of the electrical fire, but that the same still subsists in those particles, till they communicate it to something else, and that it is never really destroyed."

He observed that fire-light discharged the shot, but not sun-light. He supposed that particles from the candle took the charge away, in the same manner as sand; and that the rarefied hot air allowed the electric fluid to pass more easily.

Schuster has remarked that if he had exposed clean zinc instead of a shot to sun-light, he would have discovered the photo-electric effect.

Franklin then states that "the electrical fire was not created by friction, but collected, being really an element diffus'd among, and attracted by other matter, particularly by water and metals."

He had observed that: "(I) A person standing on wax and rubbing the tube, and another person on wax drawing the fire, they will both of them (provided they do not stand so as to touch one another) appear to be electrized to a person standing on the floor; that is, he will perceive a spark on approaching each of them with his knuckle. (II) But, if the persons on wax touch one another during the exciting of the tube, neither of them will appear to be electrized. (III) If they touch one another after exciting the tube, and drawing the fire as aforesaid, there will be a stronger spark between them, than was between either of them and the person on the floor. (IV) After such strong spark, neither of them discover any electricity.

"These appearances we attempt to account for thus: We suppose, as aforesaid, that electrical fire is a common element, of which every one of the three persons above mentioned has his equal share, before any operation is begun with the tube. A, who stands on wax and rubs the tube, collects the electrical fire from himself into the glass; and his communication with the common stock being cut off by the wax, his body is not again immediately supply'd. B, (who stands on wax likewise) passing his knuckle along near the tube, receives the fire which was collected by the glass from A; and his communication with the common stock being likewise cut off, he retains the additional quantity received. To C, standing on the floor, both appear to be electrised: for he having only the middle quantity of electrical fire, receives a spark upon approaching B, who has an over quantity; but gives one to A, who has an under quantity. If A & B approach to touch each other, the spark is stronger, because the difference between them is greater. After such touch there is no spark between either of them and C, because the electrical fire in all is reduced to the original equality. If they touch while electrising, the equality is never destroy'd, the fire only circulating. Hence have arisen some new terms among us: we say B (and bodies like circumstanced) is electrised *positively*; A, *negatively*. Or rather B is electrised *plus*; A, *minus*. And we daily in our experiments electrise bodies *plus* or *minus*, as we think proper. To electrise *plus* or *minus*, no more needs to be known than this, that the parts of the tube or sphere that are rubbed, do, in the instant of the friction, attract the electrical fire, and therefore take it from the thing rubbing: the same parts immediately, as the friction upon them ceases, are disposed to give the fire they have received, to any body that has less. Thus you may circulate it, as Mr. Watson has shewn; you may also accumulate or subtract it upon, or from any body, as you connect that body with the rubber or with the receiver, the communication with the common stock being cut off."

These passages from Franklin's first letter on his researches may be compared with the quotations from Dufay and Watson. They show that Franklin already had a clearer insight into electricity than his predecessors. In this letter he wrote of *positive* and *negative* electricity for the first time in history. When this terminology is compared with Dufay's *vitreous* and *resinous* electricity, and Watson's more advanced view that the two sorts of electrification were due to an excess or defect of one sort of electricity, it is seen that Franklin has introduced precise, quantitative or mathematical terminology into the subject.

This sort of achievement is a mark of the highest type of scientific mind. In addition, the argument is presented with perfect analytical clarity.

The social aspect of the experiment by which he proves the existence of positive and negative electricity is important. The experiment could not easily have been performed without the help of several intelligent persons. Franklin found these in his Junto society. Thus the existence of the Junto helped the discovery of positive and negative electricity. As Franklin had partly derived the idea of the Junto from Freemasonry, one sees a connection between this movement and electrical theory. Franklin experimented with Leiden jars and analysed their mode of operation in terms of his quantitative electrical conceptions. He found that "The whole force of the bottle, and power of giving a shock, is in the GLASS ITSELF; the non-electrics in contact with the two surfaces serving only to *give* and *receive* to and from the several parts of the glass; that is, to give on one side, and take away from the other.

"This was discovered here in the following manner: Purposing to analyze the electrified bottle, in order to find wherein its strength lay, we placed it on glass, and drew out the cork and wire, which for that purpose had been loosely put in. Then taking the bottle in one hand, and bringing a finger of the other near its mouth, a strong spark came from the water, and the shock was as violent as if the wire had remained in it, which shewed that the force did not lie in the wire.

"Then, to find if it resided in the water, being crouded into and condensed in it, as confin'd by the glass, which had been our former opinion, we electrified the bottle again, and, placing it on glass, drew out the wire and cork as before; then, taking up the bottle, we decanted all its water into an empty bottle, which likewise stood on glass; and taking up that other bottle, we expected, if the force resided in the water, to find a shock from it; but there was none. We judged then, that it must either be lost in decanting, or remain in the first bottle. The latter we found to be true, for that bottle on trial gave the shock, though filled up as it stood with fresh unelectrified water from a teapot. To find, then, whether glass had this property merely as glass, or whether the form contributed anything to it; we took a pane of sash-glass, and, laying it on the stand, placed a plate of lead on its upper surface; then electrified that plate, and bringing a finger to it, there was a spark and shock. We then took two plates of lead of equal dimensions, but less than the glass by two inches every way, and electrified the glass between them, by electrifying the uppermost lead; then separated the glass from the lead, in doing which, what little fire might be in the lead was taken out, and the glass being touched in the electrified parts with a finger, afforded only very small pricking sparks, but a great number of them might be taken from different places. Then dexterously placing it again between the leaden plates, and compleating a circle between the two surfaces, a violent shock ensued. Which demonstrated the power to reside in glass as glass, and that the non-electrics in Contact served only, like the armature of a loadstone, to unite the force of the several parts, and bring them at once to any point desired; it being the property of a non-electric, that the whole body instantly receives or gives what electrical fire is given to, or taken from, any one of its parts."

These experiments demonstrated the fundamental importance of the dielectric or insulator in electrical action, and are direct ancestors of the discovery of radio-waves. They provided the foundation for Faraday's further analysis, and proofs that the seat of electrical action is in the dielectric. From this conception Maxwell elaborated the modern theory of electricity, and deduced the probable existence of radio-waves. The Leiden jar has provided much of the inspiration for modern electrical theory, as Franklin used it to show the importance of activities in dielectrics, and Hertz first proved the existence of radio-waves with its help in 1887. The discharge of the jar is oscillatory, and the surging backwards and forwards of the electricity in the spark sends out radio-waves, as waves radiate from the place where a pebble has dropped into water.

The last paragraph of the quotation from Franklin's explanation of the action of the jar shows that he clearly understood the nature of non-electrics or electrical conductors.

The next paragraph in Franklin's letter continues:

"Upon this we made what we called an *electrical battery*, consisting of eleven panes of large sash-glass, arm'd with thin leaden plates. . . ."

Here Franklin introduced the term "electrical battery" into literature.

In 1749 he wrote that "The electrical matter consists of particles extremely subtile, since it can permeate common matter, even the densest metals, with such ease and freedom as not to receive any perceptible resistance." He considered that the experience of a shock through one's body showed that electricity might pass through, and not merely along the surfaces, of substances.

He ascribed the divergence of the rays in brush discharges to the mutual repulsion of the particles of electricity.

Franklin believed electricity was of one sort only. The positive and negative states described the presence or absence of electricity. This one-fluid theory would not explain why negatively electrified bodies, i. e., bodies without electricity, repelled each other. But the necessary logical modifications are simple.

Franklin's thought and terminology is modern. Of eighteenth-century investigators Franklin could have accommodated his ideas to the modern electron theory of matter with least revision. Franklin supposed that a charged body was surrounded by an atmosphere of electrical particles. He supposed that the appearance of the corona in the dark marked the shape of this atmosphere.

"The force with which the electrified body retains its atmosphere . . . is proportioned to the surface over which the particles are placed . . . so a blunt body presented (to a charged body) cannot draw off a number of (electrical) particles at once, but a pointed one, with no greater force takes them away easily, particle by particle."

Franklin writes that he is not entirely satisfied with these explanations, but as he has nothing better to offer he does not cross them out, "for even a bad solution read, and its faults discovered, has often given rise to a good one."

He says that if there were "no other use discover'd of Electricity this however is something considerable, that it may *help to make a vain man humble*" by deceiving him into false speculations.

He thinks his letter on the Leiden jar "may contain nothing new" or worth reading because the European investigators have probably discovered his results already.

"Nor is it of much importance to us, to know the manner in which nature executes her laws; 'tis enough if we know the laws themselves, 'tis of real use to know that china left in the air unsupported will fall and break; but *how* it comes to fall, and *why* it breaks, are matters of speculation.

"To know this power of points may possibly be of some use to mankind, though we should never be able to explain it."

He then considers the analogy between an electrified cloud and an electrified body.

"I say, if these things are so, may not the knowledge of this power of points be of use to mankind, in preserving houses, churches, ships & cont. from the stroke of lightning, by directing us to fix on the highest parts of those edifices, upright rods of iron made sharp as a needle, and gilt to prevent rusting, and from the foot of those rods a wire down one of the shrouds of a ship, and down her side till it reaches the water? Would not these pointed rods probably draw the electrical fire silently out of a cloud before it came nigh enough to strike, and thereby secure us from that most sudden and terrible mischief?

"To determine the question, whether the clouds that contain lightning are electrified or not, I would propose an experiment . . ."

He describes how electricity might be drawn from an electrified cloud by a pointed rod fixed on the top of a tower or steeple. The experiment was successfully made by Dalibard in Europe. Later, Franklin himself drew electricity from the upper atmosphere with a kite.

The success of the lightning experiments established Franklin's popular fame. He had shown that one of the most mysterious phenomena, which had been associated with supernatural powers since the beginning of human intelligence, was of a material nature, and could be imitated on a small scale in the laboratory.

This was a great contribution to the emancipation of the human imagination, and, as such, of far greater value than the utility of the lightning conductor, which is not very high, as ordinary conductors are inadequate to the discharge of the huge forces released in strokes of lightning.

Franklin invented many other interesting electrical contrivances and theories. He made an electrostatic motor which would run for half-an-hour, driven by the discharge from two Leiden jars. He worked out theories of thunderstorms, and the origin of atmospheric electricity. But sufficient has been given to illustrate his genius.

He transformed the study of electricity into a branch of modern science when he introduced the mathematical terms *plus* and *minus*, or *positive* and *negative*.

This theoretical innovation, and the brilliant experiments from which it was deduced, secured for him the deep respect of the greatest of his intellectual contemporaries, and is the solid basis of his scientific fame.

His spectacular theories and experiments on lightning are of even more cultural than scientific interest. They brought hitherto mysterious phenomena within the range of human reason. Their contribution to modernity was their chief importance.

Incidentally, they gave Franklin a popular, semi-magical fame, which was of enormous assistance to him as a diplomat.

His accounts of his researches were exquisitely modest. He was absolutely without the jealousy common among discoverers. Finally, his scientific writings are composed in an almost incomparably lucid and spacious style.

Rutherford has remarked that the lucidity of Franklin's writings is in marked contrast to the turbidity of the writings of some of his scientific contemporaries, and it is not unreasonable to suppose that Franklin's lucidity is a fair index to the state of his conceptions of electrical actions, and the turbidity of his contemporaries to the state of theirs.

The combination of the qualities and circumstances of Franklin's electrical researches made an overwhelming impression on his generation, for just reasons.

3. LATER LIFE

THE Speech of Polly Baker was published in *The Gentleman's Magazine* in London in the year in which Franklin started his electrical researches, and in the period when his intellect was at the maximum of its creative power. After his youth he rarely dispensed with an urbane style in his writings, and only on occasions when he was deeply moved. He wrote with the plainest directness, and without urbane maneuvers, in some of his dispatches from Paris to America, at the worst crises in the War of Independence. A similar plainness is seen in the style of the *Speech*.

Jefferson writes that Franklin said he wrote it to fill up space in a newspaper when news was slack. It has not been found in Franklin's own newspaper. "The Speech of Miss Polly Baker before a Court of Indicature, at Connecticut near Boston in New England; where she was prosecuted the fifth time, for having a Bastard Child: Which influenced the Court to dispense with her Punishment, and which induced one of her Judges to marry her the next Day—by whom she had fifteen Children." This satire contains the most pointed expression of Franklin's advanced conceptions of personal relationships and morals.

By 1746, at the age of forty, Franklin had virtually retired from business. He received a considerable income from the wealth he had acquired from his holdings in various printing and other businesses. These had provided him with the means and leisure to pursue scientific researches. Thus Franklin's fortune became a little Rockefeller Foundation, whose director combined equal financial and scientific genius. His foundation also enabled him to become a politician and statesman. He vehemently agitated for the creation of militia and defenses in Philadelphia, and his "Plain Truth" pamphlet contains appeals to the people to protect their "persons, fortunes, wives, and daughters" from "the wanton and unbridled rage, rapine, and lust of negroes, mulattoes, and others, the vilest and most abandoned of mankind." He writes that the rich have the means to fly, and may lodge their fortunes in distant and safe places, but "we, the middling people, the tradesmen, shop-keepers, and farmers," cannot. Therefore they must arm, in spite of their Quaker citizens' "mistaken principles of religion, joined with the love of worldly power."

In 1749 Franklin writes that he does not like negro servants and he proposes to sell the two he has at the first good op-portunity. Franklin's later attitude to the negroes is shown in a letter to Condorcet written in 1774. He writes, "the negroes, who are free, live among the white people, but are generally improvident and poor. I think they are not deficient in natural understanding, but they have not the advantages of education. They make good musicians."

The electrical researches of 1746 stimulated his general scientific imagination. He mentions his discovery of the track of the northeast storms which frequently blow on the North American coast. In the same letter to Jared Eliot he comments on the strata of sea shells on the tops of mountains and writes "It is certainly the *wreck* of a world we live on! . . . Farther, about mountains (for ideas will string themselves like ropes of onions)" . . . Some mountains appear to be "divided by nature into pillars," as he saw "somewhere near New Haven."

In 1747 he is "satisfied we have workmen here who can make the apparatus" for electrical experiments "as well to the full as that from London; and they will do it reasonably."

He was elected a member of the Pennsylvania Assembly in 1748.

During 1750–1751 the relations between the English and the French concerning North America were strained. The colonists were anxious about the attitude of the Indians if war should start. Franklin considered this problem, and discussed what sort of population was desirable, and what laws govern the growth of populations, in his "Observations Concerning the Increase of Mankind and the Peopling of Countries." He concluded that in America the "people must at least be doubled every twenty years," as there is "no bound to the prolific nature of plants or animals, but what is made by their crowding and interfering with each other's means of subsistence." He argues that "the labor of slaves can never be so cheap here as the labor of working men is in Britain," and that Americans purchase slaves because they cannot leave their jobs, whereas "hired men are continually leaving their masters (often in the midst of his business) and setting up for themselves.

"Slaves also perjorate the families that use them; the white children become proud, disgusted with labor, and being educated in idleness, are rendered unfit to get a living by industry."

In the same pamphlet he observes that:

"The prince that acquires new territory, if he finds it vacant, or removes the natives to give his own people room," the legislator that promotes trade and agriculture, "and the man that invents new trades, arts, or manufactures, or new improvements in husbandry, may be properly called fathers of their nation."

This pamphlet forestalled the chief conclusion of Malthus' "Essay on Population," besides containing very suggestive contributions to other branches of social science. In it, Franklin used the notion of "natural selection," in connection with population problems; and referred to war as "a plague of heroism."

In 1753 he commented on the laziness of "the poorer English laborers" who came to America, compared with the Germans. He suggested it may be due to "the laws peculiar to England, which compel the rich to maintain the poor." He had observed that the Indians could not be civilized because of their former experience of the easy life of the woods, where food may be collected with very little labor, "if hunting and fishing may indeed be called labor, where game is so plenty." From this he deduces the origin of civilization. "I am apt to imagine that close societies, subsisting by labor and art, arose first not from choice but from necessity, when numbers being driven by war from their hunting grounds, and prevented by seas, or by other nations, from obtaining other hunting grounds, were crowded together into some narrow territories, which without labor could not afford them food."

He is in favor of workhouses, which, he hears, are being established in England. "I should think the poor would be more careful, and work voluntarily to lay up something for themselves against a rainy day, rather than run the risk of being obliged to work at the pleasure of others for a bare subsistence, and that too under confinement." The connection between individualist competition and biological notions of the survival of the fittest, which became prominent in the nineteenth century, are seen here in embryo.

Franklin afterwards foresaw that the high wages paid in America would tend to increase the wage-level in other countries. "The independence and prosperity of the United States of America will raise the price of wages in Europe, an advantage of which I believe no one has yet spoken." He contended that the principle of reducing wages in order to increase exports was mistaken. Exports should be increased by decreasing the price of goods, not by decreasing the wages of the workmen who made them.

"The price of labor in the arts, and even in agriculture, is wonderfully diminishing by the perfection of the machinery employed in them."

He explains that improved machinery and "judicious subdivision of labor" will reduce the costs of production, and hence the price. These principles do not have any logically necessary connection with low wages. High wages attract the best workmen, who spoil fewer tools and material, work faster, and produce the best goods. "The perfection of machinery in all the arts is owing, in a great degree, to the workmen." They make the inventions and improvements.

Low wages are not "the real cause of the advantages of commerce between one nation and another"; but are "one of the greatest evils of political communities."

"Wages in·England are higher than in other parts of Europe, owing to more efficient machinery and labour organization. In America wages are still higher, owing to the special circumstances of high demand for labour in a new country whose population and agriculture are expanding rapidly. The expansion of the American market will increase the demand for goods, and hence increase wages, in Europe. Emigration to America will decrease the number of workmen in Europe, and increase the wages of the remainder through competition."

Franklin discusses the argument that improved technique will not necessarily increase wages, because the very small number of "proprietors and capitalists" will keep wages as low as possible, owing to the operation of forces "inherent in the constitutions of European states." He suggests that "the causes, which tend continually to accumulate and concentrate landed property and wealth in a few hands" may be diminished by political action inspired by the success of the Americans in securing independence and liberty. "The remains of the feudal system might be abolished," the mode of taxation changed, and commercial regulations amended.

The problems of defense against the French and Indians were the occasion for an assembly of commissioners from the various colonies at Albany. Franklin represented Pennsylvania. The question of union had been ardently discussed in the colonies, so Franklin, without instructions from his assembly, presented to the commission a plan containing *Short Hints towards a Scheme for Uniting the Northern Colonies.* Other unauthorized plans were also submitted, but Franklin's was approved.

The scheme consisted of a governor-general, a soldier appointed and paid by the King, and a council containing delegates from the assemblies. The council was to propose acts, which would be carried out, or vetoed, by the governor-general. Its funds were to be drawn from an excise duty on strong liquors.

Franklin said that the assemblies found the scheme gave

too much power to the crown, and the British Government thought it too democratic.

The scheme was the first plan of union of the American colonies which received official discussion. It contained no suggestion of American independence.

The colonists considered the plan gave the crown half the power, whereas "in the British constitution, the crown is supposed to possess but one third, the lords having their share."

As the choice of the commissioners "was not immediately popular, they would be generally men of good abilities for business, and men of reputation for integrity; and that forty-eight such men might be a number sufficient."

Later in 1754 Franklin was asked by Governor Shirley of Pennsylvania to report secretly on a suggestion of the British to nominate members of the proposed grand council and to tax the colonies. John Adams said that "this sagacious gentleman and distinguished patriot, to his lasting honor, sent the governor an answer in writing" which powerfully opposed the suggestion of taxing the colonists "by act of Parliament, where they have no representation," and "excluding the people" "from all share in the choice of the grand council." This answer was published in England twelve years later.

The disputes on taxation became serious by 1757, so Franklin was sent by the Pennsylvania Assembly as their Agent to London to negotiate their disputes with the Penn family, the proprietors of Pennsylvania, and the British Government.

While waiting to embark at New York, he wrote to a friend his reflections on the production of cold by evaporation, of which he had just heard from Professor Simson of Glasgow. He has supposed electricity to be a fluid, and considers heat is also a fluid. Heat expansion is due to the filling of the pores of bodies with the fluid. Melting and evaporation are due to the forcing apart of the constituent particles; "a damp moist air shall make a man more sensible of cold, or chill him more, than a dry air that is colder, because a moist air is fitter to receive and conduct away the heat of his body."

The fluid fire is attracted by plants in their growth and is consolidated with the other materials of which they are formed. When bodies burn, the fluid fire and air escape again.

"I imagine that animal heat arises by or from a kind of fermentation in the juices of the body, in the same manner as heat arises in the liquors preparing for distillation, wherein there is a separation of the spirituous from the watery and earthy parts. And it is remarkable that the liquor in a distiller's vat, when in its highest and best state of fermentation, as I have been informed, has the same degree of heat with the human body—that is, about 94 or 96.

"Thus, as by a constant supply of fuel in a chimney you keep a room warm, so by a constant supply of food in the stomach, you keep a warm body." Clothing does not give a man warmth, but prevents the dissipation of his natural heat. He supposes that mixtures of snow and salt cool because they are better conductors than the constituents. This would explain why the snow and salt appear to dissolve into water, at the low temperature, without freezing.

In another letter he refers to the ancient knowledge in the East of cooling by evaporation. Water flasks were cooled by wrapping in wet woollen cloths. Water in unglazed pots was cooled by evaporation through the pores. The evaporation of sweat therefore explained how the human body kept cool in hot weather, and why the temperature of a live body kept below high summer temperatures, whereas a corpse acquired them. Evaporation explained why reapers in Pennsylvania were liable to drop dead if they did not drink freely. If they did not drink freely, they did not sweat, and so could not be cooled to a healthy temperature. Plants probably remain cool in the sunshine by evaporation. Franklin concludes by suggesting that painful inflammations would be cooled better by rags soaked in spirit than in water, because the spirit evaporates more quickly.

Soon after Franklin arrived in England he sought his relatives and ancestors, showing the characteristic American interest in genealogy.

He took rooms in the house of Mrs. Stevenson of Craven

Street, by the Strand. She had a charming daughter, to whom he enjoyed giving lessons in, and writing letters on, science and learning. In one of these, which has already been quoted, he described experiments by which he had compared the power of different colored bodies to absorb heat radiation from the sun. In another, he summarized the utility of insects to man, and concluded his remarks:

"The knowledge of nature may be ornamental, and it may be useful; but if, to attain an eminence in that, we neglect the knowledge and practice of essential duties, we deserve reprehension. For there is no rank in natural knowledge of equal dignity and importance with that of being a good husband or wife, a good neighbour or friend, a good subject or citizen— that is, in short, a good Christian."

The end of the war between England and France was approaching in 1760. Some in England were in favor of leaving Canada to the French, and taking territory in the West Indies. Franklin combated this view in a pamphlet. He discussed the future of North America, and the need for controlling the unsettled lands of the Mississippi, in the interests of England. The English were jealous of the rise of manufactures in America, because it would damage their export trade. Franklin wrote: "Manufactures are founded on poverty. It is the multitude of poor without land in a country, and who must work for others at low wages or starve, that enables undertakers to carry on a manufacture, and afford it cheap enough to prevent the importation of the same kind from abroad, and to bear the expense of its own exportation.

"But no man, who can have a piece of land of his own, sufficient by his labor to subsist his family in plenty, is poor enough to be a manufacturer, and work for a master. Hence, while there is land enough in America for our people, there can never be manufactures to any amount or value." It was therefore to the interest of England to retain the unsettled lands of Canada, and the West.

He explains that the establishment of industrialism in a sparsely populated country is complicated and cannot be introduced in parts, owing to the subdivision of labor. A complete set of skilled workmen cannot be persuaded to leave their own country. Countries rarely lose established industries, except by bad police oppression or religious persecution. "They sometimes start up in a new place" "like exotic plants," but do not pay "until these new seats become the refuge of the manufacturers driven from the old ones." The presence of manufacturing in any place is not due to soil, climate, or freedom from taxes.

As Agent for Pennsylvania Franklin had to negotiate with the British Government concerning the numerous disputes between the Proprietaries, who had been presented with the land of the province by Charles the Second, and the inhabitants represented by the Assembly. His experiences inclined him to think in 1764 that "the cause of these miserable contentions is not to be sought for merely in the depravity and selfishness of human minds." He suspected "the cause is radical, interwoven in the constitution, and so become the very nature, of proprietary governments; and will therefore produce its effects, as long as such governments continue. And, as some physicians say, every animal body brings into the world among its original stamina the seeds of that disease that shall finally produce its dissolution; so the political body of a proprietary government contains those convulsive principles that will at length destroy it."

In another discussion of proprietary troubles he remarks: "Such is the imperfection of our language, and perhaps of all other languages, that, notwithstanding we are furnished with dictionaries innumerable, we cannot precisely know the import of words, unless we know of what party the man is that uses them."

Franklin returned to America in 1762. In the same year his son William was appointed Governor of New Jersey, at the age of thirty-one years. William Franklin had been born in 1731, the year after Franklin was married, but his mother was not Franklin's wife. He was carefully educated and pushed by his father. Franklin said the appointment was not solicited, and opponents of the British Ministry suggested it was an indirect bribe to embarrass him in his work as Colonial Agent. Thomas Penn, one of the Proprietaries of Pennsylvania, wrote: "I am told you will find Mr. Franklin more tractable, and I believe we shall, in matters of prerogative; as his son must obey instructions, and what he is ordered to do his father cannot well oppose in Pennsylvania." William Franklin became an ardent Royalist. He resolutely resisted the insurgents in the War of Independence, and retired to England with a pension and reparation from the British Government. He died in 1813 at the age of eighty-two years. His son William Temple Franklin was also illegitimate. Franklin took the youth with him to Paris, to act as private secretary, and afterwards repeatedly solicited Congress to give him a place in the diplomatic service. Congress evaded these solicitations. The grandson was of mediocre ability. He was unhappy in America, after living with Franklin for many years in Paris, and finally returned to his father in England, and died at Paris in 1823.

The great wars by which England captured the colonies of France in Canada and India were ended in 1763. The British Government had difficulty in finding the money to pay for the wars, so they decided to tax the American colonies. They considered the Americans owed their protection against France chiefly to the British navy and army, and therefore the Americans should contribute to their cost. The size of the contributions was to be decided by the House of Commons, and not by the colonial assemblies. An act was passed, by which all business and legal transactions in America were declared invalid without stamps. These could be purchased with gold or silver money only. The colonists violently opposed the act, as they disliked paying increased taxes, had real difficulty in finding gold to send to England, owing to the drain on it to pay for imports from England, and disputed the right of the House of Commons to tax them when unrepresented. They contended that taxation without representation was contrary to the principle of British political liberty. At the beginning of this agitation Franklin was again sent to England to protest against the stamp proposals, and to petition for the recognition of Pennsylvania as a crown colony. Nevertheless, the Stamp Act was passed, and the petition failed.

The Stamp Act excited riots in America, and even demonstrations against Franklin's relatives. His wife describes how she prepared to protect her house with firearms against demonstrators.

Franklin was consulted in London by the British authorities on the causes of the uproar. His brilliant advocacy of the colonies' case when examined before members of the House of Commons and explanations to other important persons, weakened the influence of the British Ministry, and helped to force it to resign. The new ministry repealed the act in 1766.

In the summer of 1766 Franklin visited the Continent of Europe with Sir John Pringle, the physician and scientist. They visited Paris in 1767, and Franklin became personally acquainted with many eminent Frenchmen. This contact proved of great importance later in his career. Pringle was elected President of the Royal Society in 1772. When the struggle between the British Ministry and the colonies became acute, George III, in his annoyance with Franklin and the Americans, ordered that the lightning conductors on Kew Palace should have blunt knobs instead of sharp points. Franklin, the inventor of conductors, had directed that the points should be sharp, so that an overcharge of electricity might be dispersed silently and without explosion . . . the question of blunt and sharp conductors became a court question, the courtiers siding with the King, and their opponents with Franklin. The King asked Sir John Pringle to take his side, and give him an opinion in favor of the knobs. To which Pringle replied by hinting that the laws of nature were not changeable at Royal pleasure. It was then intimated to him by the King's authority that a President of the Royal Society entertaining such an opinion ought to resign, and he resigned accordingly.

This incident inspired the epigram:

While you, great George, for safety hunt,
And sharp conductors change for blunt,
The nation 's out of joint.
Franklin a wiser course pursues,
And all your thunder fearless views,
By keeping to the point.

During the discussions concerning the right to tax Americans not represented in the House of Commons, the supporters of taxation argued that many Englishmen who were not represented were nevertheless taxed. Franklin commented: "Copy-holds and lease-holds are supposed to be represented in the original landlord of whom they are held. Thus all the land in England is in fact represented. . . . As to those who have no landed property in a county, the allowing them to vote for legislators is an impropriety. They are transient inhabitants, and not so connected with the welfare of the state, which they may quit when they please, as to qualify them properly for such privilige."

In 1767 Franklin wrote to Lord Kames: "Upon the whole, I have lived so great a part of my life in Britain, and have formed so many friendships in it, that I love it, and sincerely wish it prosperity; and therefore wish to see that union, on which alone I think it can be secured and established. As to America, the advantages of such a union to her are not so apparent. She may suffer at present under the arbitrary power of this country; she may suffer for a while in a separation from it; but these are temporary evils which she will out· grow. Scotland and Ireland are differently circumstanced. Confined by the sea, they can scarcely increase in numbers, wealth, and strength, so as to overbalance England. But America, an immense territory, favoured by nature with all advantages of climate, soils, great navigable rivers, lakes, &c., must become a great country, populous and mighty; and will, in less time than is generally conceived, be able to shake off any shakles that may be imposed on her, and perhaps place them on the imposers. In the meantime every act of oppression will sour their tempers, lessen greatly, if not annihilate, the profits of your commerce with them, and hasten their final revolt; for the seeds of liberty are universally found there, and nothing can eradicate them. And yet there remains among that people so much respect, veneration, and affection for Britain, that, if cultivated prudently, with a kind usage and tenderness for their privileges, they might be easily governed still for ages, without force or any considerable expense. But I do not see here a sufficient quantity of the wisdom that is necessary to produce such a conduct, and I lament the want of it."

In 1767 Franklin wrote a pamphlet against the British Government's embargo on the exportation of corn. He supported the farmers' complaint that the price of corn was reduced. "You say poor laborers cannot afford to buy bread at a high price unless they had higher wages." "I am for doing good for the poor; but I differ in opinion about the means. I think the best way of doing good to the poor is, not making them easy *in* poverty, but leading or driving them *out* of it." "More will be done for their happiness by inuring them to provide for themselves, than could be done by dividing all your estates among them."

In 1767 he wrote against the impressing of seamen; "there being no slavery worse than that sailors are subjected to." Franklin contended that conscription should apply to all citizens, or none. If volunteers could not be attracted, "the end might be answered by giving higher wages."

In 1768 he wrote to his son complaining that an editor of an English paper, "one Jones, has drawn the teeth and pared the nails of my paper, so that it can neither scratch nor bite. It seems only to paw and mumble. . . . I am told there has been a talk of getting me appointed undersecretary to Lord Hillsborough; but with little likelihood, as it is a settled point there that I am too much of an American."

The Parliamentary changes were accompanied by an election. "Great complaints are made that the natural interest of country gentlemen in their neighbouring boroughs is overborne by the moneyed interests of the new people, who have got sudden fortunes in the Indies, or as contractors. *Four thousand pounds* is now the *market price* for a borough. In short, this whole venale nation is now at market, will be sold for about two millions, and might be bought out of the hands of the present bidders (if he would offer half a million more) by the very Devil himself.

"The crown has *two millions a year in places and pensions to dispose of,* and it is well worth while to engage in such a seven years' lottery, though all that have tickets should not get prizes."

Franklin witnessed the scenes of Wilkes' election for Middlesex. The mob smashed the windows of all who refused to illuminate their houses in Wilkes' honor "for an outlaw and an exile, of bad personal character, not worth a farthing." He writes that "property and even life is little more secure in London than on the disturbed American frontiers." The condition of London weakened confidence in the American argument for more democratic government, and direct rule of the colonies under the crown, without the control of the House of Commons. "Mobs patrolling the streets at noonday, some knocking all down that will not roar for Wilkes and liberty; courts of justice afraid to give judgment against him; coal-heavers and porters pulling down the houses of coal merchants that refuse to give them more wages; sailors unrigging all the outward-bound ships, and suffering none to sail till merchants agree to raise their pay; watermen destroying private boats and threatening bridges; soldiers firing among the mobs and killing men, women, and children, which seems only to have produced a universal sullenness, that looks like a great black cloud coming on, ready to burst in a general tempest."

Franklin wrote many years later, in 1781, that "if George the Third had had a bad private character, and John Wilkes a good one, the latter might have turned the former out of his kingdom."

During the tense Anglo-American disputes, and the Wilkes excitements, Franklin made some experiments in hydrodynamics. He and Pringle had observed in Holland that canal boats sailed less quickly in shallow than in deep water. The phenomenon was well-known to the water-men, who knew that a dry summer would slow down canal traffic. Not having found any references to the effect "in our philosophical books," Franklin constructed a hydrodynamical model of a canal, "fourteen feet long, six inches wide, and six inches deep, in the clear, filled with water within half an inch of the edge." The model boat was "six inches long, two inches and a quarter wide, and one inch and a quarter deep. When swimming it drew one inch water. To give motion to the boat I fixed one end of a long silk thread to its bow, just even with the water's edge, the other end passed over a well-made brass pulley of about an inch diameter, turning freely on a small axis; and a shilling was the weight. Then placing the boat at one end of the trough, the weight would draw it through the water to the other."

Franklin measured the time taken by the boat to sail from end to end with water 1½, 2, and 4½ inches deep. The times were respectively 101, 89, and 79 units. He concluded that if "four men or horses would draw a boat in deep water four leagues in four hours, it would require five to draw the same boat in the same time as far in shallow water. . . . Whether this difference is of consequence enough to justify a greater expense in deepening canals, is a matter of calculation, which our ingenious engineers in that way will readily determine."

At the same date he advised a friend to learn to swim by "choosing a place where the water deepens gradually, walk coolly into it till it is up to your breast, then turn round, your face to the shore, and throw an egg into the water between you and the shore. It will sink to the bottom, and be easily seen there. . . ." Franklin gives an elaborate account of how the learner should retrieve the egg, so that he learns to swim during the retrieval.

He describes how he used kites to draw him through the water when he was a boy, and suggests they might be used to assist swimmers trying to cross the English channel from Dover to Calais. He adds that "the packet-boat, however, is still preferable."

In one of the many articles written in 1769 on the Anglo-American dispute, Franklin discusses "the excellency of the invention of colony government, by separate, independent legislatures. By this means, the remotest parts of a great empire may be as well governed as the center; mis-rule, oppressions of proconsuls, and discontents and rebellions thence arising, prevented. By this means the power of a king may be extended without inconvenience over territories of any dimensions, how great soever. America was thus happily governed in all its different and remote settlements, by the crown and their own assemblies, till the new politics took place, of governing it by one Parliament, which have not succeeded and never will."

In another pamphlet he remarks: "ought the rich in Britain, who have made such numbers of poor by engrossing all the small divisions of land, and who keep the laborers and working people poor by limiting their wages,—ought those gentry to complain of the burden of maintaining the poor?"

He visited a large coal mine near Whitehaven in Cumberland during the summer. He noticed the impressions of fossil ferns of coal in seams deep under the sea, and wrote to the French philosopher Dubourg: "I am persuaded, as well as you, that the sea coal has a vegetable origin, and that it has been formed near the surface of the earth; but, as preceding convulsions of nature had served to bring it very deep in many places, and covered it with many different strata, we are indebted to subsequent convulsions for having brought within our view the extremities of its remains, so as to lead us to penetrate the earth in search of it."

Franklin continues to repeat during 1770 his arguments concerning the encroachments of the Lords and Commons on the prerogative of the sovereign. "By our constitutions he is, with his plantation parliaments, the sole legislator of his American subjects." "Let us, therefore, hold fast our loyalty to our

King, who has the best disposition towards us and has a family interest in our prosperity; as that steady loyalty is the most probable means of securing us from the arbitrary power of a corrupt Parliament."

Franklin was deeply interested in the introduction of new industries, such as silk-worm cultivation, into America. In 1771 he quotes Ogilby's description of silk-worm cultivation in China. "They prune their mulberry-trees once a year, as we do our vines in Europe, and suffer them not to grow up into high trees, because through long experience they have learned that the leaves of the smallest and youngest trees make the best silk, and know thereby how to distinguish the first spinning of the threads from the second, viz.: the first is that which comes from the young leaves, that are gathered in March, with which they feed their silkworms; and the second is of the old summer leaves. And it is only the change of food, as to the young and old leaves, which makes the difference in the silk. The prices of the first and second spinning differ among the Chineses. The best silk is that of March, the coarsest of June, yet both in one year."

Franklin comments: "I have copied this passage to show that in Chekiang they keep the mulberry-trees low; but I suppose the reason to be the greater facility of gathering the leaves."

There are other examples in Franklin's writings of his notice of the biological and other aspects of nutrition. He had read reviews of Lind's book on the diseases of seamen. In 1757 Lind published accounts of simple scientifically controlled experiments on the administration of plant products to seamen suffering from scurvy. His experiments showed that dried spinach was useless, as it lost during drying "something contained in the natural juices of the plant" which "no moisture whatever could replace." This is the earliest scientific evidence for the existence of vitamins.

Franklin introduced rhubarb cultivation into America.

In 1771 he corresponded with T. Percival, the chief founder of the Manchester Literary and Philosophical Society. He suggested that a drop of rain may often grow while falling, "attracting to itself such (drops) as do not lie directly in its course by its different state with regard either to common or electric fire."

Differences of common fire, or heat, cause coagulation, as the moisture in warm air coagulates with the walls of a glass containing cold water.

"An electrified body, left in a room for some time, will be more covered with dust than other bodies in the same room not electrified, which dust seems to be attracted from the circumambient air."

Franklin suggests that rain drops may coagulate through a similar electrical process of precipitation, as "we know that the drops of rain are often electrified"; and the falling of hail on hot days shows that great differences of temperature exist in the atmosphere. Hence differences in temperature and electrical charge may explain the growth of rain drops.

In November 1771 he advises his friend Mrs. Hewson (formerly Mary Stevenson, whom he had hoped would have married his son) how to manage her baby. "Pray let him have every thing he likes. I think it of great consequence while the features are forming; it gives them a pleasant air, and, that being once become natural and fixed by habit, the face is ever after the handsomer for it, and on that much of a person's good fortune and success in life may depend. Had I been crossed as much in my infant likings and inclinations as you know I have been of late years, I should have been, I was going to say, not near so handsome, but as the vanity of that expression would offend other folk's vanity, I change it out of regard to them and say a great deal more homely."

Franklin made a tour in Ireland and Scotland in 1771. He was appalled by the contrast between the opulence of the wealthy and the wretchedness of the poor. He writes with reference to the condition of the bulk of the population: "Had I never been in the American colonies" "where every man is a freeholder, has a vote in public affairs, lives in a tidy warm house, has plenty of good food" "but were to form my judgment of civil society by what I have lately seen, I should never advise a nation of savages to admit of civilization; for I assure you that, in the possession and enjoyment of the various comforts of life, compared to these people, every Indian is a gentleman."

In 1772 Franklin visited various English towns and called on Joseph Priestley at Leeds. On July 1st Priestley wrote: "I presume that by this time you are arrived in London, and I am willing to take the first opportunity of informing you that I had never been so busy, or so successful in making experiments, as since I had the pleasure of seeing you at Leeds." Priestley then describes his discovery that sprigs of mint could restore the quality of air rendered noxious by breathing, and other experiments which preceded his discovery of oxygen.

On August 19th, 1772, Franklin described to his son how he was cultivated by the diplomatic corps in London, and treated as an unofficial member, and that his company was so much desired that he rarely dined at home in winter. Learned and ingenious foreigners make a point of visiting him, "for my reputation is still higher abroad than here."

Three days later he was elected one of the eight foreign members of the French Academy of Sciences.

In September he describes his system of *moral or prudential algebra* to Priestley. "Divide half a sheet of paper by a line into two columns; writing over the one *pro* and over the other *con;* then during three or four days' consideration, I put down under the different heads short hints of the different motives, that at different times occur to me, *for* or *against* the measure. When I have thus got them all together in one view, I endeavour to estimate their respective weights; and, where I find two (one on each side) that seem equal, I strike them both out. If I find a reason *pro* equal to some two reasons *con*, I strike out the three. If I judge some two reasons *con*, equal to some three reasons *pro*, I strike out the five; and thus proceeding I find at length where the balance lies; and if, after a day or two of further consideration, nothing new that is of importance occurs on either side, I come to a determination accordingly."

He remembers that the weight of reasons cannot be determined with mathematical exactitude, but he finds the comparative study of the collected reasons improves his judgment, and restrains rashness.

In December, 1772, he observes in a letter: "The people seldom continue long in the wrong, when it is nobody's interest to mislead them."

Franklin performed tolerably well on several musical instruments. He had noticed the sweet tone emitted by rubbing the fingers on wet glasses. He devised an armonica consisting of a series of glass dials on which melodies could be played with clean, damp fingers. These musical interests led him to consider the explanation of the popularity of Scottish and other folk airs. He was an anti-modernist, and criticized advanced contemporary music as cacophonous.

In 1772 the President of the Board of Trade, Lord Hillsborough, drew up a report on the petition of Walpole, Franklin, Sargent and Wharton for permission to make a settlement on the Ohio River. He opposed the petition, but the arguments and influence of Franklin and his friends caused the permission to be granted. Hillsborough was headstrong, and resigned in anger when his advice was not accepted. In his report it is stated that "The great object of colonizing upon the continent of North America has been to improve and extend the commerce, navigation, and manufactures of this kingdom, (Great Britain) upon which its strength and security depend." He quotes the commander-in-chief of the British forces in America: "Let the savages enjoy their deserts in peace."

Hillsborough and the anti-American party did not conceive colonization as the creation of new countries and nations in hitherto savage countries, and could not appreciate Franklin's conception of an empire consisting of self-governing dominions under one crown.

In 1773, Franklin wrote to Dubourg that "as to the magnetism which seems produced by electricity, my real opinion is that these two powers of nature have no affinity with each other, and that the apparent production of magnetism is purely accidental." He considered magnetism due to the movements of a magnetic fluid. In another letter to the same philosopher concerning the nature of death he comments on the preservation of food and of living animals, and remarks that the invention of processes for doing this would be valuable for transporting "those delicate plants which are unable to sustain the inclemency of the weather at sea." He recalls that he has "seen an instance of common flies preserved." "They had been drowned in Madeira wine, apparently about the time when it was bottled in Virginia to be sent hither. (London.) At the opening of one of the bottles at the house of a friend where I then was three drowned flies fell into the first glass that was filled. Having heard it remarked that drowned flies were capable of being revived by the rays of the sun, I proposed making the experiment upon these. They were, therefore, exposed to the sun upon a sieve which had been employed to strain them out of the wine. In less than three hours two of them began by degrees to recover life. They commenced by some convulsive motions of the thighs, and at length they raised themselves upon their legs, wiped their eyes with their forefeet, beat and brushed their wings with their hind feet, and soon after began to fly, finding themselves in Old England, without knowing how they came thither.

"I wish it were possible, from this instance, to invent a method of embalming drowned persons in such a manner that they may be recalled to life at any period, however distant; for having a very ardent desire to see and observe the state of America a hundred years hence, I should prefer to any ordinary death the being immersed in a cask of Madeira wine with a few friends until that time, to be then recalled to life by the solar warmth of my dear country! But since in all probability we live in an age too early and too near the infancy of science to hope to see such an art brought in our time to its perfection, I must for the present content myself with the treat which you are so kind as to promise me of the resurrection of a fowl or a turkey-cock."

Franklin had been in London as Agent of Pennsylvania for seventeen years. Massachusetts and other colonies had also appointed him agent. He was now sixty-seven years old, and thought of retiring. A young Bostonian, named Arthur Lee, who had been educated at Eton, was appointed Agent-designate for Massachusetts. Lee disagreed with Franklin in temperament and opinions, and did not disguise his anxiety for Franklin's return. Franklin refers to this in a letter to a Boston clergyman.

To another Boston clergyman he remarks: "Providence seems by every means intent on making us a great people." While he was noting the growing strength of America, he noted the increasing obstinacy of the King.

In 1773 he writes to his son: "Between you and me, the late measures have been, I suspect, very much the king's own, and he has in some cases a great share of what his friends call *firmness.*"

Franklin wrote to Dr. Percival concerning the high death-rate in Manchester. He considered that the manufacturing life appeared to be unwholesome, owing to lack of housing space, poverty and drinking. "Farmers who manufacture in their own families what they have occasion for and no more, are perhaps the happiest people and the healthiest."

He does not believe that colds are due to damp clothes, moist or fresh air, but over-eating in proportion to exercise. He compared the loss of weight by perspiration when a man is naked, and when he is clothed. A young physician was engaged to sit naked for one hour. His perspiration loss was compared with the loss when clothed, and was found to be almost doubled. Franklin concluded that the notion that common colds are due to stopping pores or obstructing perspiration are ill founded.

Franklin astonished his friends in 1773 by calming the waves on Derwent Water, in the British Lake District, with oil. The report of this experiment raised much interest, so Franklin wrote an account of the subject for the Royal Society. He writes: "I had, when a youth, read and smiled at Pliny's account of a practice among the seamen of his time, to still the waves in a storm by pouring oil into the sea . . . it has been of late too much the mode to slight the learning of the ancients. The learned, too, are apt to slight too much the knowledge of the vulgar. The cooling by evaporation was long an instance of the latter. The art of smoothing the waves by oil is an instance of both.

"In 1757, being at sea in a fleet of ninety-six sail bound against Louisberg, I observed the wakes of two of the ships to be remarkably smooth, while all the others were ruffled by the wind, which blew fresh. Being puzzled with the differing appearance, I at last pointed it out to our captain, and asked him the meaning of it. 'The cooks,' said he, 'have, I suppose, been just emptying their greasy water through the scuppers, which had greased the sides of those ships a little.' And this answer he gave me with an air of some little contempt, as to a person ignorant of what everybody else knew. In my own mind I at first slighted his solution, though I was not able to think of another; but recollecting what I had formerly read in Pliny, I resolved to make some experiments of the effect of oil on water, when I should have opportunity." He was at sea again in 1762, and noticed "the wonderful quietness of oil on agitated water in the swinging glass lamp" "made to hang up in the cabin." "This I was continually looking at and considering as an appearance to me inexplicable. An old sea captain, then a passenger with me, thought little of it, supposing it an effect of the same kind with that of oil put on water to smooth it, which he said was a practice of the Bermudians when they would strike fish, which they could not see if the surface of the water was ruffled by the wind. This practice I had never before heard of, and was obliged to him for the information; though I thought him mistaken as to the sameness of the experiment, the operations being different as well as the effects. In one case the water is smooth till the oil is put on, and then becomes agitated. In the other it is agitated before the oil is applied, and then becomes smooth."

The sea captain also told him that the fishermen of Lisbon reduced the surf on the bar of the river by pouring oil on the water. A person who had often been in the Mediterranean informed him "that the divers there, who, when under water in their business, need light, which the curling of the surface interrupts by the refractions of so many little waves, let a small quantity of oil now and then out of their mouths, which rising to the surface smooths it, and permits the light to come down to them. All these informations I at times revolved in my mind, and wondered to find no mention of them in our books of experimental philosophy.

"At length being at Clapham (London), where there is, on the common, a large pond, which I observed one day to be very rough with the wind, I fetched out a cruet of oil, and dropped a little of it on the water. I saw it spread itself with surprising swiftness upon the surface; but the effect of smoothing the waves was not produced; for I had applied it first on the leeward side of the pond, where the waves were greatest; and the wind drove my oil back upon the shore. I then went to the windward side where they began to form; and there the oil, though not more than a teaspoonful, produced an instant calm over a space several yards square, which spread amazingly, and extended itself gradually till it reached the lee side, making all that quarter of the pond, perhaps half an acre, as smooth as a looking-glass.

"After this I contrived to take with me, whenever I went into the country, a little oil in the upper hollow joint of my bamboo cane, with which I might repeat the experiment as opportunity should offer, and I found it constantly to succeed.

"In these experiments, one circumstance struck me with particular surprise. This was the sudden, wide, and forcible spreading of a drop of oil on the face of the water, which I do not know that anybody has hitherto considered. If a drop of oil is put on a highly polished marble table, or on a looking-glass that lies horizontally, the drop remains in its place, spreading very little. But, when put on water, it spreads instantly many feet round, becoming so thin as to produce the prismatic colors, for a considerable space, and beyond them so much thinner as to be invisible, except in its effect of smoothing the waves at a much greater distance. It seems as if a mutual repulsion between its particles took place as soon as it touched the water, and a repulsion so strong as to act on other bodies swimming on the surface, as straw, leaves, chips, etc., forcing them to recede every way from the drop, as from a centre, leaving a large clear space. The quantity of this force, and the distance to which it will operate, I have not yet ascertained; but I think it is a curious inquiry, and I wish to understand whence it arises.

"In our journey to the north . . . we visited the celebrated Mr. Smeaton, near Leeds. Being about to show him the smoothing experiment on a little pond near his house, an ingenious pupil of his, Mr. Jessop, then present, told us of an odd appearance on that pond which had lately occurred to him. He was about to clean a little cup in which he kept oil, and he threw upon the water some flies that had been drowned in the oil. These flies presently began to move, and turned round on the water very rapidly, as if they were vigorously alive, though on examination he found they were not so. I immediately concluded that the motion was occasioned by the power of the repulsion above mentioned, and that the oil, issuing gradually from the spongy body of the fly, continued the motion. He found some more flies drowned in oil, with which the experiment was repeated before us. To show that it was not any effect of life recovered by the flies, I imitated it by bits of oiled chips and paper, cut in the form of a comma, of the size of a common fly; when the stream of repelling particles issuing from the point made the comma turn round the contrary way. This is not a chamber experiment; for it cannot be well repeated in a bowl or dish of water on a table. A considerable surface of water is necessary to give room for the expansion of a small quantity of oil. In a dish of water, if the smallest drop of oil be let fall in the middle, the whole surface is presently covered with a thin greasy film (and when the film) has reached the sides of the dish, no more will issue from the drop, but it remains in the form of oil; the sides of the dish putting a stop to its dissipation by prohibiting the farther expansion of the film."

Franklin then discusses the mode of the calming action of the oil.

"There seems to be no natural repulsion between water and air, such as to keep them from coming into contact with each other. Hence we find a quantity of air in water; and if we extract it by means of the air pump, the same water again exposed to the air will soon imbibe an equal quantity.

"Therefore air in motion, which is wind, in passing over the smooth surface of water, may rub, as it were, upon that surface, and raise it into wrinkles, which, if the wind continues, are the elements of future waves.

"The small first-raised waves, being continually acted upon by the wind, are, though the wind does not increase in strength, continually increased in magnitude, rising higher, and extending their bases, so as to include a vast mass of water in each wave, which in its motion acts with great violence.

"But if there is a mutual repulsion between the particles of oil, and no attraction between oil and water, oil dropped on water will not be held together by adhesion to the spot whereon it falls; it will not be imbibed by the water; it will be at liberty to expand itself; and it will spread on a surface that, besides being smooth to the most perfect degree of polish, prevents, perhaps by repelling the oil, all immediate contact, keeping it at a minute distance from itself; and the expansion will continue till the mutual repulsion between the particles of the oil is weakened and reduced to nothing by their distance.

"Now I imagine that the wind, blowing over water thus covered with a film of oil, cannot easily *catch* upon it, so as to raise the first wrinkles, but slides over it, and leaves it smooth as it finds it.

"The wind thus prevented from raising the first wrinkles,

that I call the elements of waves, cannot produce waves, which are to be made by continually acting upon, and enlarging those elements," and thus the water is calmed.

"We might suppress the waves in any required place, if we could come at the windward place where they take their rise. This in the ocean can seldom if ever be done. But perhaps something may be done on particular occasions, to moderate the violence of the waves when we are in the midst of them, and prevent their breaking where that would be inconvenient.

"For, when the wind blows fresh, there are continually rising on the back of every great wave a number of small ones, which roughen its surface, and give the wind hold, as it were, to push it with greater force. This hold is diminished, by preventing the generation of those smaller ones. And possibly too, when a wave's surface is oiled, the wind in passing over it may rather in some degree press it down, and contribute to prevent its rising again, instead of promoting it."

Franklin, Banks, Solander, Carnoc and Blagden with Captain Bentinck experimented off the shore near Portsmouth in a blustering wind, to see whether the surf could be reduced by pouring oil on the sea from a large stone bottle. The experiment failed, for the surf on the shore was not sensibly reduced. Franklin suggested they had not used sufficient oil, and had not started pouring the oil sufficiently far from the shore. He thanked his colleagues for their assistance in an experiment that might have contributed to "the improvement of knowledge, such especially as might possibly be of use to men in situations of distress."

No important improvement on Franklin's experiments was made for more than one hundred years. Then, in 1891, Miss Agnes Pockels, an untrained German amateur experimenter, began the investigations of the properties of water surfaces which directed Lord Rayleigh to the conception of unimolecular layers. W. B. Hardy, I. Langmuir, and others have in the last quarter of a century widely extended these researches, which now have the highest practical significance.

The theory of the chemistry and physics of surfaces was

founded by Franklin and still includes his ideas. It is of fundamental importance in many industrial and biological processes, and is one of the most important branches of modern science.

Franklin proposed *An Abridgment of the Books of Common Prayer* in 1773. He had noticed the declining attendance at church, so he prepared a shorter and simpler scheme of common prayer. He rationalized the Prayer Book. The proposal failed completely. Franklin apparently forgot that men do not expect intelligible religion. They do not go to religion for persuasion, but for emotional support. The incident shows he was extremely non-mystical.

Franklin had become an established figure in London since his arrival in 1757. Owing to his skilful representation of the interests of the colonies he gradually became their mouthpiece in England. His discreet personality attracted a group of social friends, and his contributions to science and social philosophy secured him a much respected position in the circles of the Royal and other learned societies.

Faÿ has emphasized the value of his connection with the Freemasons. This consolidated his position.

Its full strength was suddenly revealed in 1774, by the affair of the Hutchinson letters. These had been written by born Americans, urging the British Government to force their countrymen to accept taxation by the House of Commons, without representation in that body. Hutchinson wrote that "there must be an abridgment of what are called English liberties; for a colony cannot enjoy all the liberty of a parent state."

Franklin obtained these letters by means which have never been explained, and sent them to New England, for confidential inspection by a few of the leading politicians. A knowledge of their contents spread, and presently they were published, contrary to Franklin's instructions. Franklin said he thought that if the American protestors knew some influential American-born citizens were advising the British Government

to use force against them, they would become more patient
with the British Government, recognizing that it had been
misled by some of their own people. The event did not promote peace, as Franklin had expected, but raised fury on both
sides of the Atlantic. The Americans were furious with the
machinations against them, and the British Government were
furious that the contents of such secret documents had become
public.

The British Government made Franklin submit to a public
examination concerning his conduct in the affair. He was
called before the Privy Council, consisting of the Lord President, the Secretaries of State, and many other Lords. A number of distinguished visitors such as Edmund Burke and
Joseph Priestley were in the public audience. The examination
was conducted by the Attorney-General, Wedderburn, with
the extremest personal abuse, and the President did not trouble
to preserve decorum among the members of the council, who
laughed and clapped at the Attorney-General's witticisms.

Franklin wore "a full-dress suit of spotted Manchester velvet, and stood conspicuously erect, without the smallest movement of any part of his body. The muscles of his face had been
previously composed, so as to afford a placid, tranquil expression of countenance, and he did not suffer the slightest
alteration of it to appear during the continuance of the speech."

This event destroyed Franklin's hopes for the creation of
an empire of British commonwealths. It finally convinced him
that the governing classes of Britain were not to be persuaded
into a progressive imperial policy. Further, the personal insults
showed that he could no longer hope to be personally assimilated into the British upper classes. His recognition of the
permanency of his exclusion from those classes helped to in-
tensify that part of the Anglo-American conflict which involved
struggles between different social classes. Britain's snub to
Franklin was not only a snub to America, but from a merchant-
landowner class to a class of relatively small property owners.
The bitterness of the Anglo-American contest was increased by

the psychology of class conflict. The American governing classes resented the assumption of superior social status by the English governing classes as much as the English attempts to tax their property. If the Americans had been allowed to feel that the contest was between two groups of gentlemen of equal status for a rich prize, they would perhaps have compromised without independence. But the English would not accept the American leaders as gentlemen. This class division added class hatred to the other motives for dispute, and made the combatants far more implacable.

Franklin felt he had been stupidly and unjustly treated, as indeed he had, even from the point of view of the British governing classes, and the collapse of his political and social aspirations converted him into a relentless enemy.

The British Government withdrew their recognition of his status as a colonial agent, and dismissed him from his position of Deputy Postmaster General of the colonies.

Franklin described to Joseph Priestley in 1774 his recognition of the existence of marsh gas. When passing through New Jersey in 1764 friends told him that if a lighted candle were applied near the surface of certain rivers, "a sudden flame would catch and spread on the water, continuing to burn for near half a minute."

His philosophical friends in England were incredulous. Finley of New Jersey sent the following letter to the Royal Society in 1765: "A worthy gentleman, who lives a few miles' distance, informed me that in a certain small cove of a mill-pond, near his house, he was surprised to see the surface of the water blaze like inflamed spirits. I soon after went to the place, and made the experiment with the same success. The bottom of the creek was mudded, and when stirred up, so as to cause a considerable curl on the surface, and a lighted candle held within two or three inches of it, the whole surface was in a blaze, as instantly as the vapor of warm inflammable spirits, and continued, when strongly agitated, for the space of several seconds. It was at first imagined to be peculiar to that place; but upon trial it was soon found that such a bottom in other places exhibited the same phenomenon. The discovery was accidentally made by one belonging to the mill."

The letter was read to the Royal Society in 1765, but deemed beyond credulity, so it was not printed.

Comparisons of the chemical constitutions of olefiant gas and marsh gas gave John Dalton valuable inspiration in his development of the atomic theory of chemistry. He showed that the marsh gas contained exactly twice as much hydrogen as the olefiant gas for equal contents of carbon. This whole-number relation suggested to him that ultimate particles of marsh gas contained one atom of carbon, and two of hydrogen, while the ethylene particle contained one of each.

Marsh gas occupies an important position in the history of chemical theory, because its constitution could be easily compared with that of other gases containing the same constituents in different proportions, and led to the discovery of the chemical Law of Multiple Proportions; that if two elements combine to form more than one compound, then the weights of one of those elements that combine with a fixed weight of the other bear a simple ratio.

The nature of the origin of marsh gas was also important. As it was found in ditches and marshes, it was particularly apt to interest the self-taught meteorologist, and observer of the country-side, John Dalton. He extracted a large part of the atomic theory out of marsh gas because it came from phenomena of the country-side with which he had a profound acquaintance. His discovery of the Law of the Partial Pressures of Gases arose out of his prolonged studies of the properties of the air, in connection with the weather.

Franklin and Dalton surpassed the London fellows of the Royal Society in being able to recognize the reality of peculiar phenomena. Franklin's recognition that the "will o' the wisp," or flame that flitted over marshes, was an example of gaseous combustion and not a strange illusion, is a parallel to his recognition of the material nature of the flashes of lightning. It is interesting to note that he twice detected the material reality under natural flame phenomena, with lightning, and with marsh gas. He had the power of viewing common things without common illusions, which is one of the rarest intellectual gifts.

Franklin's capacious intellect could advance and follow all these matters, even in the midst of increasing political tension, and political labors. He could still find energy to keep contact with the formative personalities of the time, besides the established politicians and scientists. Tom Paine made his acquaintance, and sailed for America in 1774, with introductions from him. Franklin became the world's intellectual exchange in the third quarter of the eighteenth century.

The dispute between England and America deepened. The English insisted on the Americans accepting tea subject to an import duty from the East India Company. This company had at least seventy nominees who had been bribed into membership of the House of Commons. The Americans preferred not to consume tea which had been taxed without their consent, so they boycotted English tea, and either went without tea, or obtained it from smugglers. The effects of the boycott on the East India Company, and thence on British commerce generally, were profound. The company was left with four million pounds' worth of tea in its warehouses, and the price of its stock fell from 280 to 160, occasioning private bankruptcies and distress. The Government then arranged for the company's tea to be sold duty-free in certain American ports, but without technically repealing the tax. A consignment of tea arrived in Boston. The infuriated population, led by some of the richest citizens, prevented it from being landed, and a number of persons in disguise threw the tea into the harbor.

These events were followed by military actions against the Bostonians by the forces of the British Government.

War between England and the colonies became imminent. Franklin made a last effort to move all influences for peace. He succeeded in meeting Chatham, who had evaded him for eighteen years. The Imperialist statesman considered that the unity of the empire was ultimately more valuable financially and in every way, than the disputed interests of the moment.

He was quite willing to allow considerable self-government to the constituent colonies, but was absolutely against independence.

Franklin helped Chatham with the notes for his speeches against British military compulsion. They complimented each other on their similar ideals for the future of the British Empire, and Franklin assured him that he had never met anyone in America, drunk or sober, who desired independence. It is impossible to believe that Franklin did not deceive Chatham on this point. But Chatham would not proceed without the assurance, so Franklin gave it, and hoped for the best.

He drew up schemes of reconciliation for the secret consideration of the British Government. One of these contained a series of articles, of which the twelfth is particularly interesting. This concerns the conditions of appointment of judges. These were formerly appointed by the crown and paid by the assemblies. The duration of the appointment was decided by the crown, and the duration of the salary by the assemblies. It had been urged against the assemblies that they exerted undue influence over the courts of justice through their control of judges' salaries. The assemblies replied that making them dependent on the crown for the continuance of their places allowed the crown an undue influence; "that one undue influence was a proper balance for the other." The assemblies would grant permanent salaries to the judges, if the crown would consent to retain judges only during *good behavior.*

This passage shows the notion of a balance of forces was included in the mechanism of the proposed administrative arrangements.

Chatham moved in the House of Lords of January 20th, 1775, that the British army should be removed from Boston in order to "allay ferments and soften animosities." Franklin writes that he "was quite charmed with Lord Chatham's speech in support of his motion. He impressed me with the highest idea of him, as a great and most able statesman." He informed Chatham that "he has seen, in the course of life, sometimes eloquence without wisdom, and often wisdom without eloquence; in the present instance he sees both united, and both, as he thinks, in the highest degree possible." It is said that Chatham concluded his speech: "If the ministers thus persevere in *misadvising* and *misleading* the king, I will not say that they can alienate the affections of his subjects from his crown, but I will affirm that they will make the crown *not worth his wearing.* I will not say that the king is betrayed, but I will pronounce that *the kingdom is undone.*

"The motion was rejected. Sixteen Scotch peers, and twenty-four bishops, with all the lords in possession or expectation of places, when they vote together unanimously, as they generally do for ministerial measures, make a dead majority, that renders all debating ridiculous in itself." Chatham was ill, and had lost favor, and was at the end of his career. His last actions showed that his former evasion of Franklin had been an evasion of the American problem, and that his judgment of that problem had been profoundly faulty.

After this, Franklin could do little more, so he sailed for America, not without fear of arrest, and announcing that the death of his wife in 1774 required his return for the settlement of his affairs. They had been parted for nearly ten years. Franklin had corresponded with her loyally, but not very ardently. He had not seemed to mind whether she was in America or England. While he had quite liked her, he was probably not sorry that she had not encumbered his European diplomatic movements.

When he arrived in America he was welcomed by his daughter Sarah, who had become the head of his household. She had married Richard Bache in 1767. The sole surviving descendants of Franklin came through her line. She looked after him during his last years.

The colonies had organized a congress at Philadelphia of leading representatives to discuss what should be done. When Franklin arrived, he was appointed a delegate for Pennsylvania.

He had spent part of his time on the journey over the Atlantic observing the temperature and appearances of the water in the Gulf Stream.

Shortly before his arrival in America, fighting between English soldiers and Americans started at Lexington. Franklin threw himself into the work of defense. *Chevaux-de-frise* were constructed in the River Delaware according to his design, which retarded the advance of the British ships for two months.

The Congress declared the Independence of the United States of America in 1776. They needed aid desperately, for they were fighting the most formidable power in the world. They naturally decided to send Franklin, their most famous citizen, to solicit aid. He sailed again for Europe, to collaborate with Deane and Lee in the negotiation of a treaty of commerce and friendship with France. The success of the American insurrection depended on French aid, and therefore on Franklin, who was the leading personality among the commissioners. He was nearly seventy years old when he set forth on this tremendous task.

The commissioners struggled against the lack of confidence of the French in the future of the United States. The French wanted their traditional enemy to be weakened, but were anxious not to support a losing cause. Unofficial methods of helping the Americans with money were devised by Beaumarchais, but the French would not give more official assistance until they could see more clearly how the contest would end. Franklin, Deane and Lee lived in the midst of a clash of social forces which were to determine the paths of empires and of English and French cultures. Their status was not recognized, and they had little money to finance their activities.

The influence of personalities on the direction of social affairs is often exaggerated, but in some situations it may be great. The balance of social forces in an unstable equilibrium provides such a situation. The French could not make up their minds whether to support the Americans as full allies. While they were trying to decide, the extraordinary personality of

Franklin was constantly before them, as an advertisement of a nation. He was even more famous among French than among other scholars. His electrical researches had at first been appreciated better in France than in England. Besides his fame, he possessed extraordinary vitality. His mind was twenty years younger than his age. He behaved with extreme discretion and modesty, he had social charm, and adapted himself apparently without effort to the manners of the French. Yet the structure of his culture was different from that of the French or the English. Talleyrand said he was remarkable in conversation because of his simplicity and the evident strength of his mind.

Franklin was the first important ambassador of a new nation, and he appeared to be a superman. Presumably other supermen might be found in the place where he came from, so the people he represented were not to be abandoned without much deliberation.

Franklin was the living advertisement of the present and future greatness of America. He fascinated the French while they deliberated. After nearly two years, Washington captured Burgoyne's army at Saratoga. The French now had courage to give the Americans full support. Franklin's rôle and task became more normal. He had to deal with exceedingly complicated diplomatic maneuvers, spying, and intrigue, but it was no longer necessary for him to appear as a magician or superman. His long experience of difficult negotiations, his mastery of journalism and Freemasonry, his intellectual prestige, his understanding of a wide variety of special subjects, enabled him gradually to solve the diplomatic problems.

Franklin's difficulties in Paris were vastly increased by difficulties with his colleagues. The complicated diplomatic and financial maneuvers were beyond Deane's comprehension. Deane could not give a satisfactory account of the financial arrangements, and was suspected of peculation. Arthur Lee was the son of Virginian slave-owners, and had been educated at Eton. He was a member of the governing classes by birth, and was separated by the traditions of class behavior from

Franklin, who had been born in the lower middle class, and had become a member of the governing classes through inherent ability, and not through the possession of traditional governing class position and habits. Lee wished to conduct American affairs in Paris like a man accustomed to government, with aristocratic manners. His class sensitivity was increased by a morbidly suspicious temperament. He suspected the discreet and subtle habits that Franklin had had to acquire in order to rise to power. He believed that Franklin was liable to sell the United States to England or France, and communicated his suspicions to powerful groups in Congress. He even directly suggested that Franklin should be recalled, in favor of himself.

The efficiency of the British spying system in Paris was remarkable. A large fraction of the American Commissioners' acquaintances were in English pay. Great efforts were made after Saratoga to persuade Franklin and his colleagues to accept peace terms which would concede nearly everything except independence and alliance with France.

George III and his advisers sent peace commissions to America partly to avoid negotiating with Franklin. The king wrote to his prime minister, "The many instances of the inimical conduct of Franklin towards this country makes me aware that hatred of this country is the constant object of his mind, and therefore I trust that, fearing the rebellion, colonies may accept the generous offers I am enabled by Parliament to make them by the Commissioners now to be sent to America; that his chief aim in what he has thrown out is to prevent their going. . . . Yet I think it so desirable to end the war with that country, to be enabled, with redoubled ardor, to avenge the faithless and insolent conduct of France, that I think it may be proper to keep open the channel of intercourse with that insiduous man."

Franklin's hatred of the British governing classes was born during his abuse before the Privy Council by Wedderburn.

When he went to Versailles to sign the treaty with France, he wore the "full-dress suit of spotted Manchester velvet," which he had not worn after he had been insulted in it, and he never wore it again after the occasion of the signature of the treaty.

Franklin continued his philosophic interests in the midst of his great diplomacy. He attended the Academy of Sciences regularly. He read a paper on the *Aurora Borealis* in 1779. He ascribed it to the action of electricity in the upper atmosphere, which, being at a low pressure, would be a good conductor of electricity. He supposes the electricity is brought into the polar regions on the raindrops of clouds, which drift there with the hot air rising from the tropics and falling near the poles. Atmospheric electricity is normally able to escape in lightning discharges, but cannot so escape in the polar regions, he believes, because those regions are covered with ice, which is a non-conductor. The melting of the ice-cap in summer would explain why the *Aurora* is weaker in summer than in winter.

He supposes that the polar air owing to its extra density offers more resistance to the electric matter passing through it, and thus makes it visible.

"The rays of electric matter issuing out of a body, diverge by mutually repelling each other, unless there be some conducting body near to receive them; and if that conducting body be at a greater distance, they will *first diverge*, and then *converge*, in order to enter it. May not this account for some of the varieties of figure seen at times in the *motions* of the luminous matter of the aurorae?"

Franklin is here using the notion of lines of force.

About the same time he wrote to the *Journal of Paris* about *An Economical Project*. This was a suggestion of systematic early rising in order to use daylight fully and save the cost of illumination. He calculates "that the city of Paris might save every year by the economy of using sunshine instead of candles" the sum of $25,000,000,000, or £5,000,000.

He proposes to make the people rise early by taxing window shutters, restricting the sale of candles, stopping vehicular traffic after dark, and ringing church bells at dawn.

The plan of advancing time by the clock, as in the modern

systems of Summer Time, apparently did not occur to him. The proposal of systematic daylight saving by the son of a candle maker is an example of the influence of industrial experience on the conception of inventions for the improvement of the organization of social life.

In 1779 Franklin issued a general order to the captains of American ships to give a safe passage to Captain Cook, whose return from his last world voyage was expected. Franklin believed science, medicine, and even all productive labor should be exempt from interference during war. He persuaded the Congress not to put an embargo on the import of English scientific instruments and learned books, and was proud of incorporating a similar provision in the Constitution of Pennsylvania.

Franklin's interest in economics procured him the friendship of the French physiocrats and economists. His belief in the superiority of farming to industry as a foundation of society agreed with that of the physiocrats. As Faÿ remarks, the French liberal economists drew him away from the ideas of the British mercantile economists. But Franklin had emancipated himself before he met them. The French economic thinkers did not provide him with principles, but added enthusiasm to them. Franklin showed more optimistic belief in humanity after his contact with the French, but not a new economic philosophy.

He wrote from France in 1779 concerning the liquidation of the national debt by the depreciation of paper money:

"This effect of paper currency is not understood on this side the water. And indeed the whole is a mystery even to the politicians, how we have been able to continue a war four years without money, and how we could pay with paper that had no previously fixed fund appropriated specifically to redeem it. This currency, as we manage it, is a wonderful machine. It performs its office when we issue it; it pays and clothes the troops and provides victuals and ammunition; and when we are obliged to issue a quantity excessive, it pays itself off by depreciation."

Franklin's remarks on "managed currency" and its value in social crises have a modern air.

Franklin continued to correspond with Priestley, Price and other English protestant philosophers.

"Dr. Priestley, you tell me, continues his experiments with success. We make daily great improvements in *natural*—there is one I wish to see in *moral*—philosophy: the discovery of a plan that would induce and oblige nations to settle their disputes without first cutting one another's throats."

He writes to Priestley: "I always rejoice to hear of your being still employed in experimental researches into nature, and of the success you meet with. The rapid progress *true* science now makes, occasions my regretting sometimes that I was born so soon. It is impossible to imagine the height to which may be carried, in a thousand years, the power of man over matter. We may perhaps learn to deprive large masses of their gravity, and give them absolute levity, for the sake of easy transport. Agriculture may diminish its labor and double its produce; all diseases may by sure means be prevented or cured, not excepting even that of old age, and our lives lengthened at pleasure even beyond the antediluvian standard. O that moral science were in as fair a way of improvement, that men would cease to be wolves to one another, and that human beings would at length learn what they now improperly call humanity!"

"The greatest discovery made in Europe for some time past is that of Dr. Ingenhousz's relating to the great use of the leaves of trees in producing wholesome air."

Then he describes Rochon's invention of a range-finder based on the double refraction by Iceland spar.

The anti-Catholic Gordon riots occurred in London in 1780. Franklin wrote to a friend: "The beginning of this month, a mob of fanatics, joined by a mob of rogues, burned and destroyed property to the amount, it is said, of a million sterling." After these riots Gibbon wrote: "Our danger is at an end, but our disgrace will be lasting, and the month of June 1780 will ever be marked by a dark and diabolical fanaticism which I had supposed to be extinct, but which actually subsists in Great Britain perhaps beyond any other country of Europe."

Franklin and Gibbon were in some agreement on the Gordon riots, but on each other, they were not. Franklin once found that Gibbon was staying in an inn at which he had just arrived. He sent an invitation to Gibbon, who was upstairs, to spend the evening with him, and received the answer that it was impossible to converse with a "revolted subject." Franklin replied that when "the decline and fall of the British Empire should come to be his subject," he "would be happy to furnish him with ample material which was in his possession."

Franklin objected to religious tests for citizenship and appointments. "I think they were invented not so much to secure religion itself as the emoluments of it."

Some experiences with the swelling of mahogany wood in Europe drew his attention to the humidity of the air. He remarks: "The greater dryness of the air in America appears from some other observations. . . ."

Veneer woods which were durable in Europe "never would stand with us," the thin sheets shrank, and "were for ever cracking and flying."

"In my electrical experiments there, it was remarkable that a mahogany table, on which my jars stood under the prime conductor to be charged, would often be so dry, particularly when the wind had been some time at northwest, which with us is a very drying wind, as to isolate the jars." . . . "I had a like table in London . . . but it was never so dry as to refuse conducting the electricity."

In 1781 Franklin found himself "rather inclined to adopt that modern" view "which supposes it best for every country to leave its trade entirely free from all incumbrances."

During a visit to Hanover, he met an educated man, who subsequently applied to him for a place as a soldier. He remarked that he could not "conceive what should reduce him to such a situation as to engage himself for a soldier."

The difficulties of the American commissioners in their negotiations and between themselves became almost unmanageable. Lee was recalled and Franklin offered to resign. Deane was recalled owing to misunderstandings of his affairs. Franklin's offer was not accepted, and Adams and Jay were sent to join Franklin and Lee as commissioners with authority to make peace with England when permissible. The quarrels continued almost as ferociously. Adams was a very able man. The appointment of Washington as commander-in-chief of the American Army was chiefly due to him, and he was probably the most influential politician in Congress. Though extremely honest, Adams was introspective and sensitive. He was little and fat, and was unable to carry off his appearance without looking slightly comic. Paris could not imagine that he could be more important in American home politics than such an immense personality as Franklin. Adams did not receive very much notice. He felt slighted. He was also inexperienced in the technique of European diplomacy. When he asserted himself the French objected to his diplomatic manners. This increased his anger, and his introspective suspicions. His psychological state had put him in sympathy with Lee. Further, his principles of social philosophy were far nearer to Lee's than to Franklin's.

A measure of Franklin's discretion and diplomatic subtlety is given by his skilful management of this very difficult situation. Adams was perhaps the most powerful American of the moment, but Congress decided that Franklin must become the sole American ambassador to France, while Adams was appointed to Holland, and Jay to Spain.

Franklin had always been susceptible to attractive women. His amiability was an essential factor in his marvelous success at Paris. He was very friendly with the widow of the philosopher Helvetius, and may have proposed to her when he was seventy-five. In one of his letters to her, he discussed why her house was one of the most distinguished and frequented salons in Europe. He ascribed it to her power of making everyone feel happy there.

Mrs. John Adams, who in her own style was also a charming woman, wrote of a visit to Mme. Helvetius: "She entered the room with a careless, jaunty air; upon seeing ladies who were strange to her, she bawled out, 'Ah! mon Dieu, where is Franklin? Why did you not tell me there were ladies here?' You must suppose her speaking this in French. 'How I look!' said she, taking hold of a chemise made of tiffany, which she had on over a blue lute-string, and which looked as much upon the decay as her beauty, for she was once a handsome woman; her hair was frizzled; over it she had a small straw hat, with a dirty gauze half-handkerchief round it, and a bit of dirtier gauze than ever my maids wore was bowed on behind. She had a black gauze scarf thrown over her shoulders. She ran out of the room; when she returned, the Doctor entered at one door, she at the other; upon which she ran forward to him, caught him by the hand, 'Helas! Franklin'; then gave him a double kiss, one upon each cheek, and another upon his forehead. When we went into the room to dine, she was placed between the Doctor and Mr. Adams. She carried on the chief of the conversation at dinner, frequently locking her hand into the Doctor's, and sometimes spreading her arms upon the backs of both the gentlemen's chairs, then throwing her arm carelessly upon the Doctor's neck.

"I should have been greatly astonished at this conduct, if the good Doctor had not told me that in this lady I should see a genuine Frenchwoman, wholly free from affectation or stiffness of behaviour, and one of the best women in the world. For this I must take the Doctor's word; but I should have set her down for a very bad one, although sixty years of age, and a widow. I own I was highly disgusted, and never wish for an acquaintance with any ladies of this cast. After dinner she threw herself upon a settee, where she showed more than her feet. She had a little lap-dog, who was, next to the Doctor, her favourite. This she kissed, and when he wet the floor she wiped it up with her chemise. This is one of the Doctor's most intimate friends with whom he dines once every week, and she with him. She is rich, and is my near neighbour; but I have not yet visited her. Thus you see, my dear, that manners differ exceedingly in different countries. I hope, however, to find amongst the French ladies manners more consistent with my ideas of decency, or I shall be a mere recluse."

Franklin was informed of the defeat of Cornwallis, and the virtual collapse of the British campaign, in the autumn of 1781. The long negotiations for the final peace commenced. Of the English he wrote: "though somewhat humbled at present, a little success may make them as insolent as ever. I remember that, when I was a boxing boy, it was allowed, even after an adversary said he had enough, to give him a rising blow. Let ours be a douser."

He took shares in the newly-formed National Bank.

He restrained Congress from asking too much of the French. "This is really a generous nation, fond of glory, and particularly that of protecting the oppressed. Trade is not the admiration of their noblesse, who always govern here. Telling them their *commerce* will be advantaged by our success, and that it is their interest to help us, seems as much as to say, 'Help us, and we shall not be obliged to you.' Such indiscreet and improper language has been sometimes held here by some of our people, and produced no good effects."

A friend sent him a copy of Cowper's poems. "The relish for reading poetry had long since left me; but there is something so new in the manner, so easy and yet so correct in the language, so clear in the expression, yet concise, and so just in the sentiments, that I have read the whole with pleasure, and some pieces more than once."

In 1782, Franklin wrote to Priestley that he would rejoice if he could recover the leisure to search "into the works of nature; I mean the *inanimate*, not the *animate* or moral part of them; the more I discovered of the former, the more I admired them; the more I know of the latter, the more I am disgusted with them. Men I find to be a sort of beings very badly constructed, as they are generally more easily provoked than reconciled, and more disposed to do mischief to each other than make reparation. . . ." He suggests that as Priestley grows older he may "repent of having murdered in mephitic air so many honest, harmless mice, and wish that, to prevent mischief, you had used boys and girls instead."

A few days later he writes to another friend "I have been apt to think that there has never been, nor ever will be, any such thing as a *good* war, or a *bad* peace."

The peace negotiations between America, England and France dragged on and on, and were conducted with suspicion and clumsiness by every participating government.

At the age of seventy-six years, Franklin had to exert intellectual direction over the conflicting political forces. His mental alertness and vigor in these affairs were quite extraordinary, but few persons, especially his American colleagues, understood that his physical lassitude, partly due to gout, and partly to "diplomatic illnesses" for bluffing negotiators, did not reflect the activity of his political intelligence. He was accused of apathy in his country's cause.

Franklin's colleague Jay was of Huguenot descent, and like Adams a Puritan. He had an excellent character, but his traditions excited suspicion against the French Catholic monarchist politicians. Though his temperament was more amiable than Adams', his political principles were fundamentally similar. He is reported to have said in negotiations with an English peace commissioner concerning security for the guarantee of peace that "he would not give a farthing for any parchment security whatever. They had never signified anything since the world began, when any prince or state, of either side, found it convenient to break through them. But the peace he meant was such, or so to be settled, that it should not be the *interest* of either party to violate it. This, he said, was the only security that could be proposed to prevent those frequent returns of war, by which the world was kept in continual disturbance."

Almost at the same moment, Franklin was assisting a poor peasant from Provence to publish schemes for making peace treaties durable, and was trying to have privateering outlawed in warfare between nations.

The lawyer Jay had no faith in international law, while Franklin hoped that the cruelty of war might be mitigated by the gradual extension of agreed prohibitions on violence against civilians.

Franklin continued to follow his scientific interests. He discussed the reports of live toads being found in stone, and how long they might have been there. Pringle had written to him in 1780:

> "Sir:—Last year I had the honor to inform you that two of those large moths called Muskitoe Hawks, which appear about September, and disappear about the beginning of December, lived seventy-one days after I had cut their heads off with a pair of scissors."

In 1782 he outlined a nebular theory of the origin of the earth, to account for the facts of geology, such as buried coal strata. "I should conceive, that, all the elements in separate particles being originally mixed in confusion, and occupying a great space, they would (as soon as the almighty fiat ordained gravity, or the mutual attraction of certain parts, and the mutual repulsion of others, to exist) all move to their common centre.

"The original movement of the parts towards their common centre would naturally form a whirl there." He is pleased to hear of the "ferruginous nature of the lava which is thrown out of the depths of our volcanoes.

"It has long been a supposition of mine that the iron contained in the surface of the globe has made it capable of becoming, as it is, a great magnet; that the fluid of magnetism perhaps exists in all space; so that there is a magnetical north and south of the universe as well as of this globe, and that, if it were possible for a man to fly from star to star, he might govern his course by the compass; that it was by the power of this general magnetism this globe became a particular magnet."

He supposes the shape of the earth may have been changed by shifts of the axis. As the equatorial diameter is many miles greater than the polar, this would produce flooding by the seas, and the laying of new strata on the tops of old mountains.

The contact of water and fire under the earth may produce explosive shocks that send waves through the "internal ponderous fluid." These waves will pass under all countries, and shake them.

"Men cannot make new matter of any kind."

In 1783 he corresponded with the Italian scholar Filangieri on the principles of the American Constitutions. According to Bigelow, it is said that the correspondents became impressed by the American concern to place restrictions on the popular will, while the European philosophers and democrats wished to abolish such restrictions.

The quarrel between Adams and Franklin became public in 1783. Adams abused the intentions of the French minister de Vergennes, even in front of English ministers, and had for years been attacking Franklin through his friends and relatives in Congress. Franklin had hitherto ignored these attacks, but at last he had to warn the Congress against Adams' attacks. He summarized their nature, and then delivered an immortal judgment of his able colleague:

"I am persuaded, however, that he means well for his country, is always an honest man, often a wise one, but sometimes, and in some things, absolutely out of his senses."

In spite of the most distracting political quarrels, and his age, he preserved his interest in science.

The Brothers Montgolfier demonstrated their hot-air balloon in 1783. The invention excited great interest, and later in the year Saint Fond, the Roberts, and Charles constructed a varnished silk balloon filled with hydrogen manufactured by treating iron filings with weak sulphuric acid. The diameter of the balloon was twelve feet. It was released in Paris before an enthusiastic crowd of five thousand persons, including Franklin. An attached note requested the finder to return the balloon. It fell twelve miles distant, and was reported to contain some ice.

Franklin sent lively descriptions of the experiments to Sir Joseph Banks, the President of the Royal Society, and subscribed to funds for further experiments. He immediately considered that the invention "may pave the way to some discoveries in natural philosophy of which at present we have no conception." He thought that persons might bound across the country attached to small balloons, so that they would press the earth with a weight of not more than ten pounds. Horses might be assisted in the same way. Water might be frozen by hauling it up to a captive balloon, and persons might be given a view of the country from a height of one mile, for a guinea, etc.

"A few months since the idea of witches riding thro' the air upon a broomstick, and that of philosophers upon a bag of smoke, would have appeared equally improbable and ridiculous.

"These machines must always be subject to be driven by the winds. Perhaps mechanic art may find easy means to give them progressive motion in a calm, and to slant them a little in the wind.

"Beings of a frank and *Sic* nature far superior to ours have not disdained to amuse themselves with making and launching balloons, otherwise we should never have enjoyed the light of those glorious objects that rule our day and night, nor have had the pleasure of riding round the sun ourselves upon the balloon we now inhabit."

Franklin sent an admirable description of the ascent of Charles and Robert to Banks. "Never before was a philosophical experiment so magnificently attended."

A small balloon fell in a direction contrary to that of the ground wind. Franklin remarks that a knowledge of the different directions of winds at different heights "may be of use to future aërial voyagers."

He wrote to Ingenhousz that ballooning appears "to be a discovery of great importance, and what may possibly give a new turn to human affairs. Convincing sovereigns of the folly of wars may perhaps be one effect of it, since it will be impracticable for the most potent of them to guard his dominions. Five thousand balloons, capable of raising two men each, could not cost more than five ships of the line, and where is the prince who can afford so to cover his country with troops for its defense as that ten thousand men descending from the clouds might not in many places do an infinite deal of mischief before a force could be brought together to repel them?" Franklin's previsions of the possibilities of aërial warfare have been fulfilled brilliantly. The military experiments of landing hundreds of troops behind the supposed enemy's lines by parachutes are today familiar to the newspaper reader.

He reports to Ingenhousz that Morveau has proposed filling the balloons with gas "made from sea coal"—coal-gas.

Owing to his interest in balloons, he received "a letter in France, the first through the air, from England." Thus Franklin received the first Anglo-French air-mail delivery.

Meanwhile the definitive peace treaties between all the belligerent powers were signed at last, in September, 1783.

News from America that the people are remiss in paying taxes prompts him to express his conception of property.

"All property, indeed, except the savage's temporary cabin, and other little acquisitions absolutely necessary for his subsistence, seems to me the creature of public convention. Hence the public has the right of regulating descents, and all other conveyances of property, and even of limiting the quantity and uses of it. All the property that is necessary to a man, for the conservation of the individual and the propagation of the species, is his natural right, which none can justly deprive him of; but all property superfluous to such purposes is the property of the public, who, by their laws, have created it, and who may therefore by other laws dispose of it, whenever the welfare of the public shall demand such disposition. He that does not like civil society on these terms, let him retire and live among savages. He can have no right to the benefits of society who will not pay his club towards the support of it."

Franklin was visited in 1783 by Baynes and Romilly, who were then young men. Bigelow quotes Baynes' notes of their conversations. Franklin discussed the plans of Price and others for a general peace in Europe. He thought it would be difficult to persuade the various sovereigns to send delegates to one place "but if they would have patience, I think they might accomplish it, agree upon an alliance against all aggressors, and agree to refer all disputes between each other to some third person, or set of men, or power. Other nations, seeing the advantage of this, would gradually accede; and perhaps in one hundred and fifty or two hundred years, all Europe would be included."

Franklin's lower limit for the date of a successful league of nations was 1933. The event showed his estimate was partially correct; perhaps by 1983 it will have become adequately verified.

Samuel Romilly, the English legal reformer, wrote in his diary: "Of all celebrated persons whom in my life I have chanced to see, Dr. Franklin, both from his appearance and his conversation, seemed to me the most remarkable. His venerable patriarchal appearance, the simplicity of his manner and language, and the novelty of his observations, at least the novelty of them at that time to me, impressed me with an opinion of him as one of the most extraordinary men that ever existed."

Franklin read to him some passages from the American Constitutions, and expressed surprise that the French Government had allowed them to be published. They made a "very great sensation in Paris, the effects of which were felt many years afterwards."

The psychologist and charlatan, Mesmer, appeared in Paris in 1784. He became very fashionable, and was supported by Lafayette, and other eminent persons. The Academy of Sciences was requested by the King to report on Mesmer's claims. Franklin and Lavoisier were appointed members of the committee of investigation. Mesmer refused to make any experiments under expert observation, but his disciple Desson offered to make demonstrations. These were done at Franklin's garden at Passy. The investigators easily proved that Desson consciously or unconsciously attempted to deceive the audience. Franklin pointed out in an unpublished paragraph of the report the relation between the emotionalism of the Mesmerists and eroticism. Mesmer fled, discredited, but his pupil de Puysegur demonstrated some of the phenomena of hypnosis, such as controlled automatism and insensibility to pain, in 1785. Franklin helped to expose the mistakes, or swindling in Mesmerism, but he did not help the recognition of its valuable part, which was an important psychological discovery.

Franklin was interested in the improvement of the technique of printing. French printers had proposed that type containing groups of letters should be used in order to save time in composition. Franklin devised his own scheme of "logography," as it is called. John Walter, the founder and printer of the London *Times*, discussed logography with Franklin and originally printed the journal with such type. The experiment was expensive, and unsuccessful, as the time saved in composition was lost in distributing the type.

Franklin was asked in 1784 by the American astronomer Rittenhouse to describe his speculations on the nature of light and matter. His reply contained expressions of scientific faith which form an interesting parallel with the famous address given by Faraday at the Royal Institution in 1846. A lecturer was unable to fulfil his engagement, so at the last moment Faraday offered some extempore "Thoughts on Ray-vibrations." One of these consisted of the electro-magnetic wave-theory of light: "The view which I am so bold as to put forth considers, then, radiation as a high species of vibration in the lines of force, which are known to connect particles and also masses of matter together. It endeavours to dismiss the ether, but not the vibrations."

Franklin suggested that "universal space, as far as we know it, seems to be filled with a subtile fluid, whose motion, or vibration, is called light.

"The power of man relative to matter seems limited to the dividing it, or mixing the various kinds of it, or changing its form and appearance by different compositions of it, but does not extend to the making or creating of new matter, or annihilating the old. Thus, if fire be an original element, or kind of matter, its quantity is fixed and permanent in the world."

The germs of the theories of the conservation of mass and energy are seen in these notions.

Franklin suggested in 1784 for the first time in Europe or America the use of water-tight bulkheads in the construction of ships. He had had some part in the management of the packet or postal and message boat service between England and America, so he had had some professional interest in ships. When the French proposed to start a packet service after the peace, he advised that "as these vessels are not to be laden with goods, their holds may, without inconvenience, be divided into separate apartments after the Chinese manner, and each of those apartments caulked tight so as to keep out water. In which case if a leak should happen in one apartment, that only would be affected by it, and the others would be free; so that the ship would not be so subject as others to founder and sink at sea. This being known would be a great encouragement to passengers."

Franklin invented bifocal spectacles. He describes in 1785 how he was prompted to do so. "I had formerly two pair of spectacles, which I shifted occasionally, as in travelling I sometimes read, and often wanted to regard the prospects. Finding this change troublesome, and not always sufficiently ready, I had the glasses cut, and half of each kind associated in the same circle. By this means, as I wear my spectacles constantly, I have only to move my eyes up or down, as I want to see distinctly far or near, the proper glasses being always ready. This I find more particularly convenient since my being in France, the glasses that serve me best at table to see what I eat not being the best to see the faces of those on the other side of the table who speak to me; and when one's ears are not well accustomed to the sounds of a language, a sight of the movements in the features of him that speaks helps to explain; so that I understand French better by the help of my spectacles."

Franklin left Europe in 1785. His health had become weak, as he suffered from gall-stones. He could not walk much, nor ride on horseback, or in an ordinary carriage. On his departure he received magnificent expressions of regard and honor, and was carried in the Queen's litter to his ship.

At Southampton he was met by his son, who had recently revived relations with him. His reply to his son's letter contains expressions of his views on the involuntary nature of human opinions, and the relations between personal and political duties. He wrote that the meeting would be very agreeable to him. "Indeed, nothing has ever hurt me so much, and affected me with such keen sensations, as to find myself deserted in my old age by my only son."

But "our opinions are not in our own power, they are formed and governed much by circumstances that are often as inexplicable as they are irresistible." He considered his son might have remained neutral in the struggle, and not have taken up arms against his father's countrymen, as there "are natural duties which precede political ones, and cannot be extinguished by them."

Though he was seventy-nine years old, and departing from Europe gloriously, he was not distracted from work during the voyage by the multitudes of memories that must have risen in his mind, as he watched the ocean.

He wrote long descriptions of various scientific matters which he had not been able to describe before, owing to lack of time.

He described a boat he had seen on the Seine, driven by air-screws turned by hand.

He made the first scientific study of the Gulf Stream, with numerous measurements of the temperature of the water.

"This stream is probably generated by the great accumulation of water on the eastern coast of America between the tropics, by the trade winds.

"I find that it is always warmer than the sea on each side of it, and that it does not sparkle at night." The differences of temperature were about $6°$ F.–$10°$ F. and the water was frequently warmer than the air above.

He suggests that it warms the air above, and forms "those

tornados and waterspouts frequently met with and seen near the stream." The condensation of the moisture in this warm air by the cold water of Newfoundland produces the fogs there. The drift of the stream is sufficient to retard a sailing vessel sixty or seventy miles in a day. Franklin drew a chart of the stream from information supplied him by American sea-captains. The temperature of water at various depths was obtained by letting down corked bottles. At thirty-five fathoms the cork was stove in by the water pressure. When hauled to the surface the temperature of the water in the bottle was 6° F. lower than that of the surface water.

He records more of his ideas on fireplaces and ventilation. He complains that architects "have no other ideas of proportion in the opening of a chimney than what relates to symmetry and beauty, respecting the dimensions of the room, while its true proportion, respecting its function and utility, depends on quite other principles; and they might as properly proportion the step in a stair-case to the height of a story instead of the natural elevation of men's legs in mounting."

This contains the statement of the principle of modern functionalist architecture. "In time, perhaps, that which is fittest in the nature of things may come to be thought handsomest." "Some, I know," are "so bigoted to the fancy of a large, noble opening, that rather than change it, they would submit to have damaged furniture, sore eyes, and skins almost smoked to bacon."

Franklin was opposed to the abolition of capitals for nouns in printing. He considers it less easy to understand the meaning of passages without capitals. The modern functionalist printers do not use capitals, so he would not have been in agreement with them on that point. He disliked gray printing and preferred black.

He describes experimental models by which the ventilation of buildings could be investigated.

He suggests that mines could be ventilated by tall chimneys, which commonly produce vertical draughts through temperature differences between the walls and the air inside.

If the chimney be painted black it will absorb more heat from the sun's rays, and hence produce more draught.

His physical infirmity prompted him to invent an instrument for lifting books off high shelves in his library. This consisted of two thin laths on the end of a stick. The laths could be inserted round the desired book, and then clapped tight by a string.

In 1787 Franklin, who had introduced Tom Paine to America, gave him an introduction to Rochefoucauld, asking him to assist the development of Paine's invention of the iron bridge. The pamphleteer was the first to suggest that bridges should be built of iron, and made a model to illustrate his idea.

Franklin was in favor of free-trade, but considered direct taxes impracticable in a sparsely populated country. He agreed in 1787 with his friend Morellet that "liberty of trading, cultivating, manufacturing, etc." is preferable "even to civil liberty, this being affected but rarely, the other every hour."

Franklin was elected a delegate to the Convention for the new Constitution. He was eighty-one years old, and had little influence on the deliberations. It is said that friendly guards were set to watch him in company, and prevent him from giving away the Convention secrets.

He did not approve of the Constitution, but proposed that it should be signed unanimously, for the sake of unity. According to Jefferson, in his proposal of the general signature, Franklin said that it did not fully accord with his sentiments, but he had lived long enough to have experienced that one should not rely too much on one's own judgment. He had often found himself mistaken in his favorite ideas. He repeated that he materially objected to certain points, but as the Constitution was the best possible under the circumstances, it should go forth with united signatures.

He informed his French friend Veillard that he did not consider two chambers of representatives necessary. He hoped the Congress would soon improve the Constitution. He believed his countrymen "are *making experiments* in politics," as he wrote to Rochefoucauld.

His faculties waned in extreme old age. He was unable to perceive the genius of John Fitch, who built the first steamboat. Fitch's boat plied on the Delaware River in 1788. Franklin saw it and described the sight in letters to friends. But he would not subscribe for the continuation of Fitch's experiments. When the inventor called on him, he was offered six dollars as a charitable gift, which was not to be accepted as a subscription for the boat. He declined the offer, and was quietly infuriated. Fitch was unlettered and uncouth. His boat broke down, and he was considered crazy. He emigrated to Kentucky, and committed suicide near the Ohio River, after having prophesied that some day the Ohio would be navigated by steamboats, and men more powerful than he would gain riches and fame from his invention.

Franklin's popularity declined with his powers. As he approached death, his acquaintances became fewer, and when he died in 1790, the younger generations were not keenly moved. To them he appeared rather gross and grasping. He was not universally mourned. The French celebrated his memory magnificently, and the United States House of Representatives observed official mourning, but the Senate did not.

III

Science and the American Constitution

SCIENTIFIC IDEAS HAVE HAD AN EXCEPTIONAL influence on the history of America, more, perhaps, than on the history of any other country, except the U.S.S.R. The structure of the American Constitution has provided one of the channels for the exertion of this influence. At the present time, the Constitution is more than ever the center of American political thought. The contentions between the executive, the houses of Congress, and the Supreme Court, affect the foundations of American life. If the form of the Constitution is partly due to the influence of certain scientific ideas, science has had a part in the rejection or delay, for good or ill, of social plans such as the New Deal.

As Franklin was the first great American scientist, and a member of the Convention that devised the Constitution, it is necessary to enquire whether the aspects of the Constitution which show the influence of certain scientific ideas were due to him.

In 1814 John Adams wrote a letter to John Taylor concerning the nature of different types of government. Taylor had enquired whether the differences between monarchy, aristocracy and democracy were numerical or characteristic. Were they merely different ways of partitioning power among the members of the population, so that the one, or the few, or the many were sovereign; or were they reflections of qualitative differences between the members of the population? Did kings possess some higher quality not possessed by nobles, and did nobles possess some quality not possessed by the ordinary man?

According to the first notion the differences between king, noble and citizen are merely due to size. One governs because it has more power than the others. According to the second notion, one governs because it possesses power of a higher type, not merely more power than the others. It will be noticed that the first notion appeals to the ideas of arithmetic and mechanics, where one quantity is bigger or smaller than another, but not different in nature. Power in a system of government consisting of reactions between larger or smaller powers, all of the same nature, depends on the balance between the various powers. As Taylor wrote, it is "complicated with the idea of a balance."

The second notion involves characteristic differences between king, nobles and citizens. For instance, the king may be supposed to be divine, while the others are not. He rules because he possesses a higher quality that places him above others, and gives him a higher order of wisdom. His power overcomes that of others not because it is merely larger, but because it is of a higher type.

The notion of the divine right of kings is derived from a dangerous extrapolation of biological observation. The differences between men and animals are very great, and appear to be qualitative; to the primitive observer man seems to possess qualities fundamentally different from those of animals. Every man has been dependent on his parents or elders, and at an early age acquired an impression that they possess powers qualitatively superior to his own. The notion of divine right is derived from the belief in the qualitative differences between men, and between men and animals. It is interesting to note that Taylor illustrates the notion of king, nobles and citizens as qualitatively different by a biological example: the characteristic differences between "the calyx, petal, and stamina of plants."

Taylor denounces both the mechanical and the biological notions of the system of government, and says that "they have never yet . . . been used to describe a government deduced from good moral principles."

Adams replied that the Constitution of the United States was certainly not deduced from good moral principles, but asks:

"Is not the constitution of the United States 'complicated with the idea of a balance?' Is there a constitution upon record more complicated with balances than ours? In the first place eighteen states and some territories are balanced against the national government, whether judiciously or injudiciously, I will not presume at present to conjecture. . . . In the second place, the house of representatives is balanced against the senate, and the senate against the house. In the third place, the executive authority is in some degree balanced against the legislative. In the fourth place, the judiciary power is balanced against the house, the senate, the executive power, and the state governments. In the fifth place, the senate is balanced against the president in all appointments to office, and in all treaties. This, in my opinion, is not merely a useless, but a very pernicious balance. In the sixth place, the people hold in their own hands the balance against their own representatives, by biennial, which I wish had been annual elections. In the seventh place, the legislatives of the several states are balanced against the senate by sextennial elections. In the eighth place, the electors are balanced against the people in the choice of the president. And here is a complication and refinement of balances, which, for any thing I recollect, is an invention of our own, and peculiar to us."

John Adams continues:

"However, all this complication of machinery, all those wheels within wheels, these *imperia* within *imperiis* have not been sufficient to satisfy the people. They have invented a balance to all balances in their caucuses. We have congressional caucuses, state caucuses, county caucuses, city caucuses, district caucuses, town caucuses, parish caucuses, and Sunday caucuses at church doors; and in these aristocratical caucuses *elections are decided.*

"Do you not tremble, Mr. Taylor, with fear, that another balance to all these balances, an over balance of all 'moral liberty,' and to every moral principle and feeling, may soon be invented and introduced: I mean the balance of corruption? Corruption! Be not surprised, sir. If the spirit of party is corruption, have we not seen much of it already? If the spirit of faction is corruption, have we seen none of that evil spirit? If the spirit of banking is corruption, . . . have you ever heard or read of any country in which this spirit prevailed to a greater degree than in this? Are you informed of any aristocratical institution by which the property of the many is more manifestly sacrificed to the profit of the few?"

Students of constitutional law, such as Woodrow Wilson and W. A. Robson, have cited this passage as an early exposition of the degree in which the notions of "checks and balances" entered into the structure of the Constitution.

Wilson writes that "the government of the United States was constructed upon the Whig theory of political dynamics, which was a sort of unconscious copy of the Newtonian theory of the universe. In our own day, whenever we discuss the structure or development of anything, whether in nature or society, we consciously or unconsciously follow Mr. Darwin, but before Mr. Darwin they followed Newton."

Wilson brilliantly argues that under Newtonian influence any system, including that of government, is conceived as a system of bodies moving according to the laws of mechanics and gravitation, in which action and reaction are equal and opposite, and all bodies are nicely poised by a balance of the forces acting on them. He writes that the Whigs tried to give England a balanced constitution. They did not destroy the King, but offset his power by a system of checks and balances, which would regulate his course, or at least make it calculable.

Wilson considers that the English politicians, true to their habits, did not clearly apprehend what they were doing, and the nature of their actions was first clearly explained by Montesquieu. He writes that "the admirable expositions of the *Federalist* read like thoughtful applications of Montesquieu to the political needs and circumstances of America."

Wilson comments "that government is not a machine, but

a living thing. It falls, not under the theory of the universe, but under the theory of organic life. It is accountable to Darwin, not to Newton." It should be subject to the laws of adaptation, and its organs should not be offset against each other, but coöperate quickly in the interests of life, and provide a "ready response to the commands of instinct or intelligence." Wilson, like Taylor, invoked biological illustrations in contrast to the purely quantitative principles of the Whig theory of government.

Wilson's comments on the Newtonian characteristics of the Constitution are important and interesting, and exhibit an intellectual originality with which he has not commonly been credited.

There are also parallels between the "checks and balances" of the American Constitution, and the mental conflicts, or "checks and balances," in puritan psychology. The psychological frustrations of an Adams are related to the principles of the Constitution. It is significant that Franklin, who was free from complexes and frustrations, was philosophically opposed to the Constitution.

It is well-known that the Constitution was devised by fifty-five statesmen, during four months' secret sessions of a special convention. Franklin was a member of the convention, though eighty-one years old. He expressed his opinion of the new Constitution in 1789, in a letter to a friend. He wrote that the provision of two houses, of representatives and senators, was a device for giving superior influence to the rich. He asked, "Is it supposed that wisdom is the necessary concomitant of riches?" "Private property is a creature of society, and is subject to the calls of that society, whenever its necessities shall require it, even to its last farthing." The payment of taxes does not confer a benefit on the public, but discharges a social obligation. "The combinations of civil society are not like those of a set of merchants," or board-meetings, in which the holder of the majority of shares decides policy. The important ends of civil society are personal securities and liberty, and the poorest has as much right to these as the richest. He regretted that there was a disposition to create an aristocracy of the rich.

He doubts whether the division of the English legislature into two or three branches was a product of wisdom, and suggests it arose from historical necessity, owing to the pre-existence of an odious feudal system. Notwithstanding its division of powers, the English Government had become an absolute monarchy, owing to bribery of the people's representatives by the king. He considered two houses defective in practice. A bad motion might be passed by one house because the persons who understood the matter best happened to be in the other house. This provoked contentions between the houses, which would never have arisen if all representatives had been in one house, so that those with special knowledge could have explained defects in the motion as soon as it had been proposed.

Franklin disagreed with the Constitution, but proposed that all delegates should sign it, as a better was not to be had, and he hoped it might soon be amended and improved by Congress. He thought that any form of government might serve, if operated by suitable men.

It is evident that the Newtonian notions of checks and balances, and mechanical equilibrium, were not introduced into the Constitution by Franklin, though he was a scientist. They were introduced by philosophic statesmen and lawyers who were not scientists. The incident provides an example of the dangers of the misapplication of scientific ideas by politicians who do not properly understand them. Mistakes of the same sort are occurring at present in various countries, where political oppression is excused by false biological theories of the nature of human beings. The most perfect statement of the principles which inspired the Constitution was made by James Madison in the tenth number of the *Federalist*. He wrote that "the diversity in the faculties of men, from which the rights of property originate, is not less an insuperable obstacle to a uniformity of interests. The protection of these faculties is the first object of government. From the protection of different and unequal faculties of acquiring property, the possession of different degrees and kinds of property immediately results; and from the influence of these on the sentiments and views of the prospective proprietors, ensues a division of the society into different interests and parties.

"The latent causes of faction are thus sown in the nature of man; . . . but the most common and durable source of factions has been the various and unequal distribution of property. Those who hold and those who are without property have ever formed distinct interests in society. Those who are creditors, and those who are debtors, fall under a like discrimination. A landed interest, a manufacturing interest, a mercantile interest, a moneyed interest, with many lesser interests, grow up of necessity in civilized nations, and divide them into different classes, actuated by different sentiments and views. The regulation of these various and interfering interests forms the principle task of modern legislation, and involves the spirit of party and faction in the necessary and ordinary operations of the government."

Madison conceived the Constitution as a machine for the regulation of the various interfering interests. The struggles between the classes of society were to be nicely balanced by the machinery of the Constitution so that the wheels of society revolved for ever in an equilibrium comfortable to those who have the greatest faculty for acquiring property.

In the view of Madison's explanation, it is astonishing to read in James Bryce's chapter on the Origin of the Constitution, in his book on *The American Commonwealth*, that among the creators of the Constitution "There were no questions between classes, no animosities against rank and wealth, for rank and wealth did not exist."

The chief engineer of the construction of the Constitutional machine was Alexander Hamilton, of coarser but more powerful genius than Madison. Hamilton passionately believed in the superiority of the rich and well-born. As Bertrand Russell has remarked, this belief may have been strengthened by reaction from the feeling of inferiority due to his illegitimate birth. Hamilton's belief appears to have been partly a psychological rationalization. He had much opportunity to become rich, but died poor. It seems that an unconscious motive of his action was not to become rich, but to receive the approbation of the rich and well-born, to achieve respectability.

A similar motive probably inspired the royalist sentiments of Franklin's son, and the aristocratic sentiments of his grandson, both of whom were illegitimate.

The complications of the checks, balances, and equilibria of the Constitution are an extreme form of the Whig theory of political dynamics. In some degree, they also are an expression of reaction against illegitimacy. The American revolutionaries were anxious to remove any appearances of loss of respectability produced by recent highly unrespectable activities. They sought to do this by adopting political theories which were an extension of orthodox British theories. In a sense, they were more royalist than the King. Some of the sources of the mechanical theories incorporated in the Constitution have been indicated by John Adams in his *Defence of the Constitutions*. His order of discussion of the subject-matter was influenced by that of Montesquieu in his *Spirit of Laws*. Montesquieu's book contains examples of Newtonian modes of thought, and was analysed by D'Alembert, the famous master of theoretical mechanics and author of D'Alembert's principle. In his section on Monarchy, Montesquieu writes:

"It is with this kind of government as with the system of the universe, in which there is a power that constantly repels all bodies from the center, and the power of gravitation that attracts them to it. Honour sets all the parts of the body politic in motion, and by its very action connects them; thus each individual advances the public good while he only thinks of promoting his own interest."

Adams quotes examples of the notion of balances from various authors. He gives passages from Machiavelli, where the possibility of the perpetual revolution of government through the forms of monarchy, aristocracy and democracy is discussed. Machiavelli wished to discover how such "revolutions of infinity" may be prevented. He is appealing to the notion of stabilizing a machine. He wished to provide the social machine with an automatic speed regulator or governor. Adams' most interesting quotation is from Harrington: "empire follows the balance of property, whether lodged in one, a few, or many hands." In his *Oceana* he conceives the perfect government as an equilibrium between the king, nobility and people, which cannot exist unless they are duly balanced against each other.

Adams discusses the views of various philosophers, including those of Franklin, on government. He assumes that Franklin was opposed to the notion of balances. In the Constitutional Convention Franklin had said that the notion of balancing two assemblies, such as a house of representatives and a senate, against each other reminded him of the practice of certain drivers of wagons drawn by four oxen. When they had a heavy load and came to a steep hill, they took a pair of oxen off, and chained them to the rear of the wagon, and drove them up hill, so that the rate of the descent of the wagon was moderated. Adams reprobated this oracular parable on balances, and proceeds: "The president of Pennsylvania might, upon such an occasion, have recollected one of Sir Isaac Newton's laws of motion, namely,—'that reaction must always be equal and contrary to action,' or there can never be any *rest*. He might have alluded to those angry assemblies in the heavens, which so often overspread the city of Philadelphia, fill the citizens with apprehension and terror, threatening to set the world on fire, merely because the powers within them are not sufficiently balanced."

Thus the lawyer Adams began to quote Newton against the scientist Franklin.

Several suggestive conclusions may be drawn from Adams' remarks. Adams and other American lawyers were fascinated by ideas supported by the authority of Newtonian mechanics. They, who were not scientists, were ready to brandish Newton's authority against their opponents.

Franklin, who was a scientist, was the only important member of the Constitutional Convention who was not impressed by conscious and unconscious appeals to Newtonian ideas.

Woodrow Wilson has made illuminating comments on the influence of Newtonian ideas on the formulation of the Constitution. But the notion of a constitution as a balanced mechanism is older than Newton. Machiavelli, who could conceive a constitution as a safety device, or speed regulation of social change, died in 1527. Harrington published *Oceana* in 1656. Newton did not publish the *Principia* until 1687.

The study of the American Constitution helps to show that "Newtonian" ideas are older than Newton. As Hessen has explained, Newton's mechanics grew out of the social movement named the Renaissance and Reformation. The chief feature of this movement was the development of trade, and the growth of the political power of the trading classes. As trade became more and more the basis of power, money and the production of goods became more and more important and interesting. The extension and refinement of production stimulated the study of the number and properties of goods. Improvements in the technique of arithmetic and physics, the sciences which describe the number and properties of things, followed. Some authorities state that the early Italian merchants introduced a symbol for zero into arithmetic. The merchants at first used a dot as the symbol of zero. Some of their slicker competitors swindled accounts by juggling with the dots, so large and unconcealable hexagons were introduced. The O is a degeneration of a quickly drawn hexagon.

With the progress of the Renaissance, men looked less and less to heaven and more and more to multiplication of money and goods as the source of power. The belief in government by divine right began to weaken. The respect for hieratic systems of qualities decayed. Before the Renaissance the intrinsic differences in quality between men, and between things, were considered the basis of understanding; after the Renaissance, the quantitative differences were considered more important.

Galileo and Newton discovered their system of mechanics,

because the progressive social thought of their time, that of the rising trading classes, already interpreted phenomena quantitatively rather than qualitatively. Newton refined and deepened a mode of thought already in existence, for example, in Harrington's theory of government. This is an important part of the explanation why Newton appeared in the seventeenth century, and not in the Dark Ages. Even his prodigious intellectual gifts would have been quite unable to work out the system of mechanics, if the general notions had not been implicit in contemporary thought. Newton was more indebted to society for the provision of a suitable intellectual background to his investigations, than society has been indebted to Newton for his brilliant extensions of an accepted mode of thought. The mechanics named Newtonian owe less to Newton than to the combined contributions of his predecessors, not only in the sphere of scientific thought, but in the sphere of general thought, and its characteristic attitudes towards the concept of nature.

Woodrow Wilson's diagnosis of the Constitution as Newtonian is only partly correct. He did not notice that Newton was inspired by a preceding system of ideas to which "balanced" and mechanical theories of government were related. When Newton announced his laws of nature, he adopted the word "law" from contemporary theories of government, which were more or less consciously those of a mercantile society. Thus Newtonian mechanics is indebted to Whig or mercantile theories of government. In the environment of such theories, and allied systems of thought, he produced his mechanics. These, in turn, were adapted to give more precise expression to the theories of government suitable to trading classes. Thus there was a continual interaction between notions of government and scientific ideas.

The mutual interaction between the ideas in Newton's intellectual environment and his scientific thought was recognized by Macaulay. In a discussion of the state of England in 1685, he notices the remarkable work of the Royal Society in the application of science to practical affairs. Its members had given formal instructions to farmers on the best methods of planting, and had done much work on the production of new vegetables, the use of new manures, and the adaptation of foreign plants to cultivation in England.

The wide interest in experiment and theory provided an atmosphere in which the intellect of a Newton might flourish. Macaulay writes that

"Perhaps in the days of Scotists and Thomists even his intellect might have run to waste, as many intellects ran to waste which were inferior only to his. Happily the spirit of the age on which his lot was cast, gave the right direction to his mind; and his mind reacted with tenfold force on the spirit of the age."

The influence of Utilitarianism on Macaulay is emphasized in this passage by his repetition of the phrase "running to waste," and his implied dismissal of the work of the Schoolmen as worthless. His suggestion that Newton had ten times as much influence on the spirit of the age as that spirit had on him is an exaggeration, but also an admission that Newton's intellectual achievements were an offspring of the culture which existed when he was born. He bred and polished the rough ideas which he found in a favorable environment, until they acquired a far grander appearance and power, though their nature still remained the same.

The influence on political thought of the system of ideas extended and refined by Newton has been discussed by Carl Becker in his study of the Declaration of Independence.

The political philosophies to which the Declaration of Independence and the Constitution appeal for justification are not the same, but nevertheless have many common features. They were derived from a system of ideas which had acquired wide prestige during the eighteenth century. Some parts of this system are invoked with particular emphasis and clarity in the Declaration.

The first paragraph states that a people may be entitled to independence by "the laws of nature and of nature's God." The second paragraph begins with the statement that "We hold these truths to be self-evident, That all men are created equal, that they are endowed by their creator with certain unalienable rights . . ."

These statements express very definitely the political philosophy of the natural rights of man.

This philosophy was the intellectual weapon used by those who achieved the independence of the United States, and it was as important as any other weapon used in the struggle. A complete explanation of why the United States succeeded in gaining independence cannot be given without counting the help received from the philosophy of the natural rights of man. Why did this philosophy have such strength and prestige in the last quarter of the eighteenth century?

A general tendency to research and exploration had been a feature of the human movement of the Renaissance. Men visited distant countries, examined the Bible, and made innumerable other investigations, and obtained interesting results which could be adapted to their own advantage. The activity of investigation was gradually systematized, and in some countries had begun to acquire the form of science. Investigation acquired prestige because it had brought riches and religious independence to many men. Success helped to create in men a deep respect for an activity which brought so much. As ships were the means of investigation in foreign trade, and continents were the source of interesting finds, so the reason was the means of investigation in intellectual affairs, and nature was the source of interesting finds. With the success of investigation, the prestige of reason and nature rose, and constituted Macaulay's "spirit of the age." Their prestige was considerable when Newton began to study, but it was greatly increased by his marvelously successful use of the concepts of reason and nature.

According to Thomas Aquinas the highest law was the Eternal Law, which was equivalent to God's mind. A portion of the Eternal Law was revealed to man through the Bible and the Church, and a further portion was accessible through the application of reason. This was natural law. Aquinas believed that the natural law accessible to reason was only a small portion of the Eternal Law. During the five hundred years following his time, more and more scope was ascribed to natural law, until, in the eighteenth century, as Becker explains, the scope of natural law was believed to cover the whole of the Eternal Law. The belief that the whole of God's mind was accessible to human reason became widely accepted. This was due to the success of the movement of which Copernicus, Galileo and Newton were leaders.

The scientists reasoned with nature, and were rewarded with remarkable answers. They therefore paid more and more respect to nature, and began to deify it, and to neglect the Bible and the Church. This did not imply that they had become irreligious. The majority of scientists were religious, and Newton was extremely religious, but they had changed their tenets.

The spectacular explanation of the laws of the solar system by Newton immensely enhanced the prestige of nature as a source of knowledge. Before his work, the belief that the natural laws which govern the behavior of objects on the surface of the earth, should also operate on the moon, and throughout all space, would have seemed impudently presumptive. The proof that this presumption was correct gave a correspondingly large encouragement to human confidence in the power of reason, and the importance of the information which nature might reveal.

Newton's spectacular results attracted attention from all men of broad interests, besides specialists. Voltaire was one of the first who expounded Newton's results to the general audience. John Locke began to study earnestly the wider implications of Newton's methods, after he had been assured by Huygens that Newton's mathematics was correct.

Becker quotes Gray's bibliography of Newton, which records that before 1789, forty books about the *Principia* were published in English, seventeen in French, three in German, eleven in Latin, one in Portuguese, and one in Italian.

Desagulier translated a popular exposition of Newton which passed through six editions by 1747, and published in 1728

The Newtonian System of the World the Best Model of Government, an Allegorical Poem. Here the influence of Newtonian science on political theory is already explicit.

A weightier exposition of Newtonian science was published by the very able Scottish mathematician, Colin Maclaurin, the author of the celebrated theorem named after him. He explains that science satisfies man's curiosity about nature, provides improvements in technique, and pleases his aesthetic feeling. But it is "subservient to purposes of a higher kind, and is chiefly to be valued as it lays a sure foundation for Natural Religion and Moral philosophy; by leading us, in a satisfactory manner, to the knowledge of the Author and Governor of the Universe."

He believed that the student would learn to admire the beauty of the "Exquisite structure and just motions" of the system of nature, and would be "Excited and animated to correspond with the general harmony of Nature."

The introduction into political philosophy of the attitudes of Newtonian scientific thought was due especially to John Locke. The natural rights philosophy of the Declaration of Independence was acquired by Thomas Jefferson largely from Locke. In the Declaration the principle of that philosophy is invoked, when it is asserted that the rights of man exist in nature, and may be ascertained from nature by the exercise of reason.

This philosophical attitude is not so prominent in the Constitution, but more use is made of methods derived from it. The notion of mechanical equilibrium developed by Newton had the same origin as the philosophy of natural rights; both were derived from the investigation of nature by reason.

The American Constitution is a product of several centuries of such interactions, and is consequently a highly developed and refined expression of a system of thought concerning government and nature which dominated those centuries.

The presence of Newtonian ideas in the Constitution was due partly to their authority, and partly to the operation of the same social forces that had brought Newtonian ideas themselves into existence. The dominant American political thinkers, such as John Adams, were fascinated by Newtonian ideas. This shows that these ideas were peculiarly sympathetic to their modes of thought. If a discussion of the representative views of Adams reveals the influence of Newton, may not a study of the ideas of Adams be used to reveal peculiarities in Newton's ideas? May not the sympathy between their modes of thought be used to analyse Newton's thought?

In his article on Franklin in the *Boston Patriot* in 1811, Adams referred to Newton as "perhaps the greatest man that ever lived." Why did Adams, who was a lawyer, and did not understand mathematical astronomy, have such awe of Newton? Probably because he conceived Newton as the law-giver to the universe. He was impressed, not by the difficulty of the scientific problems solved by Newton, but by the astonishing scope of the application of his results. Newton with pencil and paper worked out the Constitution of the Universe. This appealed to lawyers who desired to work out the Constitution of the United States of America with pen and paper.

Adams was not particularly interested or impressed by Newton's contributions to experimental science. Those seemed fiddling compared with the legislation of the cosmos. The legalistic aspect of Newton's work appealed to Adams. This was to be expected. The immense fame of Newton, as Adams wrote, was connected with "mysterious wonder" at his achievement. A large part of his fame was due to the old-fashioned pre-Renaissance, scholastic modes of thought, which Macaulay so much despised. He was regarded by many as a magician. He could predict the course of the stars, apparently by pencil and paper, and without other assistance. This appealed to the demand of the unsophisticated for magic, and to the snobbery of the governing and leisured classes, who like to be able to exert power, without appearing to work. Similar motions help to explain the vogue of certain contemporary writers, such as Jeans, whose sweeping style seems, with ease, to give laws to the cosmos. His conceptions are characteristically Newtonian. Newton's attitude and work are not entirely attractive to the twentieth-century mind, in spite of their prodigious nature. May this be due to the legalistic, scholastic qualities in his thought, which appealed to lawyers such as Adams, and are made doubly clear by the lawyer's admiration and approbation? May the slight contemporary distaste for Newton be a reflection of the modern scientists' sympathy for the contradictions of the quantum theory, and dislike of legalism?

The problem seems to become clearer from the study of the nature of Franklin's scientific work. Franklin was the most important scientist of the eighteenth century. He contributed more than any other scientist towards the establishment of the modern ideas of experimental science, and of advancing the condition of human society by experimental investigation. His greatest contribution was philosophical. He assisted the escape from the legalistic tradition that saturated the part of Newton's scientific work which received the widest public recognition, and exerted the greatest public influence.

The deepest importance of Franklin's achievement was in a large degree perceived by some of his greatest contemporaries. Joseph Priestley was directly inspired by contact with Franklin's emancipated mind. He describes how he had never thought of making discoveries by experiment until after he had met Franklin. Priestley, like Faraday, was interested in science for many years before he had the courage to believe that he might discover something new. He had thought of writing a history of electricity, and asked Franklin for advice. Franklin was very helpful and encouraging, and Priestley's career as discoverer grew out of the testing of the experiments described in the history. Priestley also records that his experiments on the properties of gases began to progress after a visit from Franklin. These experiments culminated in the discovery of oxygen, a tremendous contribution to the creation of modern science. Priestley's mind was fixed in theological habits of thought, in some ways like Newton's. Franklin emancipated him, and showed him the way to modern experimental science. He owed to Franklin the philosophical perspective that led him to his great achievements.

Priestley was aware that Franklin's work and attitude might be an advance on Newton's. He writes in the preface to his *History of Electricity:* "Hitherto philosophy has been chiefly conversant about the more sensible properties of bodies. Electricity together with chemistry and the doctrine of light and colours, seems to be giving us an inlet into their internal structure, on which all their sensible properties depend. By pursuing this new light, therefore, the bounds of natural science may possibly be extended beyond what we can now form an idea of. New worlds may open to our view, and the glory of the great Sir Isaac Newton himself, and all his contemporaries, be eclipsed by a new set of philosophers, in quite a new field of speculation. Could that great man revisit the earth, and view the experiments of the present race of electricians, he would be no less amazed than Roger Bacon or Sir Francis would have been at his. The electric shock itself, if it be considered attentively, will appear almost as surprising as any discovery that he made."

This passage shows that Priestley foresaw that experimental physics would become at least as important as mathematical astronomy. He was inspired to this vision by Franklin.

One of the reasons why Franklin had little influence on the construction of the American Constitution is now clear. The makers of the Constitution were lawyers who believed they were including in their work the supposedly imperishable ideas of Newtonian mechanics, which they did not understand. They distrusted Franklin partly because he felt he was not Newtonian. They never dreamt that he was the most confident pioneer of the next advance of science beyond Newton. Franklin was the forerunner of modern experimental scientists. He could not sympathize with lawyers in love with a scientific point of view already old-fashioned. He even tried optimistically to believe that the American statesmen were, like himself, experimentalists.

In 1788, he wrote to Rochefoucauld that "We are *making experiments* in politics; what knowledge we shall gain by them will be more certain, though perhaps we may hazard too much in *that* mode of acquiring it."

The attitude of Adams and the others was profoundly different. They had no confidence in *experiments*. Adams wrote that political experiments unfortunately could not be tried in a laboratory before being tried on the community. He implied that political experiments were, for this reason, to be avoided. They were afraid of the dangers of the popular liberties necessary for political experiments. They desired only to design and construct as quickly as possible a complicated machine, in which the people could be safely confined. The machine was to be equipped with a system of automatic governors, safety valves and balance-weights, so that when the temperature of the confined people rose, their energy would be harmlessly discharged through a temporary acceleration of the balanced mechanism, and the original relative positions of the interacting parts, or social interests or classes, would remain constant for ever.

Parton has remarked that Franklin and Adams were the spiritual fathers of the Democratic and the Republican parties. Political experimentalism, of a sort with which Franklin might have sympathized, has recently become prominent in American affairs.

This belief in political experiment seems to be particularly strong in America.

In the past, politicians have asked for power on the ground that they alone knew how to solve all social problems, and only needed power to carry out the solutions. They regarded their assertion of omniscience as essential to political prestige. A new attitude has begun to appear in America, where leaders have plainly said that they did not know beforehand the solutions to all problems, but merely wished to have power to try various experimental policies.

This valuable American belief in political experimentalism is due in part to the influence of science and of the broad teaching of science, which is such an excellent feature of American education.

Franklin could not support the makers of the Constitution because, among other reasons, their philosophy involved scientific ideas already getting out of date.

The Senate did not mourn him after he died, and the States' debts to him were left unpaid. His reputation in America declined during the next century. He was remembered as a diplomat and a philosophical Sancho Panza whose overwhelming fascination was rather incomprehensible.

Benjamin Franklin: Bibliography

The Complete Works of Benjamin Franklin. Compiled and edited by John Bigelow. 10 volumes. 1887 & cont.

The Writings of Benjamin Franklin. Collected and edited with a Life and Introduction by H. A. Smyth. 10 volumes. 1905 & cont.

Benjamin Franklin: Bourgeois d'Amérique. Bernard Faÿ. 1929.

Life and Times of Benjamin Franklin. James Parton. 2 volumes. 1892.

The Franklin Bicentennial Celebration. Philadelphia. Volume I. 1906.

Benjamin Franklin: The First Civilized American. Phillips Russell. 1927.

History of Electricity. Joseph Priestley. Fourth Edition.

Collected Works. Joseph Priestley.

The Spectator.

Joseph Henry
1797-1878

I
THE SIGNIFICANCE OF HIS CAREER

II
HIS LIFE AND WORK

III
THE SMITHSONIAN INSTITUTION

BIBLIOGRAPHY

I

The Significance of His Career

JOSEPH HENRY WAS BORN IN 1797 AND DIED
in 1878. He was descended from Scottish Puritans, and acquired from them a Calvinistic mode of thought. He grew
up in a period when the civilization of the United States was
still dominantly agricultural. He lived near Albany, which
was a center of state administration, and where the owners of
large estates still had the most powerful voice in government.

Vigorous remnants of the stratified type of social structure
appropriate to a landed aristocracy existed about Albany in
Henry's youth. In such a structure, there are elements of the
caste system; it is supposed that every person is destined to
some particular status in which he will remain all his life.
Henry was a tutor to the family of the patroon Van Rensselaer, a position equivalent to that of a clerk or scholar in
medieval feudalism. He never left the scholar caste.

The influence of these circumstances was increased by the
feebleness of his father, who was unable to earn a satisfactory
living, and died when Henry was a child. The influence of
his mother was enhanced by this event. She impressed her
religious principles into him exceptionally deeply.

Joseph Henry was tall, handsome, and magnificently
healthy. He was engaged in strenuous and successful research
when he was eighty years old. He showed the extraordinary
physical vitality of many Americans of his day. His nature
was gentle and sincere, but his Calvinistic views were harder
and more somber than his temperament. In spite of his kind
disposition, he had the fear of evil and consciousness of the

frailty of man, which was characteristic of his co-religionists. As a scholar imbued with the ideas of caste or class, in an aristocratic agricultural civilization, he was far more interested in establishing his prestige in the scholar-class, than in making money. This attitude, reinforced by his mother's theology, which emphasized the danger of damnation through riches, made him not indifferent to, but fearful of, money.

Henry received the small salary of $3,500 for directing the Smithsonian Institution, and refused, during thirty-two years, to accept an increase. As he was in Washington, he was regularly consulted by the Government on scientific questions. This involved much extra work, and the connection lasted for more than three decades, but Henry refused to accept any payment. He refused to accept payment for scientific advice to the Government during the Civil War. He refused to accept several university chairs with salaries much larger than that he received from the Smithsonian Institution, and which offered him far more free time for personal scientific research. For instance, he refused the chair of chemistry in the Medical School at the University of Pennsylvania "especially because . . . it might be supposed that he was influenced by pecuniary reasons."

Henry was the first to elucidate the principles of the design of electro-magnets. He was the first to employ electro-magnets in a successful electric telegraph system, and the first to construct a reciprocating machine driven by direct electric current. These inventions were fundamental to the development of the electric telegraph and electrical machinery, but he refused to patent them.

They were employed by Morse in his development of the electric telegraph. As is often the case, success persuaded Morse and his financial backers to assert that their predecessor had exaggerated the importance of his unpatented contributions. Henry remarked in his reply to these assertions that: "My life has been principally devoted to science and my investigations in different branches of physics have given me some reputation in the line of original discovery. I have sought however no patent for inventions and solicited no remuneration for my labours, but have freely given their results to the world; expecting only in return to enjoy the consciousness of having added by my investigations to the sum of human knowledge. The only reward I ever expected was the consciousness of advancing science, the pleasure of discovering new truths, and the scientific reputation to which these labours would entitle me."

Henry would "sell to no man, nor would he deny or delay to any man the precious knowledge drawn under the providence of God from the arcana of nature."

In 1865, when the Civil War had ended, he was sixty-eight years old, and established in Washington in a position of unique scientific distinction. He steadily followed his principles of conduct through the years of wild speculation which occurred before his death in 1878. His attitude to money was the exact antithesis of that of the majority of his later contemporaries. He remained loyal to the ethics of the scholar-class, and never modified his attitude as the prestige of the financial and capitalist classes increased.

He was forty-nine years old when he accepted the invitation to become the first Secretary, or Director, of the Smithsonian Institution. He interpreted his new duties as implying a cessation of personal research, and for the long remainder of his life he was firstly an administrator of scientific work. Under his direction, the Smithsonian Institution acquired a unique position and reputation in the encouragement of research and the popularization of science. It became the parent of the modern system of meteorological forecasting by telegraph, of the United States National Museum, the Bureau of American Ethnology, the National Zoölogical Park, the National Gallery of Art, of marine biological research stations such as Woods Hole, of a world system of exchange of scientific books and specimens between research workers, and many other first-class innovations.

During his secretaryship, Henry considered he could not give time to personal research, but he gave much time to unpaid research for the Government. All of this research was of direct economic and social value. He made first-class investigations into the acoustics of the atmosphere in connection with the fog-signal system for protecting shipping, and equally excellent researches on meteorology, the strength of building materials, ballistics, solar physics, and other subjects.

This is an immense list of achievements, but it does not include his greatest researches. These were done in the years about 1830, when he discovered electro-magnetic self-induction before Faraday, and probably also discovered electro-magnetic induction before Faraday, but did not publish it first.

In total achievement Henry was the equal of Faraday, Helmholtz, Kelvin, Maxwell, and the other great scientists of the nineteenth century. He did not discover so many important new facts and theories as Faraday, but he contributed vastly more to the organization of scientific research. As G. B. Goode has explained, Henry "did much toward establishing the profession of scientific administration—a profession which in the complexity of modern civilization is becoming more and more essential to scientific progress." This is an important remark. The creation of methods of organization is even more urgent, in the conditions of modern civilization, than the discovery of such a profound phenomenon as electro-magnetic induction. Society is being disrupted by the scientific forces which have been released within it.

The most important contributions that may be made to modern culture are discoveries of rational methods of promoting and utilizing science. Henry was a distinguished forerunner of the modern social planners, who wish to integrate science into the machinery of society.

A study of Henry's achievements shows that he was a truly great man. But an air of disappointment has always hovered around his name. His friends and countrymen regretted that though he probably discovered electro-magnetic induction before Faraday, he failed to publish it first. There is a wide opinion that if Henry had made this discovery exclusively American, he would have contributed more to the advancement of science in America by this single achievement, than by the manifold contributions that he recognizedly made. He would have given American science an inspiration which might have enabled it to dominate nineteenth-century physics. This, in turn, would have raised the standard of the whole of American culture, and have made American spiritual achievements in the period more equal to the material achievements. This argument appeals to the principle of individualist competition as the motive of progress.

Henry despised money, and the principle of competition. He despised competition in priority. He refused to gamble, even in research. This code of conduct was based on his religious and social ideas. It prevented him from making the intellectual gamble that might have won world leadership in electrical research for American physicists in 1831, and which might well have persisted.

Henry's social ideas belonged to a system in which the church would have ruled the state. They were closer to those of Calvin's theocracy at Geneva than of nineteenth-century capitalism, and have more in common with socialism than competitive individualism. By rejecting personal competition for fame and wealth, Henry rejected the principles which were beginning to dominate American life. He stood outside the main stream of the contemporary American spirit. He did not become assimilated to modern American individualism. This failure to enter into, and use, the dominating system of social ideas, helps to explain the atmosphere of effeteness and disappointment over his career and that of the Smithsonian Institution. His career, and the Institution, were great, but were not what the Americans of the day wanted. The great man who expressed their ideals in science, and whom they recognized as an indubitable genius, was Thomas Alva Edison.

In his memorial address of 1878 R. E. Withers surprised some by stating that Henry "was not a genius." This meant that his greatness was not of the Edison type. He probably believed that Henry's decision to cultivate broad interests was due to the lack of an overwhelming passion to follow a narrow, or individual interest. He did not make any over-whelming contribution in any narrow direction. He refused to exploit his circumstances and employers in order to make discoveries. He was not, like Faraday, working continuously in isolation and never assisting the work of others, and he did not sacrifice his family and social life in order to pile a pyramid of discoveries. He was always refusing, and constraining himself. He showed the continuous inhibitions of Scottish caution. The extreme modesty of his claims to priority, and his praise of others who published before him, though they had discovered after him, show symptoms of what the modern psychologist calls masochism.

He considered that science did not have any necessary connection with the ordinary affairs of human life. That it might be useful to man was a happy accident, due to a benevolent Providence.

The majority of Americans did not sympathize with Henry's ideals and program of work. He was not struggling for his own ends. He was in fact serving the interests of the proprietors of American industry and agriculture. He served the governing classes loyally, owing to his Calvinistic sense of duty, though his ideals were different from theirs. He did not conceive the government as the expression of certain dominant groups in the community. He thought it was above all particular interests, and for that reason, like God, should receive obedience. His lack of insight into the nature of the state explains why he could loyally serve classes with different ideals, and why leaders of those classes, whom he served so well, should fail to appreciate him adequately, and perceive that he was a genius.

Henry disapproved of the idea that it is permissible for a scientist to make money out of his scientific discoveries, and yet the whole of his personal energies for research, after he became Secretary of the Smithsonian Institution, was devoted to investigations of economic importance. The economic needs of the state, of American agriculture, navigation and industry, encouraged his researches in meteorology, fog-horn acoustics, ballistics, strength of building materials, etc. Problems are of interest to the state when dominant or powerful classes want to make, save or get money out of them.

Henry saw no contradiction between refusing to make money for himself, and agreeing to make money for a state dominated by the rich. While he refused to make money for himself, he did not object to being an instrument which increased the efficiency, and profitability, of agriculture and industry, by the application of science.

In the first part of his career he investigated the general problems to which post-Renaissance trade and industrial interests had directed human attention. He studied how to increase the efficiency of machinery, and how to elucidate its principles. The particular machines he studied were electro-magnets. Thus, at first, Henry was an indirect instrument of the advance of the interests of industrialism. And still he believed that the motive for scientific research is divine curiosity, or the desire for insight into the "arcana of nature."

He followed his ideals with inflexible persistence in his great administration of the Smithsonian Institution.

The ideals which prompted James Smithson to found the Institution were profoundly different. Smithson was the bastard son of an English duke and a woman of royal descent. Owing to the circumstances of his birth, he was denied the full privileges of his father's class. He bequeathed the money for the foundation of the Institution from motives of revenge due to outraged class feeling. By that means, he wrote, "My name shall live in the memory of man when the titles of the Northumberlands and the Percys are extinct and forgotten."

His father, the Duke of Northumberland, disowned him, and yet his mother, descended from King Henry VII, was of even nobler blood. He hated his father, and his desire for eternal fame, more durable than that of the Northumberlands, was increased by the psychological complex, of which Oedipus offers the most famous example.

The spectacle of the great and earnest Henry, with his Puritanic sense of duty, carrying out Smithson's will with meticulous care, and creating with conscientious solidity, through thirty-two years, the firm foundation of Smithson's eternal fame, is one of the most interesting examples in the history of science of the interactions of different class motives and psychologies.

II

His Life and Work

THE GRANDPARENTS OF JOSEPH HENRY WERE
Scottish. They landed at New York on June 16th, 1775, the
day before the battle of Bunker Hill. His grandfather had
the surname Hendrie, but adopted the form Henry, perhaps
because his new countrymen elided the dee-sound when they
pronounced his name. Henry regretted that his grandfather
had not preserved the Scottish form, as it was more distinctive.
His grandmother was surnamed Alexander. The Henry family settled in Delaware County and the Alexander family in
Saratoga. Joseph Henry's parents were living in Albany when
he was born. They were poor, as his father, William Henry,
worked as a day laborer. William Henry was apparently unable to give his family much support. When Joseph Henry
was seven years old, an uncle, who was the twin-brother of
his mother, sent him to Galway in Saratoga, where he lived
with his maternal grandmother, and attended the district
school. William Henry died about two years later, when
Joseph was nine years old. Thus from the age of nine years
Joseph Henry was a son of a widowed mother. This increased
the degree of his mother's influence on his character. She was
a small woman with delicate and beautiful features, and a
refined temperament. She lived to a considerable age. She was
a devout and strict member of the Scottish Presbyterian
Church.

Joseph Henry agreed with the view that the character is
formed before the age of seven years. His history shows that
his mother had permanently impressed Presbyterian ideals in

him. These were the foundation of his later behavior and decisions, in so far as those depended on personal principles.

While his early religious training left the deepest impress, his early education did not proceed rapidly. He was not fond of school, and did not show special aptitude for learning. His first taste for reading was stimulated accidentally. His pet rabbit ran into an opening under the village meeting-house. He crawled in pursuit through an opening in the foundation wall, and passed under the floor. He noticed light coming through a gap where the floor was broken. He was excited by the secrets of the room and decided to explore them. He climbed through the gap, and discovered an open case of books, which happened to form the village library. He picked out one, and began to read it, and was soon deeply interested. This was *The Fool of Quality*, by Henry Brooke. G. B. Goode says that Joseph Henry was about eight or ten years old when he discovered this book. The hero of the story is the despised younger son of a dissolute nobleman. The elder son was trained to the peerage while the younger was deposited in the country with a farmer's wife as foster mother. The effects of the different educations are the reverse of the intention. The elder son is ruined and the younger acquires sturdy virtues. Brooke works disquisitions on sociology, economics and religion into the story. The education of the hero is according to the precepts of Rousseau, and the views on human labor as the source of wealth are drawn from William Petty and the mercantilists. Through the experiences of the hero, Brooke speaks against the oppression of the poor. His novel was published between 1766 and 1772. He was a forerunner of the nineteenth-century Liberals. He writes that poverty arises from ignorance, and not from laziness or incapacity. He attributes the misery of Ireland, where he lived, to ignorance, and writes that in his time forty-nine out of fifty Irishmen were incapable of helping themselves because they did not know how. He compares the poverty of the English with the prosperity of the Dutch, and attributes the latter to knowledge of the technique of water transport. He

recommends the construction of canals for increasing the prosperity of England. Ten years after Brooke published his novel
the first English industrial canals were dug. Thus the neglected younger son, the Fool of Quality, left to a simple
Rousseauean rearing, becomes the protagonist of progress. It
is significant that such a book should have interested a boy
of eight or ten years.

John Wesley admired Brooke's novel. Charles Kingsley
wrote in 1859 that "he purged . . . such passages as were
not to his mind, and then republished (it) during the author's
life-time, as the 'History of Harry, Earl of Moreland,' a plan
which was so completely successful, that country Wesleyans
still believe their great prophet to have been himself the
author of the book."

Perhaps *The Fool of Quality* was put into the Galway meeting-house library by Methodists. The different educations of
the elder and younger brothers are described in the opening
pages.

"Richard, who was already entitled my little lord, was not
permitted to breathe the rudeness of the wind. On his slightest
indisposition, the whole house was in alarms; his passions had
full scope in all their infant irregularities; his genius was put
into a hotbed, by the warmth of applauses given to every
flight of his opening fancy; and the whole family conspired,
from the highest to the lowest, to the ruin of promising talents
and a benevolent heart.

"Young Harry, on the other hand, had every member as
well as feature exposed to all weathers; would run about,
mother naked, for near an hour, in a frosty morning; was
neither physicked into delicacy, nor flattered into pride; scarce
felt the convenience, and much less understood the vanity of
clothing; and was daily occupied in playing and wrestling
with the pigs and two mongrel spaniels on the common; or
in kissing, scratching or boxing with the children of the village."

Joseph Henry's interesting opinions on education will be
explained presently. It is possible that they were influenced

by Brooke. It is possible that, as a widow's child, he sympathized with the younger son in the story, who was virtually without a father. As he played with pet rabbits, he would appreciate wrestling with spaniels. He must have read the book about 1805 or 1807. This was during the period of the ascendancy of Thomas Jefferson. Henry's mind was formed when the ideal of an agricultural society was dominant. It never lost that mark.

Henry regarded *The Fool of Quality* purely as fiction. It stimulated his taste for more. He repeatedly returned through the hole in the floor to the village library, and presently was allowed access through the usual door. He read the whole of the stock of fiction.

At the age of ten he worked as an office boy in the local store of a Mr. Broderick. He was kindly treated, and allowed to attend school during the afternoons. Broderick's store was the center of village gossip and popular discussion. Henry used to lounge around the store, listening to passing affairs, and recounting to other boys the stories he had lately read. He was tall for his age, thin, delicate and impulsively enthusiastic.

He left Galway when he was about fifteen years old, and returned to his mother in Albany, where he was apprenticed to a watch-maker and silversmith. After two years, the business failed, so he was released from his apprenticeship. During these years Henry learned the use of accurate tools and manipulation, which assisted him afterwards, when he became an experimental scientist. But his work with the watch-maker did not stimulate an interest in science or mechanics. His reading of fiction at Galway had still the chief possession of his mind. He was attracted by the theater in Albany. Between the years 1813 to 1816 there was an unusually good theater there under the management of a capable English comedian named John Bernard, whose company included several actors and actresses who became noted in America. Bernard was the author of a book on the stage, and on America between the years 1797–1811.

Henry saw as many plays as possible, and succeeded in getting behind the scenes, where he learned how stage effects were produced. He joined or organized a juvenile debating and theatrical society named the Rostrum, of which he became president. As he was without employment he gave the whole of his time to dramatizing stories, writing comedies, and translating a French play. He produced these plays, with notable ingenious stage effects, and acted in them himself. As he was tall, handsome, lively and intelligent, it seemed that he might have become a successful professional actor. His early experience of the stage probably helped him to acquire his command of public speaking, and effective, charming and persuasive address. During the period of his pursuit of the theater he had a slight accident, which kept him at home for a few days. He picked up a book which had been left on a table by a young Scotsman named Robert Boyle, who was lodging in the house. It was a collection of *Lectures on Experimental Philosophy, Astronomy and Chemistry, intended chiefly for the use of young persons*, by G. Gregory, D.D. The author was the Rector of West Ham, near London. He edited the works of the poet Thomas Chatterton, and compiled a dictionary of the sciences, besides many other books. He became Bishop of St. David's.

Boyle presented the little volume of lectures to Henry, when he observed his interest in it. The edition was published in 1808, so it was up-to-date.

Gregory discussed the scientific explanations of simple natural phenomena in a direct, conversational style. He writes: "You throw a stone, or shoot an arrow into the air; why does it not go forward in the line or direction that you give it? Why does it stop at a certain distance, and then return to you? . . . On the contrary, why does flame or smoke always mount upward, though no force is used to send them in that direction? . . . Again, you look into a clear well of water and see your own face and figure, as if painted there. Why is this? You are told that it is done by reflection of light. But what is reflection of light?"

The scientific attitude towards nature was new to Henry, and he was fascinated by it. He discovered that he could employ his imagination to investigate the mechanism of nature. When he saw that the investigation of natural phenomena provided more scope than drama for the exercise of an original imagination of a logical character, he retired from his dramatic society, after delivering a farewell address, in order to educate himself in science.

Henry wrote on a blank page of his copy of Gregory's *Lectures:*

"This book, although by no means a profound work, has, under Providence, exerted a remarkable influence on my life. It accidentally fell into my hands when I was about sixteen years old, and was the first book I ever read with attention. It opened to me a new world of thought and enjoyment; invested things before almost unnoticed with the highest interest; fixed my mind on the study of nature, and caused me to resolve at the time of reading it that I would immediately commence to devote my life to the acquisition of knowledge."

He became a pupil in the night school of the Albany Academy, and worked hard at geometry and mechanics. He was now a tall youth with a sinewy frame and strong constitution. He could work sixteen hours a day, continuously, for years, without serious fatigue. He had the Scottish intellectual characteristics of calm and clarity supported by determination, in an exceptional degree, but his early life had developed artistic qualities often neglected by Scots. His personality was more balanced than that of a native Scot.

As soon as he was able, he became a teacher in a country school, in order to save money for the cost of a fuller course at the Academy. He found that a knowledge of higher mathematics was necessary for the pursuit of science, so he resolutely learned the differential calculus.

When he had completed the academic course and passed the examinations, he was appointed tutor to the family of General Stephen Van Rensselaer, a landowner of Dutch descent, and president of the trustees of the Albany Academy. He was not expected to teach more than about three hours daily, so he had leisure for further study. He assisted Dr. Beck, the principal of the Academy, in chemical experiments, and attended courses on anatomy and physiology, with the intention of qualifying as a medical doctor. He read Lagrange's *Mécanique Analytique*. He was now receiving general encouragement, but his intense studies had impaired his health. He accepted an invitation secured through the influence of a friend, to act as engineer on a road-survey from West Point to Lake Erie. His health was restored by work in the open air, and he earned some money and much credit. He remained exceptionally healthy and vigorous for the remainder of his life. He had enjoyed the engineering, and had decided to accept the direction of the construction of a canal, when he was informed that he had been nominated for the chair of mathematics in the Albany Academy. He accepted this appointment in 1826.

He was now twenty-eight years old. He was expected to teach seven hours daily, including three and a half hours' arithmetic to a large class of boys. In his spare time he started the electrical researches which became famous.

Like many other cities at the end of the eighteenth century, Albany had a number of scientific societies. Two of these were amalgamated in 1824, to form the Albany Institute. Van Rensselaer was also the president of this organization. Scientific meetings were held in the Institute, lectures with demonstrations were given during the winter, and transactions were published. Dr. Beck's lectures on chemistry, like Humphry Davy's in London, attracted a fashionable, besides intelligent, audience.

Albany was the capital city of New York State. It was the headquarters of the state administration, and had an unusually large professional and educated population. This explains why it had a good theater, and several learned societies and institutes. It was a relatively admirable birthplace for a man of science, and Henry's scientific achievements were due in a considerable degree to the circumstance that he was born in one of the most cultivated American cities of his day. His opportunities at Albany might be compared with those of Davy at the Bristol Pneumatic Institution. Both were in provincial centers of learning. Davy had the advantage of meeting more talented men in his youth and at Bristol, before he went to the Royal Institution in London. Henry assisted Beck with the experiments, as Faraday assisted Davy. He found opportunities to make experiments of his own. His first communication to the Institute dealt with experiments on the cooling of steam by sudden, or adiabatic, expansion.

He held a thermometer in a jet of steam escaping from a boiler, and showed that as the temperature and pressure of the steam in the boiler was increased, the temperature registered by the thermometer decreased. Then he demonstrated that a jet of escaping steam will not scald the hand when exposed to it, if the original temperature of the steam is sufficiently high.

Henry's career as an experimental investigator began with research into problems that had been set by the development of the steam engine. The line of his work was determined by the growth of industrial technique.

His next paper was on the production of cold by the expansion of air. He put half a pint of water in a strong copper sphere of five gallons' capacity. Air was pumped into the remaining space, up to a high pressure. The sphere and its contents were allowed to cool to room temperature, and then the air was suddenly released. The water inside the sphere was frozen. Henry remarks that "this experiment was exhibited to the Institute within six feet of a large stove, and in a room the temperature of which was not less than eighty degrees of Fahrenheit's thermometer."

These experiments did not reveal any new principles, but they showed that Henry had acquired an excellent command of experimenting, and had learnt how to describe results clearly.

He undertook the road survey after they were published, and was appointed to the chair of mathematics when he had completed the survey. The Albany Academy was one of the institutions supervised by the Regents of the University of the State of New York. In 1825 the Regents organized meteorological observations for the State, and instruments were set up in the Academy as part of the system. Henry and others were asked in 1827 to tabulate the observations. This began a long and distinguished connection with meteorology. The observers were expected to note the climatic conditions on days when any peculiar behavior of plants and animals occurred. The influence of agricultural interests on the development of the science of meteorology is seen in this instruction.

Henry's first paper on electro-magnetism was read to the Institute on October 10th, 1827.

Simon Newcomb has remarked that no American since Franklin had made any contribution to the science of electricity, until Henry began his researches. This interregnum of seventy-five years was, in his opinion, one of the most curious features in the intellectual history of America. There had been "plenty of professors of eminent attainments who had amused themselves and instructed their pupils and the public by physical experiments," but they had not been inspired by Franklin's brilliant example to discover new knowledge of electricity. This is an important problem for the students of the history of science. Many factors contributed to the phenomenon. The absorption of American energy in pioneering and the achievement of independence, and the slow emancipation from the intellectual tutelage of Europe, are among them.

Henry explains his approach to electricity in his first paper. He remarks that although electro-magnetism is "one of the most interesting branches of human knowledge, and presenting at this time the most fruitful field for discovery," it is less understood in America than any other branch of science. The popular lecturers have not availed themselves of the "many interesting and novel experiments with which it can supply them," and little attention has been devoted to it in the "higher institutions of learning."

"A principal cause of this inattention to a subject offering so much to instruct and amuse is the difficulty and expense which formerly attended the experiments—a large galvanic battery, with instruments of very delicate workmanship, being thought indispensable."

Henry then explains that this difficulty had been removed by William Sturgeon of London, who had devised a set of instruments which would demonstrate the phenomena of electro-magnetism without requiring powerful sources of current. He achieved this by general improvements in design, and also by incorporation of his great invention, the electromagnet, into his apparatus. Sturgeon described his electro-magnet in 1825. It was capable of supporting a weight of nine pounds. Within two years Henry was following his researches, on the other side of the Atlantic. He suggested that in those apparatuses in which electro-magnets could not be used, greater sensitivity could be obtained by using coils containing many wires, after the manner of Schweigger, in his invention of the galvanometer. Henry designed elegant improvements of apparatuses such as De la Rive's ring, for demonstrating the alignment of an electrical coil across the earth's magnetic field.

The spur of the entertainment motive is prominent in the work of Sturgeon, who tried, and miserably failed, to gain a living by demonstrating and teaching electricity. His extraordinary career has not been adequately studied, though Joule wrote a sympathetic short account of it. The same motive is seen, among others, in Henry's first paper; the improvement in the efficiency and power of apparatus in order especially to increase its entertainment value.

Nowadays the spur of this motive is seen in the subsidy of laboratories for research on the technique of photography, talking machines and films, television, etc.

The deflection of a magnetic needle by a wire carrying a current was reported by G. D. Romagnosi in 1802, but his observation was overlooked. H. C. Oersted rediscovered the phenomenon in 1819 and swiftly drew adequate attention to

JOSEPH HENRY

A few years over the age of thirty

PLATE III

it. Schweigger increased the magnitude of the effect by using a coil of many turns instead of a single wire. His instrument could be used for measuring the strength of the current passing through the coil, and was named a galvanometer. Henry improved the effectiveness of Sturgeon's demonstration apparatus by the systematic introduction into the design of carefully-made coils containing many turns. Then he began the systematic improvement of Sturgeon's own invention of the electro-magnet.

Sturgeon's electro-magnet consisted of a bar of soft iron bent into a horse-shoe shape. The bar was varnished, and eighteen turns of bare copper wire were wound round it. Large gaps were left between the turns, so that no electrical short-circuiting could occur. The design was very inefficient, but the magnet would support nine pounds' weight, when the ends of the coil were connected to a large-current battery.

One evening, when Henry was sitting in his study with a friend, he arose and exclaimed after a few moments of reverie: "Tomorrow I shall make a famous experiment." He had just thought of a new way of winding electro-magnets, in the light of Ampere's theory of magnetism. "When this conception came into my brain I was so pleased with it that I could not help rising to my feet and giving it my hearty approbation." He began to construct electro-magnets in which the exciting coil was insulated, instead of the iron core. He used thin copper wire covered with silk. This enabled him to wind a very much larger number of turns around the core. Also, as the coils were very close, they lay almost at right angles to the axis of the core. This made the maximum use of the magnetizing force. In Sturgeon's electro-magnet, the loose coils had a pitch, or lay across the core at an angle of about thirty degrees. Henry exhibited a horse-shoe electro-magnet in 1829, which contained 400 turns of silk-covered wire. The coil was wound over itself in successive layers. Thus he was the first to construct a magnetic spool, or bobbin. He found that this electro-magnet would support a considerable weight when excited by a small current.

Later in 1829 he exhibited an electro-magnet wound with several short coils, instead of one long one. A half-inch iron bar was bent into a horse-shoe shape, and wound with thirty feet of tolerably fine copper wire. This bar would support 14 lbs. when excited by a small voltaic battery. Henry then wound a second coil of 30 feet, and attached its ends to the same battery. He found the bar would now support 28 lbs. With a larger battery, it would support 39 lbs., or more than fifty times its own weight. He explained that his "experiment conclusively proved that a great development of magnetism could be effected by a very small galvanic element."

With P. Ten Eyck he investigated in 1830 how an electro-magnet behaved at the end of a wire 1,060 feet, or about one-fifth of a mile long. The wire was "stretched several times across the large room of the Academy." They secured two voltaic batteries. One consisted of a single pair of large plates, and the other of twenty-five pairs of small plates. The total area of zinc in both batteries was the same. They found that the electro-magnet would support 8 ounces, when the current from the twenty-five cell battery was sent to it through the 1,060 feet of wire. It lifted only half an ounce when similarly excited by the single-cell battery. He found that when the long wire was cut out of the circuit, and the electro-magnet connected directly to the twenty-five-cell battery, the magnet lifted only 7 ounces. Henry comments on this remarkable result. He thinks it might have been due to variations in the conductivity of the battery, or to the slowing-down of the electricity in the long wire, which would enable it to go round the core more slowly when it arrived, and thus produce more magnetism in it. He would have verified the result by further experiments "had not our use of the room been limited, by its being required for public exercises." But he concludes that the coils of the magnet may either be single and long, or multiple and short; and the batteries must give a small current of high intensity, or a large current of low intensity, as circumstances require. An electro-magnet with a long single coil lifted less than when wound with several separate coils, but it had the property of being excited by a high-intensity battery through a long connecting wire. The current from a multiple-cell battery seemed to resemble that from a frictional machine. He points out that his results confirm the possibility of the construction of an electro-magnetic telegraph. Henry is therefore the inventor of the first telegraph employing electromagnets.

Henry's experiments were made before Ohm's law had been recognized, and units for voltage, amperage, and resistance had been defined.

P. Barlow had denied the possibility of the electro-magnetic telegraph, because experimenters had found that the current from low-voltage batteries did not produce sensible deflections in galvanometers at the ends of long connecting wires. As mentioned in Chapter I, electric communication through considerable distances had been achieved early in the eighteenth century with frictional electricity. W. B. Taylor remarks that Salva worked a static electric telegraph over a distance of 26 miles, between Madrid and Aranjuez, in 1798. This succeeded because the electricity produced by frictional machines is of a high-voltage, low-amperage type.

Henry and Ten Eyck proceeded to construct an electromagnet, with an iron core which weighed 21 lbs. The piece of iron to be attracted to the core, the lifter or armature, as he names it, weighed 7 lbs. 540 feet of copper bell wire were wound round the core, in nine coils each containing 60 feet. The ends of the separate coils were left projecting, and all numbered. "In this manner we formed an experimental magnet on a large scale, with which several combinations of wire could be made by merely uniting the different projecting ends."

The horse-shoe was suspended in a strong wooden frame 3 feet 9 inches high and 20 inches wide. The lifting power of various combinations of coils and batteries could be tested by hanging weights onto the armature. He found that two coils connected in series, when excited by a small battery, produced a lifting-power of 60 lbs., but when connected in parallel, the lifting-power was 200 lbs. Four coils in parallel gave a lifting-power of 500 lbs., and nine gave 650 lbs. The current from a voltaic battery, whose plates were exactly one inch square, was sufficient to produce a lifting-power of 85 lbs. when connected to the nine coils in parallel. With a larger battery he obtained a lifting-power of 750 lbs.

The existence of considerable quantities of copper bell wire in Albany in 1830 was an important condition of Henry's researches. It would be interesting to know why it was easily obtainable there, and how he obtained the money to buy it. Henry writes in his paper that Dr. L. C. Beck suggested they should use "cotton well waxed for silk thread, which in these investigations became a very considerable item of expense." Beck made a number of experiments with "iron bonnet-wire, which, being found in commerce already wound, might possibly be substituted in place of copper," but they failed, owing to what would now be described as the high resistance of the iron. The invention of less expensive methods of construction was an important feature of these researches.

Henry's improvement of the electro-magnet by systematic experiment and measurement shows the influence of industrial engineering methods on the development of physics. Some years later Joule started an investigation of the efficiency of the electro-magnetic engine, or form of electro-motor, which led to the modern conception of the conservation of energy. His first experiments, like Henry's, were directed to the improvement of the electro-magnet, and the work of both showed the influence of the spirit of the industrial engineer, who must design efficient machines in order to reduce the costs of production. When steam-power, or energy, became a market commodity, an accurate measure of it was demanded by commerce. This was the motive of the investigations which led to the saving of power, and the understanding of the theory of efficiency and conservation.

An electro-magnet capable of lifting 2,065 lbs., or about one ton, was constructed at Yale College under Henry's direction in 1831. A weight of 89 lbs. could be held without dropping, when the poles were reversed, by reversing the current. This principle was afterwards employed in the neutral relay of quadruplex telegraphy, described in Chapter III.

Henry's methods of constructing magnetizing coils were adopted by Faraday in the apparatus with which he discovered electro-magnetic induction, and powerful electro-magnets of his type were essential in the discovery of the polarization of light by a magnetic field.

In July, 1831, Henry described a method of producing reciprocating motion "by a power, which," he believes, "has never before been applied in mechanics—by magnetic attraction and repulsion." He constructed the first reciprocating electro-magnetic machine.

He suspended a bar electro-magnet horizontally by a pivot passing through its center of gravity. The north poles of permanent magnets were fixed under each end. When the current was sent through the coil of the electro-magnet, the north pole of the electro-magnet repelled the north pole of the permanent magnet, while the opposite occurred at the other pair of poles. The current was reversed by arranging that the oscillating magnet should bear connecting wires which dipped in and out of the acid of voltaic batteries, with each oscillation. The electro-magnet oscillated at the rate of 75 vibrations per minute for more than one hour.

Henry remarks that "not much importance, however, is attached to the invention, since the article in its present state can only be considered a philosophical toy; although in the progress of discovery and invention, it is not impossible that the same principle, or some modification of it on a more extended scale, may hereafter be applied to some useful purpose."

Henry soon saw that the power developed by his machine was indirectly drawn from the combustion of coal, and the machine would not supplant steam as a source of power. He did not expect it would have any application, except in circumstances where economy was of no importance.

While at Albany Henry began to construct a dynamo.

Henry slung more than a mile of wire around an upper room in the Academy in 1831. He sent a current from a multiple-cell battery through it to an electro-magnet which attracted the hammer of a bell. He demonstrated this apparatus to his classes, in order to prove that signals could be swiftly transmitted to a distance by electro-magnetism.

He was urged to patent these inventions, but refused, as he "did not then consider it compatible with the dignity of science to confine the benefits which might be derived from it to the exclusive use of any individual." In 1876, he wrote that perhaps this opinion had been too fastidious. Henry was not opposed to patent laws. He considered they provided the most equitable method of materially rewarding inventors, but he believed that patenting was beneath the dignity of a natural philosopher. W. B. Taylor remarks that if he had profited from his inventions he would have had more adequate means for extending his researches.

After Oersted had rediscovered that a wire bearing an electric current would deflect a magnetic needle, many investigators tried to discover the reverse effect, the production of an electric current in a wire through the medium of magnetism. Faraday was the first to publish a demonstration of the effect, and the experiment is usually considered his greatest single achievement. He obtained his first positive evidence of electro-magnetic induction in August, 1831, with the assistance of a ring electro-magnet whose magnetic strength had been increased by adopting Henry's system of winding with several separate coils. On September 24th he is confident that he has obtained a "distinct conversion of magnetism into electricity," and by November 4th he had confirmed his results by a variety of experiments.

During the last few years Henry had also been investigating how electricity might be obtained from magnetism. Soon after he read of Faraday's success, he wrote a description of his own researches, and published it in July, 1832.

In this paper he starts by recalling that the discoveries of Oersted, Arago and Faraday had shown the intimate connection between electricity and magnetism, and that magnetic effects, such as the deflection of a needle, were easily obtained from an electric current. This had immediately suggested that electric currents ought to be easily obtainable from magnetism, but, "although the experiment has often been attempted, it has nearly as often failed." He then writes:

"It early occurred to me, that if galvanic magnets on my plan were substituted for ordinary magnets, in researches of this kind, more success might be expected. Besides their great power, these magnets possess other properties, which render them important instruments in the hands of the experimenter: their polarity can be instantaneously reversed, and their magnetism suddenly destroyed or called into full action, according as the occasion may require. With this view, I commenced, last August, the construction of a much larger galvanic magnet than, to my knowledge, had before been attempted, and also made preparations for a series of experiments with it on a large scale, in reference to the production of electricity from magnetism. I was however at that time accidentally interrupted in the prosecution of these experiments, and have not been able since to resume them, until within the last few weeks, and then on a much smaller scale than was at first intended. In the meantime, it has been announced in the 117th number of the *Library of Useful Knowledge,* that the result so much sought after has at length been found by Mr. Faraday of the Royal Institution. It states that he has established the general fact, that when a piece of metal is moved in any direction, in front of a magnetic pole, electric currents are developed in the metal, which pass in a direction at right angles to its own motion, and also that the application of this principle affords a complete and satisfactory explanation of the phenomena of magnetic rotation. No detail is given of the experiments, and it is somewhat surprising that results so interesting, and which certainly form a new era in the history of electricity and magnetism, should not have been more fully described before this time in some of the English publications; the only mention I have found of them is the following short account from the *Annals of Philosophy* for April. . . ."

Henry quotes the statement of Faraday's discovery that if two insulated wires are laid parallel to each other, a current starting in one will induce a current in the other, in the opposite direction. Also, if a magnet is passed in and out of a coil, a current will be induced in the coil, while the magnet is in motion. Henry continues:

"Before having any knowledge of the method given in the above account, I had succeeded in producing electrical effects in the following manner, which differs from that employed by Mr. Faraday, and which appears to me to develop some new and interesting facts."

He describes how he had wound thirty feet of copper wire, covered with elastic varnish, round the soft iron armature of the electro-magnet which could lift 700 lbs. The ends of the wire were connected to a galvanometer. The coils of the electro-magnet were excited by suddenly immersing the plates of a voltaic battery, to which they were connected. Henry observed that the galvanometer needle was momentarily deflected at the instant of immersion. To his surprise, he found that a momentary deflection occurred, in the opposite direction, when the plates were suddenly lifted out of the battery, and the exciting current cut off.

He found that a current of electricity is momentarily produced in a coil surrounding a piece of soft iron, whenever magnetism is induced in the iron, "and a current in the opposite direction occurs when the magnetic action ceases, and also that an instantaneous current in one or the other direction accompanies every change in the magnetic intensity of the iron."

Henry then writes that "since reading the account before given of Mr. Faraday's method," he has made some more experiments. One of these consisted of obtaining sparks from the coil round the soft iron armature, by holding its ends near together when the electro-magnet was excited. He remarks that he has been forestalled in this experiment, as he has learned that J. D. Forbes of Edinburgh published an account of a similar experiment in March, "my experiments being made during the last two weeks of June."

Henry mentions that he has made "several other experiments in relation to the same subject, but which more important duties will not permit me to verify in time for this paper. I may however mention one fact I have not seen noticed in any work, and which appears to me to belong to the same class of phenomena as those before described." He then publishes the great discovery of self-induction.

From any point of view, this was a wonderful paper. He gives in it the first publication of the discovery of self-induction, and forestalled Faraday's repetition of this discovery by two years. He gives an independent discovery of the derivation of electric sparks from a current induced in a coil. He gives an account of a demonstration of electro-magnetic induction made before he had any knowledge of the method given in the account of Faraday's researches in the *Annals of Philosophy*.

It would be extremely interesting to know exactly when he first made this last experiment. Did he make it before he read the account of Faraday's work in the note in the *Library of Useful Knowledge?* It is not entirely clear whether his remarks concerning the "method given in the above account" refers both to this note and to the account in the *Annals of Philosophy*.

The note was appended by Roget to his article on Electromagnetism. As it is not often quoted it is given here in full:

"*Note.* Since the above was sent to the press. a paper, by Mr. Faraday, has been communicated to the Royal Society, disclosing a most important principle in electro-magnetism, of which, I regret, I can only give the following brief statement.

"By a numerous series of experiments, Mr. Faraday has established the general fact, that when a piece of metal is moved in any direction, either in front of a single magnetic pole, or between the opposite poles of a horse-shoe magnet, electrical currents are developed in the metal, which pass in a direction at right angles to that of its own motion. The application of this principle affords a complete and satisfactory explanation of the phenomenon observed by Arago, Herschel, Babbage, and others, where magnetic action appears to be developed by mere rotatory motion, and which have been erroneously ascribed to simple magnetic induction, and to the time supposed to be required for the progress of that induction. The electro-magnet effect of the elective (*sic*) current induced in a conductor by a magnet pole, in consequence of their relative motion, is such as tends continually to diminish that relative motion; that is, to bring the moving bodies into a state of relative rest: so that, if the one be made to revolve by an extraneous force, the other will tend to revolve with it, in the same direction, and with the same velocity."

Roget's article was signed Dec. 12th, 1831. Henry does not say when he first read the note. Perhaps it was about March 1832.

Henry's paper of July, 1832, and the history of its contents, have been carefully analysed by his daughter Mary A. Henry, in six articles published in 1892. She writes that the experiments described in the paper are to be divided into two groups, those done before he had any knowledge of Faraday's method, and those done afterwards. She explains that those made "since reading the account . . . of Mr. Faraday's method" were done in the last two weeks of June, 1832. The experiments in the first group, which includes the great experiment with the coil wound round the armature of the electro-magnet, were done before Henry had read the April number of the *Annals of Philosophy*, which he may have received in May. Thus the experiments were done before May. (Miss Henry does not discuss the bearing of Roget's note, but Henry may have read this in March. In that case, according to Miss Henry, he would have made the experiments before March.)

Miss Henry now points out that it is extremely unlikely that Henry had any opportunity for experiments between August, 1831 and June, 1832. The Academy's hall, where he made experiments, was occupied by other activities during that period, and Henry himself was engaged in a vast amount of teaching and lecturing. Henry's own account in the July paper suggests that he had no opportunity for experiments between August, 1831 and June, 1832. Thus Miss Henry concludes that Henry made his definitive experiment on electro-magnetic induction in August, 1831, or earlier. She explains that Henry had only one month's vacation in the year. He taught seven hours daily, largely to children, and he had no permanent room for experimenting. The America of 1830 was unable to provide a permanent room for the researches of a genius such as Henry. This illustrates the state of culture in the country at the time. It was therefore probable that he made his chief experiments during the August vacations.

In August, 1831, he was constructing a new electro-magnet. Now Henry describes his definitive experiment as made with the old electro-magnet described in 1829. It seems probable, therefore, that he made his definitive experiments in August, 1830, while he was still working with his old magnet.

Miss Henry says that her father used to mention in private conversation that he had noticed sparks from the coils of his electric telegraph in 1829, and had suspected they were due to electro-magnetic induction. He said, also, that he had anticipated Faraday by about a year in the discovery, but unfortunately had not published an account of his researches, owing to the lack of time for the preparation of a thorough description of them.

A difficulty in accepting this last explanation is raised by Henry's comments in his July paper on the slowness of the publication of Faraday's researches. He says it is surprising that experiments which "form a new era in the history of electricity and magnetism, should not have been more fully described before this time in some of the English publications." If Henry himself was in possession of the result in 1830, and had been refraining from publication for two years, it seems odd that he should rebuke others for failing to publish a detailed description within a few months.

As a daughter, Miss Henry was in an excellent position to know Henry's private opinions, but her discussions were published in 1892, sixty years after the events. This diminishes the value of evidence she may have heard verbally many years before.

The question whether Henry or Faraday was the first in time to discover electro-magnetic induction seems not to admit an absolutely final answer. The probability is that Henry was the first. Certainly, he made a definitive experiment whose style was absolutely his own.

The comparison between the careers of Faraday and Henry as investigators of electricity up to the year 1835 is in Henry's favor. He lived in Albany in America, with little time, small resources, and few intellectual companions. Faraday lived in London, in a world-center of intellectual activity, with much free time for research, and considerable resources. He was five years older.

Further, there were peculiar incidents in connection with several of Faraday's early electrical researches. Davy opposed his election to the Royal Society, on the ground that his work on electro-magnetic rotations was not original, and that the idea had been taken from Wollaston. Faraday was not generous in his recognition of Sturgeon, and he did not express his indebtedness to Henry for the technique of the design of electro-magnets very fully or exactly in his early papers. He failed to read Henry's description of self-induction in 1832. There is evidence that he was slower than Henry in recognizing the significance of experimental results in electricity.

Henry exhibits an almost morbid, or masochistic, modesty in the statement of his results and claims. He ascribes the minimum to himself, and the maximum to others.

A comparison of the early work of Henry and Faraday on electro-magnetic induction shows that Faraday has received too much praise for his contribution. Electro-magnetic induction was the least unique of his important discoveries. His greatness rests far more on his development of the idea of lines of force, and of the electro-magnetic field.

Henry never questioned Faraday's priority. No scientist has been more careful than he in matters of priority. His care did not arise from a contempt of applause, but from a desire not to receive applause for things he had not done. He considered the approbation of intellectual equals the greatest distinction in the gift of humanity, and he wished to preserve the standard of that approbation by the most exact assessment of achievement. Thus he disapproved of the slightest exaggeration of an achievement, and was inclined to ignore any claims concerning which there was vagueness or doubt.

From the perspective of the history of science, the question of personal priority is of no importance. The significant feature of Henry's great paper of July, 1832, is that the phenomenon of electro-magnetic induction was discovered, or about to be discovered, independently at about the same time in Albany, U. S. A., and in London, England. These events show that the progress of science depends far less than is generally believed on the efforts of individual geniuses. Faraday and Henry were the most advanced of a group of hundreds of investigators who assumed that if electric currents could produce magnets, then magnets should produce electric currents. The phenomenon of electro-magnetic induction is of enormous importance, but this does not necessarily imply that the experimental difficulties of discovery were very great. As Henry and Faraday made the discovery almost simultaneously, it could not have been of such a unique nature that it could occur only to one investigator of supreme genius.

Henry's achievements at Albany attracted the authorities of the College of New Jersey, or Princeton, and he was invited to occupy their chair of natural philosophy. He moved to Princeton at the end of 1832.

He had married his cousin Harriet L. Alexander in 1830. She had come to live in Albany after the death of her father, who had been a successful business man in Schenectady. They had ultimately six children, of which three daughters survived the death of their father in 1878. Mrs. Henry lived until 1882.

During the first years at Princeton Henry had little time for research. He had to organize his department and courses of lectures, and in 1833 fill in addition the chair of chemistry, mineralogy and geology, whose occupant was spending a year's leave of absence in visiting Europe. He subsequently also lectured on astronomy and architecture.

While he was struggling with his pile of routine duties, Faraday was pursuing without interruption his investigations of electro-magnetism, and published his rediscovery of self-induction. Henry was urged by his friend A. D. Bache, the great-grandson of Benjamin Franklin, who was at that time professor of natural philosophy in the University of Pennsylvania, to write accounts of his further researches.

He constructed an electro-magnet which would lift one and a half tons, and showed for the first time how "a large amount of power might, by means of a relay magnet, be called into operation at the distance of many miles." He communicated by an electric telegraph from the College to his house, across the campus grounds. The wire was extended "from the upper story of the library building to the philosophical hall on the opposite side, the ends terminating in two wells." He used earth returns immediately after Steinheil in Germany had discovered their practicability.

He extended his researches on self-induction. A strip of copper 1½ inches wide and 96 feet long was insulated with silk and rolled into a flat spiral like a watch spring. He would have made a larger spiral, but could not obtain the necessary material. Sparks resembling discharges from a Leiden jar could be drawn from this coil.

Henry was given a year's leave of absence in 1837 to visit Europe. He was accompanied by A. D. Bache. He acquired the friendship of Faraday, Wheatstone, Arago, De la Rive, and other eminent scientists. He spoke to the British Association at Liverpool on the lateral electric discharge. He described experiments which confirmed Biot's opinion that it "is due only to the escape of the small quantity of redundant electricity which always exists on one or the other side of a jar, and not to the whole discharge."

Henry also spoke to the Mechanics and Engineering Section on the great development of railways and canals in the United States, and on the improvement of river steamers, some of which could steam at fifteen miles per hour. In the discussion Dr. Lardner, the economist, expressed doubts of the accuracy of Henry's statement concerning the speed of the American boats, and made his celebrated declaration, on the basis of observations on Thames steamboats, that oceanic steam navigation was impossible.

He visited King's College, London, to join Faraday, Wheatstone and Daniell in an attempt to make a spark with current from a thermopile. The English experimenters tried it in turn and failed. Henry then attempted to increase the self-induction of the current by sending it through a long interpolar wire wrapped round a piece of soft iron. He succeeded in producing a spark. Faraday was delighted, and jumped up and shouted: "Hurrah for the Yankee experiment." Years later, Faraday and Wheatstone wrote a joint letter to the Royal Society, proposing that the Copley Medal should be awarded to Henry, but their proposal was deferred by the Council, and ultimately passed over. Mary A. Henry states that Wheatstone learned of the practical possibility of using a galvanometer for detecting a current at the end of a long telegraph wire from Henry during their London conversations in 1837.

After returning from Europe, Henry continued his researches on induction. He elucidated by experiment some of the properties of the transformer, demonstrating that currents of high voltage and low amperage could be obtained from those of low voltage and high amperage and the reverse. He proved this with a series of coils of various sizes. Pairs of coils were placed in contiguity, and the induction of currents in one from the other was examined.

He investigated the induction of currents in an exploring coil held in various places in the neighborhood of the inducing coil. In this way, he discovered how the coils should be aligned in order to induce most effectively any desired type of current; and the most effective dimensions, and design, of the coils. He found that soft iron placed in a coil could be magnetized by induction from remarkably great distances. He found that induction could be made through the walls of a room. A person in an empty room, holding the ends of a coil, might be given a shock by a current induced from another coil in an adjoining room. Henry remarks that the uninitiated sometimes imagined such shocks, without apparent cause, were due to magic.

He applied the action of induction at a distance to the graduation of the treatment of a patient suffering from a partial paralysis of the nerves of the face. The inducing coil was suspended from a pulley, and could be raised or lowered over the coil in which current was induced, so that the strength of the induced current could be varied, to give shocks of the correct intensity.

He examined the screening effect of materials placed between two coils. He found that conductors destroyed the induction, but non-conductors did not. He proved that the screening effect of conductors was due to the induction in them of eddy currents which neutralized the current induced in the screened coil. This was done by cutting a slit in the metal screening disc. The slit disc had no screening effect. The direction the current would have taken in the complete disc was discovered by connecting the edges of the slit by wires to a detecting instrument.

Humphry Davy had found in 1821 that the magnetization of needles by electric discharges was unaffected by the interposition of screens, irrespective of whether they were made of conductors or non-conductors. Henry explained that this result was due to the disposition of his apparatus. He arranged the conductor screens in such a way that they were equivalent to the slit disc, and could not contain eddy currents, and therefore could not operate as electrical screens.

The fact that the primary current could be completely neutralized by a secondary current suggested to him that secondary currents could be separated from primary currents, and used to induce a current in a third conductor. In this way, he established and investigated third, fourth, and fifth orders of induction.

He pointed out that the eddy currents induced in homogeneous conductors must reduce the efficiency of electromagnetic machines. The rings of metal which formed the sides of the spools bearing the exciting coils would "circulate a closed current which will interfere with the intensity of the induction in the surrounding wire. I am inclined to believe that the increased effect observed by Sturgeon and Calland, when a bundle of wire is substituted for a solid piece of iron, is at least in part due to the interruption of these currents." Henry published this work in 1838.

He made a long series of experiments on induction by electric currents produced from frictional electricity. He found that induction by these currents had peculiar characteristics. Savary had observed in 1826 that a frictional electric discharge current magnetized needles with alternate direction of polarity, depending on their distance from the wire conducting the discharge, and had suggested that it was due to oscillations in the direction of the discharge. This phenomenon was thoroughly investigated by Henry. In 1842 he explained that it was due to a property of the discharge of a Leiden jar which had not previously been recognized. The discharge was not correctly represented by the single transfer of electricity from one side of the jar to the other, but to "the existence of a principal discharge in one direction, and then several reflex actions backward and forward, each more feeble than the preceding, until equilibrium is obtained." Henry definitely confirmed the theory that the Leiden jar discharge is oscillatory five years before Helmholtz expressed the same view in 1847, and Kelvin in 1852.

The currents induced by the oscillatory discharges were detected by the magnetization of needles put inside small coils. These detectors could be set up at any distance from the wire conducting the primary discharge. Henry discovered that the needles were magnetized when the detectors were placed at remarkably great distances from the discharge wire. He found that a single spark discharge in a parallelogram of copper wire sixty feet by thirty, suspended by silk threads in the upper room of a building, was sufficient to magnetize needles in an identical parallelogram in the cellar, thirty feet below, and separated by two floors and ceilings, each fourteen inches thick. Henry comments: "The author is disposed to adopt the hypothesis of an electrical *plenum*, and from the foregoing experiment it would appear that the transfer of a single spark is sufficient to disturb perceptibly the electricity of space throughout at least a cube of 400,000 feet of capacity; and when it is considered that the magnetism of the needle is the result of the difference of two actions, it may be further inferred that the diffusion of motion in this case is almost comparable with that of a spark from a flint and steel in the case of light." Before commenting on this passage, two more experiments may be noted.

Henry connected one end of a coil in his study with the metal roofing on his house, and the other end to a metal plate in a deep well near the house. He found that needles put in this coil were strongly magnetized by lightning flashes which occurred "within a circle of at least twenty miles." He proposed to use this arrangement as "a simple self-registering electrometer for studying atmospheric electricity." He showed that the current produced in the house circuit by the distant lightning was oscillatory. He found that if a discharge from a battery of several Leiden jars was sent through the wire stretched across the campus in front of Nassau Hall, at Princeton, "an inductive effect was produced in a parallel wire, the ends of which terminated in the plates of metal in the ground in the back campus." The distance between the wires was several hundred feet, and the building of Nassau Hall stood in the

intervening space. Henry remarked, in 1846, that it was concluded that the "distance might be indefinitely increased, provided the wires were lengthened in a corresponding ratio."

It is evident from these accounts that Henry was unconsciously detecting induction due to electro-magnetic waves. He
had unwittingly invented the method of detecting radio waves
which depends on charges in the magnetization of a magnet.

His observations had prompted him to compare the spreading from a single spark discharge of what he described as induction, with the spreading of light from a spark made with
flint and steel. Here he was comparing what in fact were
electro-magnetic waves with waves of light. His understanding had prompted him to suspect a similarity between these
electrical effects and light, which was subsequently proved by
Maxwell and Hertz. It is now common knowledge that the
difference between radio-waves and light-waves is due to a
difference in wave-length only.

Henry's deduction of the similarity of the spreading of the
electrical disturbance with the spreading of light was based
on his simple calculation of the enormous volume of space
through which the disturbance was observable. The electric
spark could, as it were, be seen by the magnetic detector, as
a lighted match could be seen by the eye.

He did not use the word "energy," as, in its modern sense,
it had not, in 1842, been introduced into physics. But he saw
that the energy of the spreading mechanism of the electrical
disturbance, and that of waves of light, were of the same order,
and he concluded that the electrical spreading must be due
to an electrical plenum, or ether.

In 1842 Henry was unconsciously making experiments with
radio waves, and had begun to formulate qualitatively some
first rough ideas of an electrical ether which transmitted disturbances to great distances. He had started to approach the
electro-magnetic theory of light.

He remarked again, in an address in 1851, that the inductive
effects of the discharge current of a Leiden jar appeared to be
"propagated wave-fashion," and that the inductive effects,

which extend to such surprising distances, "must produce in surrounding space a series of plus and minus motions analogous to if not identical with undulations."

These speculations are to be compared with those of Faraday in his lecture of 1846, on *Ray Vibrations,* which, according to Clerk Maxwell, contains the first proposal of the electromagnetic theory of light. Faraday suggested that radiation was a species of transverse vibrations in lines of force. He believed this conception was implied by the phenomenon of the magnetic polarization of light, which he had discovered early in 1846 (with a powerful electro-magnet of the type invented by Henry).

Henry's greatest achievements were in electrical research, but he made many other interesting researches. He worked assiduously at meteorology, and his proposals for systematic world-weather observations, which were studied by the British Association in 1838, were wider than any before suggested. In 1831 he had shown that some aurorae are simultaneously visible in America and Europe, and are therefore due to general physical conditions of the globe, and not to local phenomena.

He used Melloni's thermopile in 1843 to measure the heat-radiation from the sky, and found that the vapors near the horizon were powerful reflectors of heat, but that the cloud of a distant thunder-storm was colder than the adjacent blue space.

He observed in 1839 that mercury could be siphoned through a height of three feet by a thick lead wire. Mr. Cornelius of Philadelphia, a manufacturer of bronzes, informed him that when silver-plated copper was heated to the melting point, the silver was burned away. Henry dissolved the surface from such a piece of burned copper, with acid, and revealed the silver underneath. This proved that solid silver would dissolve in solid copper.

He extended the knowledge of the production of phosphorescence by rays, especially from sparks, and showed that phosphorescent rays excited by polarized light were completely depolarized. G. G. Stokes rediscovered this effect ten years later.

He described in 1843 an electrical chronograph for determining the velocity of projectiles. In one form the projectile was to be fired through wire screens, each of which was connected through an induction coil to a metal pointer nearly touching paper wound round a revolving metal drum. When a screen was broken, an induction current produced a spark between the pointer and the drum, which left a small hole in the paper. This method had the great merit of no inertia in the working parts. Wheatstone invented a method of measuring the velocity of projectiles some time after 1834, but did not publish it until 1845.

He investigated the cohesion of liquids in 1844. He measured the tenacity of a soap-film by "weighing the quantity of water which adhered to a bubble just before it burst." The thickness of the film was determined by an observation of Newton's rings. He concluded that the molecular attraction of water for water is several hundred pounds per square inch, and equal to that of ice for ice. The strength of the soap-film is due not to an increase in molecular attraction, but to the reduction of the mobility of the molecules. Further experiments showed that the cohesion of pure water is greater than that of soapy water. He explained that the change from the solid to the liquid state was due, not to the destruction of cohesion, but to the neutralization of the polarity of molecules, which gave them "perfect freedom of motion around every imaginable axis."

He gave an address in 1844 *On the Origin and Classification of the Natural Motors*. His thoughts had been turned to this subject by some remarks by Babbage on "the economy of machinery," and by the researches of Liebig, Dumas, and Boussingault on vital chemistry. Henry writes that he believed he had brought the views of all these investigators together, in a manner that had not been done before. He concludes that the force of the burning fuel in an engine, and that developed by the moving animal, are ultimately derived from the sun's rays. He believed that the vital principle is restricted to the propagation of form and arrangement of atoms in living organisms. His views approximated to the theory of the conservation of energy.

He investigated in 1845 the relative heat-radiating power of portions of the sun's surface. A large image of the sun's disc was explored by a small thermopile. Henry found that the heat radiation from a large sun-spot was distinctly less than that from "the surrounding parts of the luminous disk." This research virtually founded a new branch of solar physics. It was extended by P. A. Secchi, who was a young professor in America at the time, and was assisted and encouraged by Henry.

After 1846, Henry's opportunities for research were again restricted by his working conditions. The account so far given describes the researches done before the age of forty-nine years. They form a great achievement, and the degree of Henry's ability is illustrated when it is considered that he was unable to start research until he was thirty years old, and had to work under very hard conditions until he was thirty-five. After he had done all this he became the first Secretary of the Smithsonian Institution, and directed its activities for thirty-two years.

III

The Smithsonian Institution

I

THIS INSTITUTION WAS FOUNDED WITH A sum of about £106,000, or $500,000, which passed into the hands of the Government of the United States in 1837, through the will of an Englishman named James Smithson, who died in 1829.

James Smithson was an illegitimate son of Sir Hugh Smithson, who became the first Duke of Northumberland.

Sir Hugh Smithson was the son of a Yorkshire baronet, or minor hereditary nobleman, who owned a small family estate. Country gentlemen of this sort usually managed their estates, and Hugh Smithson had been educated in this tradition. He was extremely handsome, energetic, capable and ambitious. These qualities enabled him to marry, in 1740, Elizabeth Percy, the heiress of the wealth and connections of the Percy family. This family had large estates in Northumberland, which contained deposits of coal. The growth of industry in the latter half of the eighteenth century had prompted the improvement of the steam engine, and following this achievement, the demand for coal swiftly increased. Numerous coal mines were sunk on Smithson's estates, and the number of miners and the general population increased rapidly. The rent from the Northumberland estates increased from £8,607 in 1749 to about £50,000 per annum in 1778. This development was primarily due to the growth of the coal trade. The working conditions of the miners at this period were shocking. Women were used to draw tubs of coal along the pit galleries. The chains by which they hauled the tubs were fastened round their necks, and passed between their legs, where they made horrible sores through friction.

Smithson spent a large part of his income on ostentation. His wife's equipages often excelled those of the Queen, and his expenditure exceeded that of any other private person. The old nobility hated his pride and wealth, and regarded him as an upstart. George III was friendly with him, and in 1766 made him a duke, as a consolation for failure to receive the highest political offices.

Smithson was one of the new class of magnates which achieved wealth by the exploitation of the opportunities created by the introduction of steam power and machinery into industry. He had the virtues besides the vices of his class. He was business-like. He drained and reclaimed his land, repaired the houses, and planted twelve hundred trees a year for twenty years. Dutens wrote that "he had great talents and more knowledge than is generally found amongst the nobility." On the other hand, Walpole wrote that "with the mechanic application to every branch of knowledge, he possessed none beyond the surface." This was the opinion of a philosopher of the pre-industrial leisure class, and shows the usual prejudice of that class, as exemplified by Plato twenty centuries ago, against mechanical knowledge.

His attention to details was interpreted as "littleness of temper," he was despised for his "sordid and illiberal conduct" in gambling, and "although his expenditure was unexampled in his time, he was not generous, but passed for being so owing to his judicious manner of bestowing favours."

The same sense, which was that of a new sort of commercial magnate, led him to oppose the repression of the American colonies. His son Algernon, who became the second duke, fought against the Americans at Lexington. He also did not approve of the repression, and soon noted that the American insurgents were far more formidable than a mob, brave, and not without military skill.

The first Duke of Northumberland was a leader of a new

social class, and had fierce struggles for equality with the old nobility.

It is not surprising that a man of such good looks and wealth, accustomed to get what he wanted, should have had illegitimate children. A widow named Mrs. Macie bore him a son in 1765, who came to be known as James Smithson. This son was at first named James Lewis Macie, and adopted the surname Smithson about 1802.

Mrs. Macie was a member of the Hungerford family in Warwickshire, and a descendant of Henry VII through Lady Jane Grey. Thus James Smithson belonged to the new industrial nobility as a son of its most prominent member, and also to the old nobility, as of royal descent on his mother's side. Through his relationships he might have acquired the most magnificent social position, if he had not been illegitimate.

His father apparently prevented him from being plainly recognized as his son, and indirectly incorporated into the new nobility. If he had desired, he could probably have secured a title for him. But the Duke opposed direct recognition of his paternity. When Macie was entered as a student at Oxford in 1782, his father's name was suppressed in the registry of names. This was a very exceptional departure from university procedure, and could have been secured through great influence only.

Macie was a remarkable student. When he left Oxford in 1786, he was reputed to know more than any other person in the university about the chemistry of minerals. His scientific and social standing were sufficient to secure his election to the Royal Society in the following year, when he was twenty-two years old. One of his five recommenders for election was the eminent Henry Cavendish, of whom he became an intimate friend. As Cavendish was very shy and extremely able, Smithson could not have gained his rare confidence without tact and intelligence.

Smithson always had money. It seems to have come from his mother's family. The fortune which he bequeathed to the United States for founding the Smithsonian Institution came from the Hungerford family. Virtually nothing came from the vast wealth of his father and the Northumberland family. Smithson was a clever analytical chemist. In his time, mineralogists confused native zinc carbonate and zinc silicate, and labeled them both calamine. He demonstrated their difference, and the first is now known as smithsonite, after his discovery. He devised methods of detecting small quantities of arsenic and mercury, which remained standard for half a century. He recognized substances combined together in definite proportions. His conception of chemistry was philosophical, and he wrote in a terse mode of expression more modern than the usual style of his day. He remarked in an early paper that "chemistry is yet so new a science . . ." that chemical knowledge consists "entirely of isolated points, thinly scattered, the lurid specks on a vast field of darkness."

He was advanced in his respect for accuracy, and complete descriptions of experimental procedure. He had the modern equalitarian attitude towards scientific facts, and did not underrate, like most of his contemporaries, the value of accurate facts not obviously related to some fashionable theory. His remark that "every man is a valuable member of society, who, by his observations, researches, and experiments, procures knowledge for men," is in this spirit.

Like Humphry Davy, and other chemists of the time, he was interested in the application of science to technology. Smithson wrote that "in all cases means of economy tend to augment and diffuse comfort and happiness. They bring within the reach of the many what wasteful proceeding confines to the few." He then describes an improved method of making coffee. He analysed the coloring matters in plants and medicinal herbs, and he experimented with the construction of lamps.

Davy's social significance as a chemist has been interpreted as the propagandist of the application of chemistry to industrial manufacture. He helped to sell science to the rising capitalist industry of the nineteenth century. Smithson was in sympathy with this tendency. He urged the application of science, especially where it was of economical value. Benjamin

Thompson (Count Rumford) had similar views. This American chemist founded the Royal Institution in London to encourage the application of science to the improvement of domestic and industrial economy. The English chemist Smithson founded an institution in America with rather similar objects.

When Smithson found himself with considerable wealth (virtually none of which came from his enormously rich father), he did not stop his scientific researches. He pursued them with much persistence. This seems to have been due to true scientific curiosity and also to a hope of intellectual fame which would surpass the social fame of the parent who had disowned him. His choice of mineralogy as an avenue to fame may be significant. Perhaps he wished to show how much more he knew about minerals than the father who had made so much money out of them. The motive might have been quite unconscious.

During the passage of years he became aware that his scientific talent was not great enough to accomplish spiritual revenge in this manner. Also, his health became feeble. He retired to Paris, where he divided his time between research and gambling. He became a close friend of Arago, who regretted "that this learned experimentalist should devote the half of so valuable a life to a course so little in harmony with an intellect whose wonderful powers called forth the admiration of the world around him." Arago tried to wean him from gambling by working out his prospective losses and gains by the laws of probability. Smithson was sufficiently impressed to restrict his stakes within his income, but he would not break the habit, because it was the only occupation which could distract him for a time from consciousness of his ailments.

Smithson had been born in France. Like many other liberal Englishmen he was sympathetic to the earlier changes of the French Revolution. He wrote from Paris in 1792: "*Ça ira* is growing the song of England, of Europe, as well as of France. Men of every rank are joining in the chorus. Stupidity and guilt have had a long reign, and it begins, indeed, to be time for justice and common-sense to have their turn . . . the office of king is not yet abolished, but they daily feel the inutility, or rather great inconvenience, of continuing it, and its duration will probably not be long. May other nations, at the time of their reforms, be wise enough to cast off, at first, the contemptible incumbrance."

When Smithson wrote his will, thirty-four years later, he was, no doubt, much less Jacobinical, but he retained a core of radicalism.

As his hope of great intellectual fame faded and his health declined, his resentment against his father, and his father's family and social class, increased. He felt that he was of a higher social class than his father, in virtue of royal descent through his mother, and yet his father disowned him, and refused even to have him established in his own upstart nobility. Smithson hated his father, and suffered from the psychological affliction described by Freud as the Oedipus complex. This complex was strengthened by the mark of old nobility and wealth he received from his mother and her family.

In his fury against those who thrust him out of the class to which he felt himself to belong, he wrote:

"The best blood of England flows in my veins; on my father's side I am a Northumberland, on my mother's I am related to kings, but this avails me not. My name shall live in the memory of man when the titles of the Northumberlands and the Percys are extinct and forgotten."

The desire to kill his father in revenge for social ostracism had been sublimated into the desire that his own fame should still live after that of his father and the Northumberlands was dead.

He conceived a method of achieving this through the bequest of his wealth. The first paragraph of his will reads:

"I James Smithson Son to Hugh, first Duke of Northumberland, and Elizabeth, Heiress of the Hungerfords of Studley, and Niece to Charles the proud Duke of Somerset . . ."

A mineralogical chemist could not have composed this without being deeply impelled by class feeling.

He bequeathed a small legacy to an old servant, and the rest of his property to a nephew. If the nephew had no heir, the property was to go "to the United States of America, to found at Washington, under the name of the Smithsonian Institution, an Establishment for the increase and diffusion of knowledge among men."

It is not known how Smithson conceived this particular idea. There is no evidence that he had any contact with the United States or with American citizens. Only two books about the United States were found among his large collection of books and papers. One of these contained an enthusiastic forecast of the future of the city of Washington. This may have suggested that city as a suitable place for the establishment whose fame was to outlast that of the Northumberlands.

There is a passage in George Washington's farewell address, which he may have read. "Promote, then, as an object of primary importance, institutions for the general diffusion of knowledge. In proportion as the structure of a government gives force to public opinion, it is essential that public opinion should be enlightened."

It is impossible to say whether Washington influenced Smithson. The probability is that both of them were influenced by the general social movement of the time for the diffusion of knowledge. Numerous societies and institutions were founded for this object at the beginning of the nineteenth century.

As a trained research worker Smithson carefully included "increase" of knowledge, and placed it before "diffusion," in the statement of his desire. He was more explicit on this point than Washington, the soldier and administrator.

Smithson's nephew died childless in 1835. The Government of the United States was informed of its right to his property, and President Andrew Jackson communicated the information to Congress. The formalities of acquiring the property were completed in two years, which at the time was extremely swift, owing to the good will of the British Government, and the energy of R. Rush, the American lawyer sent to London to prosecute the claim. Rush arrived with the bequest at New York in 1838. It was in the form of 105 bags, each of which contained 1,000 gold sovereigns, and another bag which contained 960 sovereigns, and "eight shillings and sevenpence wrapped in paper."

Congress debated desultorily for eight years as to how Smithson's will should be done. J. Q. Adams made the problem one of his special interests. He saw that if Smithson's scheme were successfully achieved, it would have a profound influence on the culture of the United States. He was anxious "to secure, as from a rattlesnake's fang, the fund and its income, forever, from being wasted and dilapidated in bounties to feed the hunger or fatten the leaden idleness of mountebank projectors and shallow and worthless pretenders to science."

Many different types of "establishment" were proposed. Some wished to found a university, others some sort of school, or museum, or astronomical observatory. The exclusion of a school from the proposals was secured only a few minutes before the end of the final debate. In the end, the fund was definitely secured for the foundation of an institute of higher learning.

The debates on the proposals reflect the attitudes of many of the leading men and classes of the United States of the 1830's towards science. John C. Calhoun opposed the acceptance of the bequest, on the ground that it was beneath the dignity of the United States to accept money from a private foreigner. He was also influenced by his principle of opposing any action which might strengthen the influence of Washington and the central authorities on the life of the United States. J. Q. Adams opposed the foundation of a school, on the ground that the education of citizens was the duty of the United States themselves, and should not be done at the expense of a foreigner's bequest. He pointed out that Smithson wrote that the institution was for the increase and diffusion of knowledge among men, and not among men of the United States only. It was to benefit all men.

John Davis firmly supported the acceptance of the bequest on the ground that "the establishment of institutions for the diffusion of knowledge" is "a vital principle of a republican government."

Joel R. Poinsett endowed the final scheme with the ideas of an important building, a national museum of art and science, its location in Washington, the main features of the adopted plan of organization, and the international exchange of books.

Robert Dale Owen (a son of Robert Owen) harmonized the proposals and prepared the first act of incorporation. He was assisted by A. D. Bache, who sought advice from Henry, and other scientists and scholars.

Henry was in England in 1837, when the Smithson bequest was definitely received by the United States. He had immediately become interested in its possibilities, and had retained his interest during the decade of debate. The board of the new institution hoped that Henry would become the first Secretary, or Director. He was persuaded to accept this position by Bache. He was asked to prepare a plan of organization, which he presented to the board in 1847.

He explains that Smithson's will indicates that the first object of the Institution must be the increase of knowledge, and the second, to diffuse it. "The Government of the United States is merely a trustee to carry out the design of the testator. The institution is private and not national. It is to serve the whole of mankind." Henry notes that Smithson has written that "the man of science has no country; the world is his country—all men his countrymen." The Institution should therefore be conducted in that spirit, and should not in its program give excessive weight to local interests.

Increase of knowledge was the first object. Henry proposed "to stimulate men of talent to make original researches by offering suitable rewards for memoirs containing new truths; and, to appropriate annually a portion of the income for particular researches, under the direction of suitable persons." To diffuse knowledge, he proposed "to publish a series of periodical reports on the progress of the different branches of knowledge; and, to publish occasionally separate treatises on subjects of general interest." The Institution should make special collections of objects and "also a collection of instruments of research in all branches of experimental science."

Henry held that specialization by the Institution on a particular branch of science was contrary to Smithson's intention. Any preference should be given to the higher and more abstract parts of science. "Incomparably more is to be expected" as to the future advancement of agriculture "from the perfection of the microscope than from improvements in the ordinary instruments of husbandry." He notes that in the United States "though many excel in the application of science to the practical arts of life, few devote themselves to the continued labor and patient thought necessary to the discovery and development of new truths." This is due, he considers, to the want, "not of proper means, but of proper encouragement." He considers that the publication of original work "will act as a powerful stimulus to the latent talent of our country, by placing in bold relief the real laborers in the field of original research."

He was much impressed by the cost of publication of scientific papers, especially those on natural history, which contained many illustrations. The difficulty of publication had a large influence on the development of the Smithsonian system of distributing literature. He thought that the award of "fifty or a hundred dollars" would often provide an investigator with the necessary books, equipment, or manual assistance.

He considered that the "principal means of diffusing knowledge must be the *Press.*" By this he meant all forms of printed publication. In his usage, *Press* did not refer only to daily newspapers. He proposed the publication of periodical reports of the progress of science, written in simple language.

Henry was personally opposed to the formation of a museum. He considered that this ought not to be undertaken at the expense of the Smithsonian bequest. But for the present, as it was incorporated in the approved scheme, he proposed

James Smithson
As a youth at Oxford

"My name shall live in the memory of man when the titles of the Northumberlands and the Percys are extinct and forgotten."

PLATE IV

that they should, firstly, collect objects which facilitated the "study of the memoirs which may be published"; secondly, objects not generally known in the United States; and thirdly, "instruments of physical research which will be required both in the illustration of new physical truths and in the scientific investigations undertaken by the Institution." He suggests as subjects of physical research, terrestrial magnetism, which has great theoretical interest, and also "direct reference to navigation, and to the various geodetical operations of civil and military life." The organization of a telegraphic meteorological service for the whole country, and in coöperation with the British Government, was desirable. This might lead to the solution of the problem of American storms. Exploration, which would provide material for a Physical Atlas of the United States, should be subsidized.

Physical constants, such as the weight of the earth, the velocity of light and electricity, should be re-determined. Soils and plants should be analysed. Statistical enquiries concerning physical, moral and political subjects should be made, and archaeology and ethnology supported.

Henry began to direct the Institution in 1846. He continued to be the director for thirty-two years. Before commenting on the nature of his policy, it will be helpful to consider in what degree it was achieved.

2

When Henry died in 1878, the Institution had a capital investment of $686,000. The value of the building and furniture was estimated at $500,000, the library at $200,000, philosophical apparatus at $5,000, the stock of its own unsold publications at $50,000, and other items, making $782,000. The total value was $1,468,000.

Thus in thirty-two years, by careful management, Henry had doubled the value of Smithson's bequest. He had paid for all building and development out of the interest on the original capital, which had not been diminished, but increased.

Henry pursued this rigidly economical policy during an exceptionally unsettled period of American economic and political history. During the first half of his secretaryship, when the Southern statesmen had the dominant power, investments and banking were under insufficient supervision and were insecure. The second half of his secretaryship began during the Civil War. He held the Institution together during that uncertain period, when it might have dissolved during the social turmoil. He conceived saving in expenditure as the basis of sound financial management. When he was appointed to the secretaryship his salary was $3,500, or about £700 per annum, with free living rooms in the building. He was urged on several occasions during his thirty-two years of service to accept an increase in salary, but he always refused. In 1846 the salary was perhaps not trivial, but in the America of 1878 it was inadequate. Henry was the chief scientific personage in the American capital. He had to entertain numerous visitors. He insisted on doing all this on the same salary in 1878 as he had received in 1846. His daughter has written that this was accomplished only by the most stringent economy in his home.

Henry prepared the Report of the Institution himself. He wrote simple summaries of recent advances in science, reprinted lectures delivered in the Institution, and interesting articles from inaccessible foreign journals.

In 1872 the edition of the Report contained 20,000 copies. It declined afterwards to ten or fifteen thousand.

The *Smithsonian Contributions to Knowledge* consisted of volumes of original papers. Henry wrote that "the real workingmen in the line of original research hail this part of the plan as a new era in the history of American science." They were published in editions of 1,000, and distributed freely among libraries, about 350 of which were in foreign countries. The volumes of *Miscellaneous Collections* dealt with reviews of the present state of knowledge in different branches of science, and with accounts of extensive collections of materials for research, reports of explorations, history of science, etc.

These also were issued in editions of 1,000 copies and distributed freely.

Besides these issues, the Institution published many volumes on special subjects, and various scientific bulletins. Under Henry's direction, the Institution developed a system of international exchange of scientific knowledge. A remarkable Frenchman named A. Vattemare, who was educated as a surgeon, and became a famous ventriloquist, retired from the stage in order to urge the exchange of duplicate books between the libraries of the world. He visited the United States in 1839 and aroused much interest in his scheme. The Smithsonian Institution adopted the idea, and also agreed to act as a clearing house for the dispatch of scientific publications from any American institution to suitable addresses in other parts of the world. The Royal Society of London obtained an order from the British Government that these packages should be admitted free of duty, and the Government of the United States similarly exempted packages addressed to the Smithsonian Institution. Various steamship companies granted concessions on the freight rates for the packages. The exchange service was used by the United States Government for distributing its own reports, of which 20,000 packages were distributed between 1851 and 1867. It grew into an international service for the exchange of books, journals and natural history specimens, assisted by the governments of many countries of the world. Isolated investigators far from libraries and colleagues could obtain books and specimens through the Smithsonian Institution. The list of addresses of correspondents had grown to 23,408 in 1895, of which 10,765 were those of libraries, and the remainder of private individuals. The aim of "diffusing knowledge" was grandly achieved.

In 1851 Henry reported on the necessity for the proper indexing of scientific knowledge. He explained that Young had compiled a valuable catalogue of scientific books, including works up to the year 1807. A new universal catalogue was now required. He started a bibliography of American scientific works and papers in 1854, and suggested to the British Association that a similar index of British and European works should be made. A committee of the British Association, consisting of Cayley, Grant and Stokes, approved the suggestion. They persuaded the Royal Society to prepare a catalogue of scientific works and papers published since 1800. The first volume of this great catalogue was published in 1867.

The bibliography of science grows in importance with the progress of science. It is becoming as important, if not more important, than any particular branch of science, as it is the key to the results of scientific research. The quick and certain finding in the literature of what has already been discovered is now as important, in some branches of science, as new discovery. An increasing amount of effort in modern research is wasted through failure to appreciate what has been done.

Henry was one of the chief founders of the bibliography of modern science. He inspired the development of one of the most important instruments which aids research.

The organization of a museum was one of the items required by the original scheme. Henry was opposed to this proposal, as he foresaw that the cost of keeping the increasing collections would ultimately exceed the resources of the Institution. But he obeyed the requirement. The collection became the nucleus for the United States National Museum, which was housed in a separate building in 1881. In 1927 the National Museum possessed ten million objects.

The Bureau of American Ethnology grew out of John W. Powell's exploration of the Grand Canyon of the Colorado, which was begun in 1867, and fostered by Henry, as the Secretary of the Institution. Henry was much interested in researches concerning the aborigines of America, and their pre-history.

His colleague and successor, Spencer F. Baird, was a zoölogist, and used the resources of the Institution to foster the study of natural history. His own specimens were the nucleus of the National Museum's natural history collections. His studies of fish and fisheries led him to the conception of the conservation of the natural fisheries, and of "fish culture," as a method of producing food, analogous to stock-raising. He inspired the foundation of Woods Hole, and many other biological research laboratories, where the knowledge necessary for the development of "fish culture," and the general advance of zoölogy, could be acquired. The details of the international exchange of books and specimens were supervised by Baird.

The magnitude of the administrative work of Henry and his colleagues is shown by the number of letters written by Henry. A fire occurred in his office and adjoining parts of the Institution in 1865, and copies of 30,000 pages of letters drafted by him were destroyed. He personally wrote a large part of the thirty-two Annual Reports issued during his secretaryship.

As W. H. Taft remarked in 1927, the Smithsonian Institution has been "the incubator of American science." C. G. Abbot said that its policy had been to "seek facts irrespective of their apparent economic value," and that "cooperation and not monopoly is the motto which indicates the spirit of the Smithsonian's operations."

The original plans for the diffusion of knowledge were carried out by Henry with extraordinary fidelity and success.

The international exchange of books and specimens was an original contribution towards the internationalization of scientific knowledge, and the unification of human culture.

The Smithsonian Institution gave birth to several of the national scientific institutions of the United States.

3

The first object of the Institution was to increase knowledge. Henry made and assisted many researches during the thirty-two years of secretaryship.

His project for obtaining simultaneous meteorological reports by telegraph from observers over a large area was established in 1849, with the assistance of five hundred observers.

The information received was plotted daily, by means of adjustable symbols, on a large map of the United States. "It was often enabled to predict (sometimes a day or two in advance) the approach of any of the larger disturbances of the atmosphere."

Henry explained the importance of this knowledge to navigation and agriculture. By his application of the electric telegraph to meteorological reports, he became the founder of modern meteorological forecasting of the weather.

This branch of the Institution's work became the nucleus of the Government's meteorological bureau, which was established in 1870.

Henry made in 1873 an arrangement with the Atlantic Cable Companies, by which information of new astronomical observations was transmitted without charge between the Institution and the chief observatories of Europe. This has been of much importance in the study of variable stars, *novae*, sunspots, and other swiftly-changing astronomical phenomena. Henry helped to persuade Lick to found the famous observatory that bears his name.

He became a member of the United States Light House Board in 1852.

The lighthouse lamps at that time used whale oil. As its cost was increasing, a cheaper substitute was desirable. Henry made accurate photometric measurements in a black room on the illuminating power of various oils. He found petroleum oil was unsafe owing to variation in quality. At low temperatures lard oil could be used successfully. It was immediately introduced into the lighthouse service, and as its cost was only one-fourth that of whale oil, it enabled a saving of about $100,000 per annum to be made.

He began a long series of experiments on the acoustics of the atmosphere, in connection with the improvement of foghorns for the protection of shipping, during sea-board fogs. He showed that gun signals were the most inefficient form of sound warning. Steam whistles were inferior to trumpets, and both were inferior to sirens. Horns were of no value beyond short distances. He used an "artificial ear," or phonometer, consisting of a Sondhauss stretched membrane sprinkled with sand, for measuring the intensity of sounds. He recommended machines operated by steam at 60–80 lbs., emitting a note of 400 vibrations per second. Under favorable conditions they could be heard at a distance of twenty miles. As a result of these researches the American fog-signal service in 1873 was far superior to that in Europe.

He discovered by observation in 1867 that a sound arriving against the wind could be heard more easily at the mast-head than on the deck. He learned that G. G. Stokes had forecast this effect in 1857, from the theory of wave-motions in fluids whose various layers moved at different velocities.

He determined the velocity of the wind at high altitudes by measuring the speed of the movement of the shadow of a cloud along the ground. This research should interest modern investigators who study the velocity of the wind at high altitudes, in order to assist airmen.

His fog-horn studies were pursued actively during the last decade of his life. He spent many weeks at sea in rough weather patiently collecting observations. His last report on them was published in 1877, when he was eighty years old. In the summary of his results he stated that the audibility of a sound at a distance depends on pitch, loudness and quantity. It is affected by the state of the atmosphere. Perfect stillness and uniform density and temperatures are most favorable to distant transmission. The most efficient cause of difference in audibility is the wind. The effect is not due to the velocity of the wind, but to refraction downwards of sound beams which otherwise would pass over the observer. Sometimes sounds are heard best against the wind. This is due to a dominant upper wind, whose direction is contrary to that of the wind at the surface. The existence of these upper winds was proved by means of balloons, and observations of the movement of the northeast storms on the coast of Maine.

The concentration of sound by concave reflectors and horns is of no value beyond a distance of three or four miles, or even less.

Experiments showed that neither fog, snow, hail nor rain materially interfered with the transmission of loud sounds. Sirens were heard at the greatest distances during fogs.

Some instances of sound shadows due to projecting land and buildings were observed.

The "belt-of-silence" phenomenon was thoroughly investigated. When a ship sails away from a siren, the sounds often suddenly become inaudible, and then become audible again, at a greater distance. These "belts-of-silence" were carefully investigated. The phenomenon was observed only when the sound was moving against the wind, and was due to the upward refraction of the sound, which carried it over the observer. The beam continued upward until it reached another layer of air-current, after which it was bent down again, and so became audible at a greater distance. Henry also gave two other explanations which hold in some cases.

The designing of the Smithsonian building and its rooms involved his interest in the problems of architecture and acoustics. He was of the opinion that "the buildings of a country and an age should be ethnological expressions of the wants, habits, arts, and feelings of the time in which they were erected." He did not consider architecture a fine art, like painting or sculpture. The temples of Egypt, Greece and Rome were intended (partly) to "transmit to posterity, without the art of printing, an impression of the character of the periods in which they were erected." The Greek architect designed temples "to gratify the tutelar deity," and "was untrammelled by any condition of utility." They were intended "for external worship, and not for internal use." But "modern buildings are made for other purposes than artistic effect, and in them the aesthetical must be subordinate to the useful; though the two may co-exist, and an intellectual pleasure be derived from a sense of adaptation and fitness, combined with a perception of harmony of parts, and the beauty of detail."

He contended that servile copies of ancient styles are "as preposterous as to endeavour to harmonize the refinement and civilization of the present age with the superstition and barbarity of the times of the Pharaohs."

Architecture should be consonant with the character of the people, climate, and "the material to be employed in construction. The use of iron and of glass requires an entirely different style from that which sprung from the rocks of Egypt," Greek marble and Roman brick.

He suggests that "the great tenacity of iron, and its power of resistance to crushing" should allow the construction of buildings of "far more slender" design, and "apparently lighter arrangement of parts."

After expressing these opinions, which, in 1856, were remarkably advanced, he discussed lecture-room acoustics. He noticed that though much research had been made into the nature of sound, there had been little practical application of the results. He described the arrangements of seats which give the best audibility, and methods of avoiding echoes and reverberation, according to theory and experiment. He proved experimentally that india rubber absorbs sound by converting part of its energy into heat. The rubber's rise in temperature, when bombarded by sound, was measured by an iron-copper thermopile buried in it.

He was consulted in 1851 on the properties of the marble used in the extension of the United States Capitol, and investigated methods of testing building materials.

Pieces of marble were cut and ground into cubes with one-and-a-half inch edges. Henry discovered that if the cubes were pressed between sheets of lead in a powerful press, they collapsed under about 30,000 lbs. pressure, whereas when in direct contact with the steel plates of the press, they resisted about 60,000 lbs. pressure. It had been expected that the lead packing would increase the resistance to pressure by distributing the load equably. Henry explained the unexpected result. "The stone tends to give way by bulging out in the center of each of its four perpendicular faces, and to form two pyramidal figures with their apices opposed to each other at the center of the cube, and their bases against the steel plates. In the case where rigid equable pressure is employed, as in that of the thick steel plate, all parts must give way together. But in that of a *yielding* equable pressure, as in the case of interposed lead, the stone first gives way along the outer lines or those of least resistance, and the remaining pressure must be sustained by the central portion around the vertical axis of the cube."

In the second part of his paper, published in 1855, Henry applied his ideas on the cohesion of liquids, which have already been mentioned, to the breakdown of metals under stress. He attributes rigidity not to direct attractive power between atoms, but to lateral cohesion, or resistance to slipping. The tensile strength of liquids and solids is of the same order, and their difference in rigidity is due to difference in the resistance of their atoms to slipping. When the "crystalline arrangement is perfect, and no lateral motion is allowed in the atoms, the body may be denominated perfectly rigid." Cast steel is an approximate example, as it ruptures with a "transverse fracture of the same size as that of the original section of the bar."

"The effect however is quite different when we attempt to pull apart a rod of lead. The atoms or molecules slip upon each other. The rod is increased in length and diminished in thickness until a separation is produced."

Henry deduced that as tenacity is due to lateral cohesion, or resistance to slip, "the form of the material ought to have some effect upon its tenacity, and also that the strength of the article should depend in some degree upon the process to which it has been subjected."

He showed that a lead rod became hollow under an appropriate tension. He attributed this to the constraint of the inner atoms by the outer atoms. The outer atoms had relatively more freedom. "The inner fibres (if I may so call the rows of atoms) give way first and entirely separate, while the exterior fibres show but little indications of a change of this kind."

He deduced "that metals should never be elongated by mere stretching, but in all cases by the process of wire-drawing, or rolling."

His theory of slip explained the production of a hollow inside an iron bar by hammering, and he concluded that many of the breakages of the axles of locomotive engines were due to shaping by hammering, instead of rolling.

Henry used the equipment of the United States Navy Yard in making these brilliant researches, and was assisted by J. A. Dahlgren, who afterwards invented the iron-clad which had such an important rôle in helping to win the Civil War for the Northern forces. It would be interesting to know whether the adoption of Dahlgren's ship was due to Henry's influence.

During the Civil War Henry became the chief adviser to the Government on scientific military inventions. He wrote several hundred reports, requiring much experimental investigation, on numerous military inventions.

The testing of materials for munitions contracts was also referred to him.

As a scientist, Henry had an essential rôle in the military organization of the Northern Government. His later career illustrates the close connection between science and military technique. The scientist is now becoming the most important unit in warfare.

4

Henry described the substance of his religious beliefs some days before his death in 1878. He wrote to Joseph Patterson that "we live in a universe of change." The wisdom of one man, and even of all men accumulated through centuries, is very small compared with the unknown. Unfathomable mysteries environ man on every side. But he believed the conception of the existence of one Spiritual Being is the simplest which gives human experience any intelligibility. This Being created man with intellectual faculties sufficient to gain, through what is named Science, some understanding of the operations of Nature.

He believed that this Being is unchangeable. The operations of Nature will always be in accordance with the same laws, under the same conditions. "Events that happened a thousand years ago will happen again a thousand years to come, provided the condition of existence is the same." He considered the existence of natural law evidence for the existence of an intellectual director of the universe.

He based the existence of a Creator on the grounds that "It is one of the truths best established by experience in my own mind, that I have a thinking, willing *principle* within me, capable of intellectual activity and moral feeling. . . . It is equally clear to me that you have a similar spiritual principle within yourself, since when I ask you an intelligent question you give me an intellectual answer. . . . When I examine the operations of Nature, I find everywhere through them evidences of intellectual arrangements, of contrivances to definite ends, precisely as I find in the operations of man; and hence I infer that these two classes of operations are results of similar intelligence . . . in my own mind, I find ideas of right and wrong, of good and evil. These ideas, then, exist in the universe, and, therefore, form a basis of our ideas of a moral universe. Furthermore, the conceptions of good which are found among our ideas associated with evil, can be attributed only to a Being of infinite perfections, like that which we denominate 'God.' "

This theology is essentially the same as that of his Scottish Puritan ancestors. It ascribes great importance to the deterministic aspects of the universe, and to the existence of law. Simultaneously, it ascribes equal importance to the "willing *principle* within."

A theology which ascribes equal importance to determinism and will is one of the least unfavorable to the progress of science. Persons who have acquired this system of thought believe that an order of nature exists, and have the confidence that it may be discovered by energetic applications of the will. The rise of modern science is intimately connected with the rise of Puritanism. Both Puritanism and modern science are connected with the rise of a new social system. It is sufficient for the present point to note that Henry was equipped in childhood with beliefs in the obedience of nature and man to law, and the importance of obedience to moral intuitions.

W. B. Taylor writes that Henry had a natural quickness of temper in his youth, and retained a high degree of sensibility. His first interests were fiction and the drama. His temperament was of the sanguine type, which, according to Pavlov, is the best. He could "forget what had been painful in his past experiences, and . . . remember only and enjoy that which had been pleasurable." He moulded the lively material of his temperament according to his theological principles, and schooled himself to obedience to his moral intuitions. Systematic exercise of will gave him remarkable self-control. In his later years casual acquaintances considered him reserved and unimpressible. They thought his sense of humor limited, partly because he would not respond to any sort of humor which involved cruel thoughts about others.

"He accepted all the appointments of nature and Providence as the expressions of Infinite Wisdom, and so in everything gave thanks."

In 1865, when he was sixty-eight years old, a great fire in the Institution destroyed the voluminous records of his correspondence on many matters and with many persons throughout the world, his lifetime's collection of unpublished notes of researches, and Smithson's own literary remains and mineralogical collection, and other irreplaceable things, and also the manuscript of his forthcoming Annual Report. He wrote to a friend, some days after this occurrence: "A few years ago such a calamity would have paralyzed me for future efforts, but in my present view of life I take it as the dispensation of a kind and wise Providence, and trust that it will work to my spiritual advantage."

Henry's sense of discipline is seen in his opinions on education. He writes that the "first remark which may be made in regard to education is that it is a forced condition of mind or body. As a general rule it is produced by coercion." It is obtained only through hard labor by the educator and the pupil. Prospects of reward, emulation, and appeals to affection may stimulate the pupil, but an ultimate resort by the educator to force must always be possible. "The child, if left to itself, would receive no proper development," and the "savage never educates himself mentally." If all educational institutions were abolished, "how rapidly would our boasted civilization relapse into barbarism." He did not believe that it was "the manifest destiny of humanity to improve by the operation of an inevitable, necessary law of progress." He considered that civilization "is a state of unstable equilibrium which, if not supported by the exertions of individuals, resembles an edifice with a circumscribed base, which becomes the more tottering as we expand its lateral dimensions, and increase its height."

It cannot be preserved without the labor of a large proportion of thoroughly educated persons, and cannot be advanced without making special provision for "the *actual increase* of knowledge, as well as for its diffusion." Rewards and honors should be given to "those who *really add* to the sum of human knowledge."

This truth was not generally appreciated, and the tendency was to "look merely at the immediate results of the application of science," and "to liberally reward and honor those who simply apply known facts rather than those who *discover* new principles."

A high state of civilization could be preserved only by the exertions of individuals actuated by "a generous, liberal, and enlightened philanthropy." Unfortunately, the increase of wealth and security tended to relax individual effort. "Man is naturally an indolent being, and unless actuated by strong inducements or educated by coercion to habits of industry, his tendency is to supineness and inaction." The growth of wealth and elementary education "without a corresponding increase of higher instruction" rendered the "voice of the profound teacher" less and less audible, and "obliged him to comply with popular prejudices." These conditions fostered charlatanism.

The growth of specialization, or sub-division of labor in research, narrowed the number of persons thoroughly conversant with any field of knowledge. These small groups of well-informed persons "are not generally the dispensers of favor," and "he who aspires to wealth or influence seeks not their approbation." Those actively engaged in the business of life have little time for profound thought. They must receive knowledge at second hand, and yet "they are not content under our present system of education with the position of students." They wish to be teachers, and become ambitious of authorship, and "impatient for popular applause." Knowledge becomes increasingly superficial in proportion to its diffusion. "In such a condition of things it is possible that the directing power of an age may become less and less intelligent as it becomes more authoritative, and that the world may be actually declining in what constitutes real moral, and intellectual greatness, while to the superficial observer it appears to be in a state of rapid advance."

Writing in 1854, he does not assert that this is the case in his own time, but he is "merely pointing out tendencies."

He complained that though his was emphatically a reading age, it was not "proportionately a *thinking* age." The world suffered from too many bad books, and ill-digested reading.

He attacked the contemporary state of copyright, which injured reputable authors by depriving them of payment. It damaged American education because unsuitable textbooks pirated from abroad were cheaper than suitable books written by Americans who understood their own conditions. He considered that the writing of elementary textbooks was specially difficult, and should not be left to superficially qualified authors. He disagreed with the view that "superficial men are best calculated to prepare popular works on any branch of knowledge."

He based his suggestions for methods of educating the

young on the observation that "memory, imitation, imagination and the faculty of forming habits exist in early life, while the judgment and the reasoning powers are of slower growth." Children should learn languages, and moral precepts. The acquisition of facility in mental operations such as speaking, writing, reading and calculation, is "the most important part of elementary mental instruction," but it is tedious to the teacher and pupil.

It is "preposterous . . . that the child should be taught nothing but what it can fully comprehend." This inverted the natural order of the evolution of the faculties of understanding, and produced "remarkably intelligent children who will become remarkably feeble men."

He laid "great stress upon the early education of the habits." Persons trained in good habits will act well in crises where they have no time to think, and also in old age, when the will is no longer strong enough to control bad habits early acquired.

Henry's views on the nature of man, and the best methods of education, also exhibit the influence of Calvinistic ideas. He believed that "the laws which govern the growth and operations of the human mind are as definite and as general in their application as those which apply to the material universe," but, "unfortunately," psychologists have made little progress towards their discovery.

Henry's tough-mindedness, and dislike of obscurantism, is seen in his contempt for spiritualism. Newcomb relates that a noted spiritualist succeeded in capturing Lincoln's interest during his presidency. Lincoln urgently requested Henry to receive him, and investigate his apparent power of drawing noise from various parts of a room. Henry observed the proceedings, and said that though he could not say how the sounds were produced, they certainly came from the spiritualist's person. Some time afterwards, Henry met a young man in a railway train, who presently told him that he was a maker of telegraph instruments, and even supplied mediums with apparatus for producing their manifestations. Henry asked which

JOSEPH HENRY
First Secretary of the Smithsonian Institution.

PLATE V

mediums he had supplied, and learned that Lincoln's acquaintance was among them. The young man explained that the manifestations were produced by apparatus fastened to the muscular part of the upper arm, which could be operated merely by contracting the muscles, without moving the joints, so that no movement was visible.

The firmness of Henry's mind is seen in his views on evolution and natural selection. The controversies on these ideas arose in the last years of his life, but, unlike the majority of earnestly religious persons, he was not antagonistic to them. He disagreed with his friend Agassiz, who denied them, and remarked that the theory of natural selection seemed to be the first genuine scientific theory that had been discovered in natural history.

Henry's genius was broad and collective. He could do innumerable things, and all of them well.

Joseph Henry: Bibliography

Smithsonian Miscellaneous Collections. Volume 21. 1881. Volume 30. 1887.

Smithsonian Contributions to Knowledge. Volume 18. 1873.

The Smithsonian Institution 1846–1896. G. B. Goode, & cont. 1897.

Sir Hugh Smithson: 1st Duke of Northumberland. The Dictionary of National Biography.

Conference on the Future of the Smithsonian Institution. W. H. Taft and C. G. Abbot. 1927.

Edith W. Stone: "Joseph Henry." *Scientific Monthly.* Sept. 1931.

Library for the Diffusion of Useful Knowledge: *Natural Philosophy.* 4 volumes. 1829–1838.

Mary A. Henry: "Joseph Henry." *Electrical Engineer.* New York. Jan. 13–March 9, 1892.

The Fool of Quality. Henry Brooke. With a preface by Charles Kingsley. 1859.

Josiah Willard Gibbs
1839-1903

I
THE PROBLEM OF GIBBS

II
THE SIGNIFICANCE OF HIS CAREER

III
HIS DESCENT AND EDUCATION

IV
THE EFFICIENT MANAGEMENT OF MIXTURES

V
THE USE OF MATHEMATICS

VI
HIS PERSONALITY

BIBLIOGRAPHY

I

The Problem of Gibbs

AFTER THE ANNUAL DINNER OF A BRITISH
scientific society, held in London within the last decade, twenty
or thirty of the members retired to a café in order to continue
informal conversations on topics of common interest. A discussion presently arose on the relative importance of various
famous scientific discoveries. Everyone became keenly interested in this many-sided question, and the arguments became
more and more earnest and involved. After a time, one of the
participants suggested that the results of the discussion might
be clearer if they could be expressed in a mathematical form,
such as a ballot. A ballot was accordingly organized, and each
member was asked to write down, in order of importance, the
names of the twenty scientists whom he conceived to be the
greatest that have appeared since the Renaissance. The orders
on the separate ballot papers were combined so as to give a
collective order. In this way, the party's collective opinion on
the names and order of the twenty greatest scientists since the
Renaissance was ascertained.

Newton was the first name on the list. Darwin was second,
and Faraday and Einstein were bracketed third. The next
name was Willard Gibbs. His very high place was due not to
a few votes which put him first, but to uniformly high placing by nearly all of the voters. Another interesting feature of
the final list was the absence of the name of any botanist.

The majority of the voters were experimental biologists,
with a few chemists, and one or two physicists and mathematicians. The high place given to Gibbs by the biologists was

probably due to their belief that the next fundamental advance in their science will be due to discoveries of a Gibbsian type. The conception of living matter as a system in equilibrium is emphasized more and more by the progress of experimental biology. The biologists felt that the next fundamental discovery in their science will be due to a deeper insight into the mechanism of the equilibria of the physical and chemical reactions in living matter. As Gibbs had virtually created an exact science of systems of substances in chemical and physical equilibrium, and had determined a perspective which had already provided several profound advances in science, they felt that the best promise of solving their immediate fundamental problem lay in the attitude of Gibbs. They looked to it for the inspiration which would reveal how the substances and surfaces in living matter operate.

Chemists were naturally prepared to give him a high place for his comprehensive theory of chemical equilibrium, and physicists on account of his contributions to vector analysis and statistical mechanics.

The high reputation of Gibbs, among scientists, of which this incident is a small illustration, is in remarkable contrast to his lack of popular fame. New York University has a hall of fame, where memorials are erected to great Americans. The choice of the men who are to be remembered is made by a ballot. Gibbs' name has twice failed to receive enough votes for election. The explanation and significance of this paradox is the chief problem in the consideration of his life and work as a factor in modern civilization.

The degree of his popular obscurity is shown by various facts and stories. Irving Fisher, one of his pupils, writes that in his day the majority of the students at Yale "did not know of his existence, much less of his greatness." Fifty years after the publication of Gibbs' greatest work, Yale still had no memorial of him, apart from a bas-relief in the Old Sloane Physics Laboratory, presented by Walther Nernst, the German physical chemist. Adequate memorials of Gibbs have been established in the United States only very recently. Ostwald wrote that when the news arrived in the United States, that Willard Gibbs had been recognized in Europe as a great genius, many Americans congratulated his namesake Wolcott Gibbs, who had done good work, but was assuredly no genius. Wolcott Gibbs' name was far better known in America, and "without enquiries, as a matter of course, he was taken for the newly-discovered star, and had to accept great ovations from his delighted countrymen, about which probably no one was more surprised than himself. The misunderstanding was not resolved for some time, and Willard Gibbs successfully withstood any attempt to make him into a popular hero."

Gibbs' reputation was for long far higher in Europe than in the United States. Irving Fisher has described how, when he went to study in Berlin in 1893, he was abashed to find that the German mathematicians had never heard of any of the professors who had taught him mathematics at Yale, but that when he mentioned that he had attended Gibbs' lectures, they exclaimed: "Geebs, Geebs, jawohl, ausgezeichnet." (Gibbs, Gibbs, oh yes, excellent.)

In his recently published memoirs J. J. Thomson writes that he does not know of any case of a more intimate connection between a man and a university, than between Gibbs and Yale, and it was long before Yale recognized that he was a great man. Thomson says that he was not a success as a teacher of elementary students. "Indeed it is said that there was at one time a movement to replace him." His greatness was not fully appreciated by Yale until 1901, two years before he died, when the Royal Society of London bestowed on him its highest honor, the Copley medal. Thomson writes that he had personal experience of how little Gibbs' work was known in the United States. "When a new University was founded in 1887 the newly elected President came over to Europe to find Professors. He came to Cambridge and asked me if I could tell him of anyone who would make a good Professor of Molecular Physics. I said, 'You need not come to England for that; the best man you could get is an American, Willard Gibbs.' 'Oh,' he said, 'you mean Wolcott Gibbs,' mentioning the prominent American chemist. 'No, I don't,' I said, 'I mean Willard Gibbs,' and I told him something about Gibbs' work. He sat thinking for a minute or two and then said, 'I'd like you to give me another name. Willard Gibbs can't be a man of much personal magnetism or I should have heard of him.' "

There are various stories which may be apocryphal and have no basis in particular fact. But such stories gain currency only because they are consonant with what is known about the personality and circumstances of the subject. They are useful, if only secondary, guides to the psychology of the subject and the public attitude towards him.

Gibbs never married, and lived the latter half of his life in his eldest sister's home. Her husband was Addison Van Name, the Librarian of the college. This was an exceptionally important position at Yale, because the college had evolved out of a library formed by a number of ministers in New Haven, so the librarian's office was older than those of the professors. It is said that one of Gibbs' sisters was in the habit of commandeering Gibbs to drive her around the shops in the morning in the family buggy, on the ground that her husband, who was a busy man, could not afford the time. Whether or not this story is true, it is not incongruous with Gibbs' character, for he could always find time to help others even in small things.

E. B. Wilson writes that Gibbs took his full share in the common duties of the home. In this connection he mentions the apocryphal story that Gibbs "always insisted on mixing the salad, on the ground that he was a better authority than the others on the equilibrium of heterogeneous substances."

He recounts the story that Gibbs was so modest that he blushed when someone referred to his letter in *Nature*, in which he had proved that an experiment proposed by Kelvin for the determination of the velocity of longitudinal waves in the ether was impossible.

Henry Adams towards the end of his life sought to introduce scientific modes of thought into the interpretation of history. He wrote that he looked about him in vain for a teacher. He thought of Gibbs, "the greatest of Americans, judged by his rank in science," who "stood on the same plane with the three or four greatest minds of his century."

As Gibbs never came to Washington, Adams had no chance of meeting him. But he heard from a friend that Gibbs had said that he had got most help in the problems of the philosophy of science from Karl Pearson's *Grammar of Science,* so he read this work. He found it interesting, but not original, and "never found out what it could have taught a master like Willard Gibbs."

The problem of Gibbs is the discovery of the explanations of his simultaneous greatness and obscurity, in terms of the condition of science in his time, the nature of his own work, the influence of his personal psychology and social environment, and the social history of the United States.

II

The Significance of His Career

GIBBS GREW UP IN AN ATMOSPHERE OF EX-
treme devotion to an institution with conservative social ideals.
The devotion which Yale could inspire is illustrated by the
example of Benjamin Silliman. Shortly after he had graduated in law, he was asked by President Dwight to become the
first professor of chemistry. He received the request as a command, and after being appointed to the chair, began to study
chemistry. Like a Japanese Samurai, he placed his career at
the service of the social institution to which he was devoted,
and went abroad to acquire training.

In his case the sacrifice proved to be pleasant, as he found
that he had natural aptitude for science, and became an influential scientist.

The chief aim of Yale education was to train a governing
class for politics, religion and commerce. It was similar to that
of Oxford, but more intense and narrow in its method. Group-
feeling was inculcated deeply, especially through the system
of the students' life.

A scientist cannot occupy an important place in the life of
Oxford University unless he has ability in academic politics.
The same phenomenon existed at Yale. Until recently, scientists at Oxford were encysted there, and, as scientists, had
little influence. The fundamental aim of the university was
not the advancement of science. A scientist educated in such
a system accepted the view that scientific discovery could not
be as important as training for government, and assumed that
work in isolation and without influence was natural.

In the most characteristic Oxford and Yale social theories, science is conceived as a product of curiosity and play. It is a means by which members of a leisure class may satisfy curiosity and find amusement.

The conventional theory of liberal education which the Yale faculty expressed so clearly in 1871, and which will be described presently, embodies this view. The same view is implied in E. B. Wilson's remark that "Gibbs was not an advertiser for personal renown nor a propagandist for science; he was a scholar, scion of an old scholarly family, living before the days when research had been *re*'search."

The old Oxford and Yale attitude towards science was natural in a pre-scientific age, but it is not appropriate when science has become an essential part of the social system. Gibbs did not perceive any contradiction between his acceptance of the social ideals of Yale and his recognition of the social value of multiple algebra, but this conflict suggests the chief explanation of the general failure to appreciate the importance of his work. He had insight into the nature of mathematics and science as social products with social uses, as he showed in his address on Multiple Algebra, but the body of persons in academic life which shared his views was not large enough to influence opinion.

He was not isolated by his academic colleagues through illwill. He was esteemed highly, but not understood. He was appointed professor before he had published a paper. His colleagues made special efforts to finance the publication of his great memoir *On the Equilibrium of Heterogeneous Substances*. He was elected a member of the National Academy of Sciences at the age of forty, when the usual age of election was fifty. The Academy awarded its Rumford medal to him in 1881, when he was forty-two.

His colleagues were proud of him. His work was neglected because they could not understand its significance.

The view that the significance of Gibbs' work was not evident at the date of its publication is mistaken. As Maxwell pointed out with clarity and brilliance, his work was of the highest significance for chemists. The majority of educated men failed to see this, not because it was obscure, but because they were prevented by their preconceptions of the rôle of science in human activities, and also, but in a lesser degree, by the difficulty of Gibbs' method.

He used the logic of scientific argument with greater power than any of his contemporaries. Though his mathematics was simple, his contemporaries could not understand him because they could not follow his extremely concise and rigorous logic. But if they had had a better understanding of the significance of science they would have quickly recognized the importance of his work, in spite of the difficulty of the logic.

The failure to recognize Gibbs' achievement may have been due to the absence of any new principle in it. He merely worked out the remotest consequences of an existing principle, the second law of thermodynamics. If the work had contained a new principle, its novelty would have been more obvious, even if the principle and the results derived from it had been less important than the results that he obtained in his memoirs.

This is confirmed by the history of Einstein's theory of relativity. Einstein, like Newton and Gibbs, is a great synthetic thinker, who has produced a theory which comprehends whole regions of phenomena. The ideas and mathematics of the theory of relativity are, perhaps, more difficult than those of Gibbs' chemical thermodynamics, and yet Einstein and his work have quickly received the fullest recognition.

The recent history of quantum mechanics provides a still more apposite illustration. Among living leaders of science, the one whose qualities of synthetic power, rigor and abstract thought most resemble those of Gibbs, is P. A. M. Dirac. He has not been isolated. He received a Nobel prize at the age of thirty-one. Men have become more sensitive to the significance of new theories since 1876, because subsequent history has made the social significance of science much more plain. A much larger number of persons are now sensitive to developments in science, and insist on trying to understand the most recondite theories. If Gibbs' work had appeared in 1926 its neglect would not have been permitted. Large groups of research students would have been set to study it, and simplified expositions would not have been left to the enthusiasm of individual leaders of investigation.

The isolation of Gibbs was probably not entirely disadvantageous. It may have assisted his originality. If he had been a member of a large research school he might have been exposed to more conventional influences, and not have been allowed to choose his own giant theme.

Nernst contends that deductive science of the Gibbsian type, in which numerous conclusions are drawn from a few fundamental assumptions, gives more mental satisfaction than empirical science. This belief undoubtedly contributes to the immense prestige of synthetic theorists such as Newton, Gibbs and Einstein. But it is questionable whether it has a sound foundation. The belief that theoretical deduction gives more mental satisfaction than experimental discovery may be based on class psychology, and may not be inherent in the psychology of individual activity. It may have been inspired by the ancient social belief that living without working is more distinguished than having to earn a living. This would predispose one to believe that discovery by deduction, without apparent manual work, is more satisfying than discovery by manual experiment. That part of Gibbs' prestige which rests on this belief may have a false basis.

Nernst said that Gibbs' calculations were of too generalized a character to be capable of direct application to particular problems. He considered that the successful application of general principles to particular cases constituted a definite contribution to science, even when the application involved no addition to theoretical ideas.

Generalized thinking is not of industrial value if it is not made available by suitable technical inventions. Gibbs' work cannot be dissociated from that of the chemists and engineers whose inventions made it fruitful. Its value cannot be considered greater than the practical work which enabled it to have value.

Another reason for the neglect of Gibbs' work was the lack of experimental chemists and engineers of the sort who could make use of it. This lack was due to backwardness of industrial technique. Competition had not yet forced chemical industry to study the efficiency of its processes, and evolve a large number of the sort of technicians who could increase it. This was the sort who could have made use of Gibbs' results.

From the point of view of industry, Gibbs' work was neglected because it was too crude. The general theory of processes was given, but without enough detail to afford help to a works manager in any particular process.

The theory of the equilibrium of heterogeneous substances was a gigantic fruit brought forth by the mental needs of industrialism, but it was abandoned by its gardener before it was ripe. Gibbs did not attempt to ripen the fruit and make it palatable to technologists. This also contributed to the neglect of his work.

His lack of interest in interpreting his work may be related to his conception of his social rôle. He did not feel called upon to give his students introductory courses which would have made his lectures more intelligible.

His attitude in this matter may be contrasted with Maxwell's. Through the whole of his career, Maxwell gave special attention to lectures to working men. Such lectures formed a considerable part of his duties at King's College, London, in the period when he invented the electromagnetic theory of light, and the statistical theory of gases. Is it possible that Maxwell's intelligibility was a reward for social conscience, and that Gibbs' unintelligibility was a penalty for the belief that he had no duty to ensure that his discoveries were understood and used?

Did Gibbs believe that he might be given by society the opportunity for research, without the obligation of explaining to those who supported him, the meaning and value of what he had found?

If he had been educated to consider that he could have no right to enjoy the opportunity of research without seeing that his results were exploited for the benefit of those who supported him, he might not have been content to see his work neglected.

The continual rediscovery of Gibbs' results since the publication of his papers is one of the most remarkable incidents in the history of science. The leaders of scientific research in the 1870's do not appear to have taken thorough notice of what others were doing. The organization of the exchange of knowledge was inefficient in the age of extreme individualist competition. The leaders of research still had much of the psychology of heroes. They were the kings of the intellectual world, without obligation to submit their work to the criticism of the intellectual democracy, or take full notice of what happened at other courts.

Through these circumstances the aesthetic qualities of Gibbs' work have come to be more important than the wonderful collection of results contained in it. Nearly all of these results were rediscovered and given social value by others. But besides this value, Gibbs' work still possesses direct use. His form of the adsorption equation is superior to that discovered later by Thomson, which was too inexplicit to be really useful. Development has been made through the use of the Gibbs form, and by careful attention to the conditions implied by Gibbs.

The tendency in the modern theory of solutions has been to go back more and more directly to the original formulation by Gibbs.

The notion of activities introduced by G. N. Lewis in 1907 are a fairly exact expression of Gibbs' chemical potentials.

The great advances in solution chemistry since 1920 have been due to the abandonment of the van't Hoff-Ostwald conceptions and a return to the original Gibbsian method of determining the potentials in solutions, without preconceived ideas. The most convenient expression of the potentials are Lewis' notion of activities.

Gibbs' work remains as a gigantic and beautiful exhibition of the power of the human intellect. The structure was not adequately used and appreciated when it was built. It is like a monument of the past which has been dug up, and reveals unsuspected human abilities. Many of the uses to which the monument might have been put are now supplied by a group of later and lesser buildings, but contemplation of it will always deepen the student's sense of what is possible to humanity.

III

His Descent and Education

JOSIAH WILLARD GIBBS WAS BORN IN NEW Haven in 1839. He was a member of a family which had been established in America by Robert Gibbs, the son of Sir Henry Gibbs, the proprietor of an estate at Honington, in Warwickshire, England. Robert Gibbs' mother was also a member of the English landed aristocracy, as she was a daughter of Sir Thomas Temple. The Temple family had been prominent in English governing circles for several generations. For reasons not known, the property of Sir Henry Gibbs was sequestrated in 1640, and his son Robert emigrated to Boston about 1658. Robert was loyal to Charles II, but subscribed to the popular religion of Massachusetts. His fourth son, Henry, graduated at Harvard in 1686, and became a minister. He showed "traits of obstinacy which seem to pretty generally characterize his descendants." Like other Harvard men of the time, he had a deplorably fanatical hatred of witches. His seventh child, Henry, graduated at Harvard in 1726, was librarian of the college in 1730, and later became a business man. His second wife was Katherine, a daughter of Hon. Josiah Willard, Secretary of Massachusetts Colony. Josiah Willard was an excellent man who earned the name of "the good secretary." His father was Samuel Willard, secretary, and in fact president of Harvard.

Henry and Katherine Gibbs had a son named Henry, who also graduated at Harvard and presently had a son whom he named Josiah Willard Gibbs. This was the physicist's father.

Josiah Willard Gibbs senior was born in 1790 and graduated at Yale in 1809. He married Ann Van Cleve. He had five daughters, and one son. His third child was Julia, born in 1836, and the fourth, his son, was born in 1839, when he was forty-nine years old.

The physicist was the last of a line of six college graduates on his father's side, and on his mother's side there were also graduates, including the first President of the College of New Jersey (Princeton). When Josiah Willard Gibbs senior was studying at Yale, theology still had a higher prestige than other subjects, so he followed the usual theological course, though the thought of devoting himself to mathematics, for which he had much aptitude, had passed through his mind. His contemporaries commented on his extreme modesty and retiring disposition. He was licensed to preach, but rarely entered the pulpit.

The standard of theological study at Harvard and Yale had been high in the early part of the eighteenth century but by the beginning of the nineteenth century it had declined. The new studies of mathematics, classics, natural science and English literature were attracting much of the intellectual energy formerly devoted almost exclusively to theology.

Gibbs felt, but did not accept, the attraction of the newer studies. As the study of theology was backward, there was scope for reviving it. The new impulse came from Germany, where Gesenius had recently stimulated the study of Hebrew. Stuart published a Hebrew grammar in the United States in 1821, which was based on Gesenius' work. As American printers had little acquaintance with Hebrew, Stuart had to set some of the type with his own fingers. Gibbs helped him with the correction of the proofs, and became infected with the enthusiasm for German scholarship, which was strong enough to inspire his teacher to learn the technique of printing. Gibbs gained a thorough knowledge of the German language and literature through his studies of German theological scholarship.

He was appointed professor of sacred literature at Yale.

His mental attitude of logical criticism was in contrast with the dominating current of doctrinal theology. He disliked forming and avowing opinions, as he felt that "men have no right to hold correct opinions with the will, in disregard of what may be alleged against them; and he disliked arbitrary judgments in respect to matters on which he had gained light only through candid and laborious study."

The style of his writings was clear. His logic was careful and his judgment sound, but he was inclined to be excessively averse to speculation. He could not manage the emotional aspects of intellectual appeal.

He had the ability of pursuing researches without intellectual companionship. He was particularly interested in the rationalistic theology of Eichorn, whose name was hardly known even to his familiar friends. On the study of words, his chief work, he could achieve eloquence, though in general he did not possess "that magnetic power which inspires dullness itself." He wrote that "the analysis of sentences in the concentrated light of Grammar and Logic . . . brings one into the sanctuary of human thought. All else is but standing in the outer court. He who is without may indeed offer incense, but he who penetrates within worships and adores. It is here that the man of science, trained to close thought and clear vision, surveys the various objects of study, with a more expanded view and a more discriminating mind. It is here that the interpreter, accustomed to the force and freshness of natural language, is prepared to explain God's revealed word with more power and accuracy. It is here that the orator learns to wield with a heavier arm the weapons of his warfare. It is here that everyone who loves to think, beholds the deep things of the human spirit, and learns to regard with holy reverence, the sacred symbols of human thought."

He became the leading American scholar of his day on comparative grammar, and it is noticeable that he speaks of the grammarian as a "man of science." If he had been less modest, and more tactful, that is, less uncomfortably critical, he might also have gained a distinguished reputation in Biblical interpretation and archaeology.

The elder Gibbs' aversion to positive opinion did not arise from lack of moral courage. He was an ardent advocate of justice for negroes. He considered that the political arrangements concerning negroes had been made in the exclusive interests of the whites "as a combination and conspiracy of the ruling race." He expected "the judgments of heaven to fall upon the country" because the rights of the dumb millions were "scarcely brought into the account."

His manners were gentle. He was often absent in thought and taciturn, but was rather fond of social intercourse with his particular friends.

The elder Gibbs seems to have been a mathematician by nature who, owing to circumstances, had become a grammarian. He was interested in words as symbols, as things for expressing other things. His initiative was too much inhibited by the nature of his temperament to allow him to escape from the more conventional studies into those for which he was probably better endowed. He had difficulty in impressing his ideas and desires on others.

His son was educated at the Hopkins Grammar School from 1849–1854, and prepared for Yale College which he entered at the age of fifteen, considerably younger than the usual age. Josiah Willard Gibbs Jr. was a very successful student. He was second in his class, and won several prizes in Latin and mathematics, and a scholarship for research. He presently wrote a thesis "On the form of the Teeth of Wheels in Spur Gearing," and received a doctorate in 1863. During this period, in 1861, his father died. After he had received the doctorate, he was appointed a tutor at Yale.

The effect on Gibbs of the undergraduate atmosphere at Yale when he was a student may be considered in relation to the account of student life given by "A Graduate of '69" in the book *Four Years at Yale*. The author was a freshman in the year that Gibbs was a tutor in natural philosophy, and student life in his class was probably not much different from what it had been in Gibbs' class. Gibbs entered Yale at the age of fifteen in 1854, and graduated in 1858.

The chief feature of undergraduate life was the system of secret societies. American first, second, third and fourth year students are named freshmen, sophomores, juniors and seniors. When Gibbs entered the college, an ordered system of societies was in existence. The freshman applied for membership in a freshmen's society. In his second year, he moved into a sophomore society, in the third, into a juniors', and in the fourth, into a seniors' society. The number of societies in each year or class multiplied. This led to competition between the societies for membership. The society representatives, or "runners," jumped onto the platforms of moving cars, fought the brakemen, and defied the police in order to meet the incoming candidates, and persuade them to pledge themselves immediately.

The initiation of a pledged man into his society occurred about a week after the commencement of term. Members in masks led him to the hall where the society held its secret meetings. He would be pushed into a dark room, where he would find other freshmen about to be initiated. When his turn came, members made up as horrific figures would blindfold him and lead him upstairs to an inquisitorial hall. After being asked nonsensical questions he was thrown into black empty space. He began to fall until he found himself caught and being tossed in a blanket. He may have been precipitated into a bucket of water, put into a pillory, laid on a mock guillotine, and then thrust into a coffin. Presently it was re-opened and he was "recalled to life," and found himself initiated. The initiation was supposed to test his nerves, but not to hurt him.

The chief freshmen's societies in Gibbs' class were Kappa Sigma Epsilon and Delta Kappa. A third society was formed by the class of '59, one year junior to Gibbs' class. This was named Gamma Nu. It was started as an open society in defiance of the character of the existing societies. It slowly gained ground, in spite of efforts to break it up, because some of the best men joined it, out of contempt for the silly aspect of the activities of the secret societies. Gibbs was educated just before the reform began, in a period when the social prestige of the secret societies was extreme.

The members of one society specialized in hard-working scholarship, another in careless literary excellence, and another in good fellowship and sociability. The societies were comprehensive in membership. The process of differentiation began after the freshmen had been in residence for some time. The most prominent freshmen were asked to pledge themselves for election to sophomore societies. As less than a half of the freshmen were eventually elected, competition for places became keen. Men helped the election of their friends by canvassing and political bargaining. These elections drew a little between "society-men" and "neutrals" who were not members.

The process of social selection continued through the elections to the junior, or third year, societies. According to the "Graduate of '69," these societies at that time were the most influential in college politics. They determined the election of the Wooden Spoon Committee and the five editors of the Yale Literary Magazine. The Committee elected the Spoon Man. They were supposed to choose the wittiest, most popular, and gentlemanly man of the class. The highest elective honor to which a student could aspire was the award of the Spoon.

The chief senior society was the "Skull and Bones," which was restricted to fifteen members.

The majority of undergraduates lived in rooms in private houses in New Haven. The strength of the societies was partly due to this. They provided social intercourse, which in universities such as Oxford, is offered by the colleges. Undergraduates formed eating clubs for taking meals.

There was considerable roughness in the period when Gibbs was a student. The sophomores sometimes broke into a freshman's rooms. They began to smoke into his face, and he was made to sing or dance, and if he refused, he was stirred up with sticks named "bangers." The best way of scattering a crowd of sophomores trying to break into a room was to fire a pistol shot through the door, after due warning. Unpopular freshmen were "brought down" by "hazing." They were overpowered, and their hair was cut off, or their faces marked with indelible ink, or they were stripped and covered with paint, and subjected to practices "which cannot be named." "Hazing" occurred less than once in each class, or year.

The sophomore and freshman classes engaged in "rushes." These consisted of mass fights in the streets.

Serious fights between young men of the town and the students occurred occasionally. Persons were killed in fights in 1854, and in 1858, the respective years in which Gibbs entered the college and graduated. In the first of these two fights the students discharged several pistol shots into the crowd. The man who was leading the crowd fell down and died in a few minutes. It was found afterwards that he had been stabbed with a large dirk-knife, and had not been shot. The crowd secured the two guns of the local artillery company, and loaded them, with the intention of discharging them at one of the colleges. The police succeeded in spiking the guns before they were discharged. The identity of the person who killed the man was never discovered. The relations between students and townsmen were tense for some time before and after this riot. Students could not walk in the streets without danger of disturbance. Gibbs was fifteen or sixteen when this happened. What effect could such violent events have on a quiet youth? Did they increase his shyness of society? In any case, they must have made subjects like the higher mathematics seem remote. They may have contributed towards the creation of Gibbs' personal and intellectual isolation.

The row of 1858 began between students and firemen, or members of the firebrigade. After the fighting had grown wild, there was a cry of "Shoot! Shoot!," and several pistol shots were discharged at the firemen. Their leader was shot, and died on the next day. He had a wife and two children, for whom five hundred dollars, or about one hundred pounds, was collected as compensation. Again, the person who killed the man was never identified. The students stood together very closely.

The progress of students' studies was tested by recitations before tutors. In mathematics recitations, the students worked at blackboards in front of the class. Many of the students devised ingenious methods of "skinning" or cheating. The "Graduate of '69" says that in his class chemistry was skinned entire, and that hardly a smattering of the science was learned by anyone.

The examinations in mathematics inspired the greatest craftiness. In 1855, during Gibbs' student period, it is said that a skinner noted there was a cellar under the floor of the examination hall. When he had learnt where he would sit in the hall, he bored a hole from the cellar through the floor by his place. He arranged for a friend to sit in the cellar under the hole during the examination, with a complete set of reference books. He copied the difficult questions onto small pieces of paper which were lowered by a strong black thread to his friend below. When the friend had solved them, he hauled up the solutions with the thread, and copied them in his own handwriting.

In 1867 two professional burglars from New York were engaged by sophomores to steal the mathematics paper, but were unsuccessful.

The "Graduate of '69" says that less than half the compositions handed in at language recitations were genuine, though, on the whole, honest work was the rule.

Literary achievement, especially by men of low position in the class, was esteemed by the students more highly than any other form of intellectual work. There were few contestants for the mathematics prizes, and their recipients were apt to be the objects of more or less good-natured chaff and banter.

The most characteristic feature of Yale college life was

Josiah Willard Gibbs
The Formative Period

PLATE VI

class-feeling and class-unity, i. e., the tendency of all the students of one year to act as a social unit. The extension of optional studies in the 1860's, which allowed students some opportunity to pursue those subjects which interested them most, was strongly opposed by many who believed it would undermine the social unity of the class. The aim was to make what were conceived to be good men with uniform social ideas, rather than good scholars or specialists of any sort. The prestige of sociability and good fellowship was higher than that of scholarship. This was reflected in the salaries of the professors, which were generally below the cost of the usual standard of living. Professors were willing to live at a financial loss for the sake of social prestige.

The Yale system of the 1850's and 1860's was a powerful machine for giving young men certain social characteristics. It was particularly suitable for training men of an active, extravert disposition for executive positions in politics, law, the church, and commerce. If the United States had not been growing and changing rapidly, and the number of Yale graduates had been larger, their history would have been different. They would have been governed by a type of politician even more thoroughly trained in clique manage-ment, and more undemocratic, than that produced by Oxford. The United States was too large, and the number of Yale men too small, for their government to pass entirely under the control of that group-loyal type. Students who passed through the system could not evade its profound influence.

Gibbs absorbed the Yale spirit completely. He accepted a set of social ideas of high value to a politician, but unsuited to a scientific discoverer. It increased his tendency to intel-lectual isolation, and at the same time, made that tendency seem natural.

He graduated just before the outbreak of the Civil War. His father died during the second year of the War, and he was able to continue research for his doctor's degree amid the excitement of the war atmosphere. He had already learned how to work in the atmosphere of the aggressive student life. During the first two years of his tutorship, and the last two years of the War, he taught Latin to undergraduates. These circumstances confirm that he was isolated from the popular social interests of his day. Though a young man, he appeared not to have been deeply moved by the profound social problems which provoked the Civil War. If he had, he would probably have taken some part in the struggle, even if too delicate to fight.

In 1865–66 he changed to tutoring in natural philosophy. He and his sisters left the United States at the end of 1866, on a three years' visit to Europe. This implies that their finances had not been destroyed by the Civil War. No doubt they had inherited some means from their father, and these had not been lost during the financial crises of the war.

Gibbs was twenty-seven years old when he sailed for Europe. He was mature enough, given the ability and training, to acquire the maximum value from his experiences. He spent the winter of 1866–67 in Paris, and then went to Berlin for a year, where he studied under Magnus, and attended lectures by Weierstrass, and others. He went to Heidelberg, whose staff included Kirchhoff and Helmholtz at the time, in 1868. He returned to New Haven in June, 1869. He does not appear to have visited England for study, and never established a close personal connection with British culture.

Gibbs' published works show that he was under predominantly German cultural influences. He regarded Clausius and Grassmann as his masters, and wrote in an abstract style more German than any other. He adopted the German manner of professorial lecturing. He gave far more attention to the logical exposition of general principles than to the acquisition of skill in the solution of particular problems, characteristic of English university teaching.

It is not improbable that Gibbs owed in a large degree to his father his receptiveness to German inspiration. The elder Gibbs was a profound scholar of German literature, and no doubt arranged that his son had had a thorough grounding in the German language. A thorough knowledge of a modern language has always been, and still is, rare among postgraduate students. Its cultural influence is not only larger, but higher in kind, than that of a general working knowledge of the language. Gibbs was probably one of the rare students with a knowledge of German sufficiently deep to receive directly, from men such as Kirchhoff, the strongest impression of the nature and style of German scientific thought.

His most famous work was on the equilibrium of heterogeneous substances, a subject which Kirchhoff had touched in 1855.

When he returned to New Haven in 1869, he was thirty years old. He was unmarried, and settled in the family of his sister Julia, who was three years his senior. The house had been built by his father, and Gibbs remained in it to the end of his life in 1903. The psychologist may see in these facts evidence of a mother-fixation. Gibbs lived in a house which was the symbol of the persistence of his father's authority, and he lived in a back room under the benevolent control of his elder sister, who was a substitute for his mother.

A psychoanalyst has pointed out to the writer that these details, if they are correct, seem to show that Gibbs had transferred a strong regard for his mother onto his elder sister. He went to Europe in a family group in which his elder sister probably had more authority, so his attitude towards her was continued and confirmed, and not broken, during his visit in Europe.

When he returned to New Haven and settled in her house, he produced his great memoir *On the Equilibrium of Heterogeneous Substances* as an act of devotion to her, a sort of spiritual child. It is possible that she was unable to understand the full greatness of the gift. If this were so, then it might be possible to explain peculiar features of Gibbs' behavior with regard to his work. He was abnormally modest about his achievements. Ostwald had considerable difficulty in arranging for the translation of his memoir into German.

Gibbs seemed scarcely to care whether or not it was translated. He allowed the American separates of it to go out of print, and did not have them reprinted, in spite of requests from distinguished scientists in various parts of the world. Wilson mentions that for the first fifteen years after the completion of the memoir, Gibbs appeared not to have lectured on chemical dynamics. One may imagine that an author might rest from the study of a subject for a year or two, after a period of the intensest effort, but one may expect that after that, he would return to it with increased interest, and talk about it with his friends and pupils. It is possible that his lack of effective interest in the future and development of the chief child of his brain may have been due to the disappointment of an unconscious psychological motive.

At the date of Gibbs' return Woolsey, the distinguished President of Yale, was near retirement. It was felt that a number of developments, which would better adapt the college to modern needs, might be initiated simultaneously with the election of a new president. Yale had been founded by clergy with conservative tendencies, who had separated from Harvard in order to resume what they considered to be the doctrinal purity of Calvinism. The charter of 1701 had stated that the college was for instruction in "the arts and sciences" suitable for the preparation of persons "for public employment, both in church and state," but the clergy retained control over the college, and "believed theology the basis, security and test of the arts and sciences." The conservative tendency at Yale has never been lost, and has prompted the observation that "Harvard on the whole is radical and progressive—Yale conservative."

The writer in the Eleventh Edition of the *Encyclopaedia Britannica* says further that the strength of Yale college feelings and traditions were due to poverty. Professors at Yale were not expected to live on their salaries, but their high social position was supposed to assist them to marry well-to-do wives.

In his discourse on *The Relations of Yale to Letters and Science* Daniel Coit Gilman observes that Yale and Harvard were shaped after Oxford and Cambridge rather than the Scottish, French and German universities, and that their "academic usages derived from medieval convents." The business of the early Harvard and Yale was to train two sets of leaders, for the church and state. Letters and science were not in their vocabulary, and religion and law were their chief subjects of study.

This system was gradually modified. At Yale a "chair of mathematics, physics and astronomy was instituted thirty years before the professorship of ancient languages." Franklin presented them with an electrical machine in 1749, and later with one of Fahrenheit's thermometers. Fahrenheit was the first to observe the super-cooling of water. He described the phenomenon in 1724. Its theoretical explanation was first given by Gibbs. Early in the nineteenth century Benjamin Silliman was appointed a professor and went to Scotland to continue his studies. He started the *American Journal of Science and Arts,* and became for a period the most influential man of science in the United States. The Yale school of mineralogy became especially famous under James D. Dana, and the observation of the return of Halley's comet by Yale astronomers several weeks before it was seen in Europe stimulated the study of astronomy in the United States. H. A. Newton, whose obituary notice was written by Gibbs, made important researches on the origin of meteoric showers, and Loomis on storms. The first chair of agricultural chemistry in the United States was founded at Yale in 1846.

Yale had had two students who became outstanding in invention: Eli Whitney and S. F. B. Morse.

But this record was not sufficient, and by 1870 still more service for modern life was necessary. The faculties prepared a statement of the *Needs of the University* which was published in 1871. The writers state that the difficulties of the College have been increased by the "increase in number of pupils, and need for more instructors, from growing demands for more perfect education," and "to the great and general advance in prices" (after the Civil War), "which has taken from the older endowments a large fraction of their original value." They prepared a long list of desirable new chairs and extensions to buildings, and mentioned that the endowment of each new professor would cost fifty thousand dollars "even with the present compensation of three thousand dollars—less by one or two thousand than the well-established churches of New Haven think necessary for their ministers." They wished to increase the scope of Yale into that of a university. They discussed the needs of the Library first, as that was the oldest institution of the college. (Gibbs' brother-in-law was the Librarian.)

Their conception of education is expounded in their statement that "Central and most conspicuous among the Institutions organized by the President and Fellows of Yale College, is the ancient school for liberal education, the Academical Department, which *is* Yale College in the restricted sense in which that name is commonly used. Its one aim is liberal culture as distinguished from preparation for specific employments and pursuits,—a thorough education by mental discipline—the education which fitly precedes the study of any liberal profession, and which is the *commune vinculum* of all such professions."

Gibbs agreed with this conception, and his acceptance of it helps to explain his detached attitude towards research. He regarded research as an activity which helped to provide "a thorough education by mental discipline," and he supposed that the subject of research was of secondary importance, and was the means to an end which was more important, mental discipline.

Though the writers express their opinion of the superiority of this sort of education, they discuss at length the importance and the needs of the Sheffield Scientific School, which is for "the study of the laws and forces of material nature; and for its distinctive method, instruction by object lessons." The object of the school is to promote the study of natural science and its practical applications, and training is given in civil and mechanical engineering, chemistry, metallurgy, agriculture, geology and natural history, and courses which "also lead to the professional pursuit of architecture, mechanics and mining."

They compiled a list of new chairs and tutorships required to extend the college teaching to the full scope of a university. In particular, they stated that:

"A division is further required in the department of Natural Philosophy and Astronomy. At present the recitations in Natural Philosophy are wholly conducted by tutors. But a field so vast as that of Physics, and one in which the onward march of science is so astonishingly rapid, demands the labors of a professor who shall be permanently and exclusively devoted to it."

The new chair of Mathematical Physics was founded in 1871, and Gibbs was appointed as its first occupant. It is notable that Clerk Maxwell was appointed the first Cavendish Professor of Experimental Physics at Cambridge, England, in 1871. Why were new chairs of physics being founded in widely separated parts of the world at the same date? The explanation is sociological. The first professorship at Yale was founded in 1755 for Sacred Theology, and the second in 1770 for Mathematics, Natural Philosophy and Astronomy. At Cambridge, England, the chairs in theology were the oldest, and chairs in mathematics and astronomy were founded in the seventeenth and eighteenth centuries.

Why were chairs of astronomy founded at Yale and Cambridge in the eighteenth century, while chairs of physics were not founded until a hundred years later, in 1871? The explanation is that mathematical astronomy was the most important science in the eighteenth century, as ocean navigation is based on it. The Atlantic civilization of the eighteenth century was primarily mercantile, and founded on the shipping trade. Astronomy was the science of greatest value to it, and therefore received the greatest prestige. All men of education believed it was important. This sense of the importance of astronomy came from the pressure of the interest of the ruling classes. The awareness of the interest in it caused its importance to be accepted without question. Many able men studied astronomy without formulating to themselves reasons why they should. Isaac Newton was one of them. Newton and his discoveries in mathematical astronomy were a product of the urge of the ruling mercantile classes to discover how they could increase their knowledge of the technique of transport, and discover new sources of wealth, and increase their freights and profits.

Elihu Yale himself was a leading figure in the mercantile age, which produced Newton as the master theorist of the mathematical astronomy on which their navigation and profits depended. He amassed great wealth as Governor of the East India Company's settlement at Madras in India.

By the middle of the nineteenth century, mathematical astronomy was no longer the chief physical science. It was supplanted by theoretical and experimental physics, concerned with heat and electricity. The mercantilists had been replaced by a new ruling class of industrial manufacturers, who made goods with machinery driven by steam engines, and conducted business communications by the electric telegraph. They wished their sons to learn something about heat and electricity, about the sciences of the steam engine and the electric telegraph.

Clerk Maxwell's chair was created in 1871 for the study of the new physics. Before that date, there had been no official courses of instruction at Cambridge on heat and electricity. The Cambridge course was now adapted to the cultural needs of the new governing class. The sociological meaning of the foundation of Gibbs' chair at Yale in 1871 is the same. It was a move towards the adaptation of education at Yale to the needs of the new governing class of industrial capitalists in the United States.

The motives for the changes in courses of education are not always clear at the time they are made. The directors of educational policy who make original changes have a sense

The house built by his father where Gibbs lived with his
sister's family

PLATE VII

of what developments are needed from the general atmosphere of their time, long before the reasons for the changes are clear.

Gibbs' specialty was thermodynamics, which is the finest cultural expression of the age of steam. This branch of science evolved directly out of the invention, use and improvement of the steam engine. The chief founder of the science was Sadi Carnot, whose famous cycle is the ghost of the disembodied steam engine. The leaders of the Industrial Revolution wanted more efficient steam engines, and higher profits. This demand created the general impression that these matters were important, so scientists began to search for the fundamental principles which govern the working of steam engines. Carnot, Mayer, Joule, Clausius, Rankine and Kelvin accomplished this task, and professors were needed to teach this practically valuable new knowledge in the universities.

Gibbs learned all that these masters had discovered. As a student of thermodynamics he was a direct cultural product of the Industrial Revolution. But he did not complete the chapters they had written. He wrote a new chapter of his own. By the middle of the nineteenth century, the efficiency of the steam engine had been considerably increased through the elucidation of its principles.

Similar refinements had not yet been made in the processes of industrial manufacture. The efficiency of steam engines, and sources of power, had been increased by applying the laws of heat to them. No parallel increase in the efficiency of industrial processes, in which mixtures of all sorts of substances are boiled and heated together, was obtained by applying the laws of heat to them. No one had investigated, beyond slight beginnings, the theory of the effects of heat on mixtures of substances. A vast amount of empirical knowledge of what happens when mixtures of particular substances are heated had been collected, by experiment and observation, in chemical factories, general industry, and research laboratories, but no theory of the phenomena had been worked out. The possibility of conducting the chemical processes of industry efficiently depends on the discovery of such a theory. An efficient chemical industry, in which huge quantities of raw materials are converted into an enormous variety of finished materials, cannot be devised without a knowledge of chemical thermodynamics. The manufacturer must know exactly how much energy is consumed at each stage of his processes, if his costs are to be reduced to the minimum. He must have a science of chemical energetics which will give him this information.

Willard Gibbs virtually created this science of chemical energetics.

IV

The Efficient Management of Mixtures

AS ISAAC NEWTON SUPPLIED THE SCIENTIFIC
needs of the merchant traders of his day, Willard Gibbs supplied the scientific needs of the rationalizing and efficiency-
hunting industrialists who have controlled Western civilization since the middle of the nineteenth century. This does
not imply that Newton and Gibbs consciously supplied the
most important cultural needs of the governing classes of
their days, though, as will appear in Section V of this chapter, Gibbs conceived mathematics as a tool for saving labor,
and thus serving human interests. He probably owed this
insight to the influence of the American general outlook on
life.

The motives which direct men's private lives are largely
unconscious. Perhaps not one-twentieth part of a man's motives for pursuing any particular course are clear to himself.
The aim of the science of psychology is to reveal another
twentieth or more to him, so that he shall understand himself better, and act more wisely.

The problems and aims of the study of the history of science are similar. Perhaps only one-twentieth part of the
reasons why a scientist of a particular type appeared at a particular time and solved particular problems are clear to himself and his contemporaries. The aim of the historian of science is to reveal another twentieth or more of the concealed
reasons why certain scientists appear at certain times and do
certain things. Such knowledge gives a better understanding
of the rôle of science in civilization, and helps to suggest the

best method of managing science for the benefit of humanity.

When James Watt began to manufacture steam-engines, he was troubled by the lack of any convenient method of measuring their horse-power. He could not give prospective customers a reliable estimate of the horse-power, and hence of the value, of the engine whose purchase they were considering. In order to obtain more precise information of the amount of work done by the steam inside the engine cylinder, he devised about 1790 an instrument that he named an "indicator," which was essentially a pressure gauge, and indicated the pressure of the steam inside the cylinder. In 1796 someone, almost certainly his assistant, Southern, thought of attaching a pencil to the gauge, which would trace a line on a sheet of paper moved by the engine. This figure, or "indicator diagram," gave an automatic graph of the changes in the pressure and volume of the steam in the cylinder, and its area was a measure of the amount of work done by the steam. The indicator diagram and its properties had not been fully investigated by scientists before they were first obtained from a steam-engine. In a large degree, indicator diagrams were invented and drawn by the *steam-engine*, and presented to scientists for their consideration afterwards. The scientists did not invent the theory of heat and indicator diagrams first, and then specify how steam-engines might be constructed according to their principles.

They derived the science of thermodynamics from the indicator diagrams and other data put before them by profit-seeking engineers.

The pressure-volume diagram was one of the foundations of the science of thermodynamics. Pressures and volumes of steam were naturally studied first because they are among the most accessible properties of a quantity of steam. The other directly accessible property is temperature. Scientists presently began to use diagrams in three dimensions, which were capable of representing simultaneously the pressure, volume and temperature of a quantity of steam. As a curve simultaneously represents pressure and volume in an ordinary indicator diagram, a surface simultaneously represents pressure, volume, and temperature in a three-dimensional diagram. Such pressure-volume-temperature surfaces were proposed and used by James Thomson in 1871.

Willard Gibbs began his original contributions to science by investigating the general theory of all such thermodynamical diagrams. Gibbs' researches grew directly out of science of the most practical character. He explains in the opening words of his first published paper: "Although geometrical representations of propositions in the thermodynamics of fluids are in general use, and have done good service in disseminating clear notions in this science, yet they have by no means received the extension in respect to variety and generality of which they are capable. So far as regards a general graphical method, which can exhibit at once all the thermodynamic properties of a fluid concerned in reversible processes, and serve alike for the demonstration of general theorems and the numerical solution of particular problems, it is the general if not the universal practice to use diagrams in which the rectilinear coördinates represent volume and pressure." He proceeds "to call attention to certain diagrams of different construction, which afford graphical methods co-extensive in their applications with that in ordinary use, and preferable to it in many cases in respect of distinctness, or of convenience."

He explains that other properties of a fluid besides pressure, volume and temperature may be used in order to specify its thermodynamic condition. One may also use the energy and the entropy of the fluid. As the existence of these properties was not known when the heat-properties of fluids were first studied, pressure, volume and temperature were naturally chosen for specifying the thermodynamic condition of fluids. But they are just as real physical entities as pressure, volume and temperature. The notion of energy is now commonly understood. Heat itself is one of its forms. Entropy, which started as a mathematical formula, is now perceived to have a physical meaning. It is known from experience that heat tends to flow from hot to cold bodies, and that the material universe tends towards a uniform temperature. As the age of the material universe increases, the various packets of heat in it become undone, and their contents are scattered and shuffled until they are spread out evenly. Entropy is the measure of the degree of this scattering process. Among the unpublished notes left by Gibbs is a heading for a proposed chapter on "Entropy as mixed-up-ness." Eddington defines entropy as "the practical measure of the random element which can increase in the universe but can never decrease." Clerk Maxwell defines the entropy of a body "as a measurable quantity, such that when there is no communication of heat this quantity remains constant, but when heat enters or leaves the body the quantity increases or diminishes."

While entropy is not an obvious property of bodies, it may be handled exceedingly conveniently by mathematics. Gibbs suggested that this quality should be exploited in thermodynamical diagrams by choosing entropy as one of the properties by which the condition of a body may be defined. One may construct entropy-temperature diagrams, entropy-volume diagrams, entropy-and-logarithms-of-temperature diagrams, etc. He systematically explored the features of a variety of these diagrams. He found that a number of problems which could not be conveniently solved with the assistance of the old pressure-volume diagram, could be solved easily with the assistance of one or other of the new diagrams.

It appears that Gibbs was not the first to discuss the entropy-temperature diagram. T. Belpaire sketched the idea in a paper published in the previous year, 1872. But Gibbs handled it far more profoundly. It was also independently discovered by Macfarlane Gray, about 1876. He was the chief engineer of the British Royal Navy, and he was interested in its value to engineers. He gave it the name by which it is now universally known, the "theta-phi diagram." Through it the second law of thermodynamics and the notion of entropy were placed at the service of average engineers, who could not understand the abstract mathematical presentation of these principles in the standard works on thermodynamics. As Gibbs said, this diagram is "nothing more nor less than a geometrical representation of the second law of thermodynamics." The lines in the old pressure-volume diagram representing temperature and adiabaticity are curves difficult to draw. New curves must be drawn for each particular problem, and the axes are the only permanent lines in the diagram. In the theta-phi diagram, the difficult curves need be drawn once only, as they are the permanent lines. The special lines which have to be drawn in order to find the solution of any particular problem are all straight, so the solution may be read off by inspection.

In addition, problems concerning wet steam and super-heated steam, of importance in connection with the performance of steam-engines, may be solved on one continuous diagram, because it applies to mixtures of fluids, besides uniform fluids. The diagram would give information about the loss of efficiency due to incomplete expansion of the steam, whereas the indicator diagram gave only the work done on the piston, and the efficiency of valves and steam passages. The energy of the steam could be determined by simple measurement, instead of having to calculate an area from a number of measurements of curves.

Gray writes that the theta-phi diagram was suggested to himself by Sadi Carnot's water-wheel argument, which implies the principle of the diagram. In 1879 he began to use the diagram as an aid in teaching. In 1880 he used it in a public lecture, and was informed afterwards that Willard Gibbs had discussed it previously. He looked up Gibbs' paper and writes that he found it a "very high-class production."

One of the diagrams now most used by engineers is Mollier's modification of the theta-phi diagram.

Gibbs showed that his entropy-volume diagram was particularly convenient for representing the thermodynamic condition of a body which consisted of a mixture of parts in different states, such as a mixture of ice, water and water-vapor.

In his second paper, he investigated the properties of

thermodynamic diagrams in three dimensions. He extended the entropy-volume plane diagram by adding a coördinate for energy, and derived geometrical surfaces whose points represented simultaneously the volume, entropy and energy of a body.

Thermodynamic diagrams and surfaces, in which entropy enters as a coördinate, have had a large part in the development of the science of low temperatures. This includes such achievements as the liquefaction of helium, and all that that has implied; and the vast technical developments of refrigeration, which depend on the efficient expansion and contraction of varieties of substances and mixtures, such as ammonia, sulphur dioxide and other refrigerants. Even the quick service of ice cream and chilled champagne, the importation into Europe of beef and apples from Australia, and the functioning of the refrigerator in the domestic kitchen, owe something to Gibbs. Through the use of entropy as a coördinate in the surfaces, he was able to give a complete representation of the relations between volume, entropy, energy, pressure and temperature for all states of the body. As Maxwell wrote: "The body itself need not be homogeneous either in chemical nature or in physical state. All that is necessary is that the whole should be at the same pressure and the same temperature." The tendency of the parts of a body, which were coexistent in different (solid, liquid or gaseous) states, to change from one state into another, could be deduced from the surfaces, or perhaps more accurately, it was possible to deduce from the surfaces the conditions in which different parts of a body, such as a quantity of water, may coexist in different solid, liquid and gaseous states, i. e., the conditions in which the body may exist as a mixture of ice, water, and water vapour. With their assistance it is possible to give the theoretical explanation of a number of well-known and peculiar phenomena. When a liquid not in contact with its vapor is heated above its boiling point, or cooled below its freezing point, or when a solution of a salt or gas becomes supersaturated, the introduction of a small quantity of water vapor to the superheated water

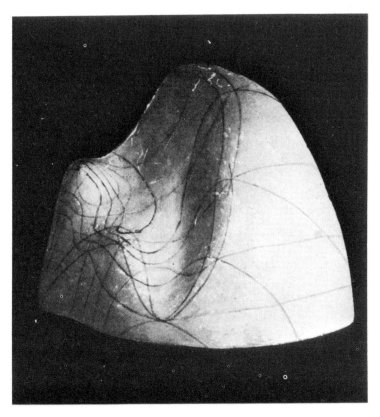

CLERK MAXWELL'S MODEL OF GIBBS' THERMODYNAMIC
SURFACE

The *Energy* axis is vertical, and stands at the back of the
model, in the middle of the picture. The *Volume* and *Entropy* axes pass from the back to the left and right front.
The model rests on the plane made by these two axes.

This model is 12 cm. high and 13.4 cm. wide.

There are two of these models in the Cavendish Laboratory. They were made by Clerk Maxwell with his own
hands. He also made a third, which he sent to Gibbs.

The illustration here is reproduced from a photograph
kindly presented by Lord Rutherford to the writer for this
book.

PLATE VIII

will produce explosive boiling, while the introduction of a small piece of ice to the supercooled water will produce explosive freezing. A particle of salt-crystal will produce explosive crystallization in the supersaturated solution of salt, and a bubble of gas will produce explosive effervescence in the supersaturated solution of gas.

This behavior of bodies in mixed states could be easily deduced from the thermodynamic surfaces, which showed that the parts of a body in one state might turn into another state suddenly. This occurred, under certain circumstances, when the parts were in two states, and in equilibrium. The introduction of a particle of the substance in the third state upset the equilibrium and produced an explosive change to a new equilibrium. The surfaces indicated the criteria which determined whether the equilibrium of the system was stable or unstable, and whether there would be a tendency for parts in one state to pass into another state.

Gibbs' researches on thermodynamic surfaces enabled him to discover a more general method of analysis. He gave all the results which appear in his first two papers in a much more general form in the third paper, on the equilibrium of heterogeneous substances. In this, he gives a discussion on the conditions of equilibrium which govern the formation of *new* bodies. The theory includes the explanation of the phenomena of superheating, supercooling, etc., in which new bodies, such as solid crystals, suddenly appear in solutions of solids. He explained that a fluid is stable if the formation of every possible new body in it, while the entropy and volume remain constant, requires an increase of energy. It is unstable if a new body could be formed having a lower energy. But it is possible that although there may be bodies which when formed in quantity would reduce the energy, so that the liquid is really unstable with respect to them, yet the formation of very small quantities would increase the energy, because an appreciable surface energy would also have to be taken into account. In that case the liquid is stable with respect to infinitesimal changes, but unstable with respect to finite changes. It will thus remain unchanged, unless one introduces some of the new body, when the necessity of the substance first appearing in an infinitesimal amount is obviated, and the way is open for a finite change to occur, which may be explosive.

Gibbs considered that the second law of thermodynamics should be placed at the beginning of the theory of heat, according to its importance, and explained that the introduction of entropy as a coördinate in thermodynamic diagrams helped to do this. He wrote that "the method in which the coordinates represent volume and pressure has a certain advantage in the simple and elementary character of the notions upon which it is based, and its analogy with Watt's indicator has doubtless contributed to render it popular. On the other hand, a method involving the notion of *entropy*, the very existence of which depends upon the second law of thermodynamics, will doubtless seem to many far-fetched, and may repel beginners as obscure and difficult of comprehension. This inconvenience is perhaps more than counter-balanced by the advantages of a method which makes the second law of thermodynamics so prominent, and gives it so clear and elementary an expression."

The two papers on graphical and geometrical methods of representing the thermodynamic properties of substances were published in 1873, when Gibbs was thirty-four years old. The authorities of Yale had appointed him a professor in 1871, when he was thirty-two, and had as yet published nothing. This shows that they had confidence in his intellectual ability, and correct judgment.

The papers were original and elegant, and their merit was at once recognized by Clerk Maxwell. It would be interesting to know how Maxwell learned of their existence, as they were published in the obscure proceedings of the Connecticut Academy. Gibbs was not inclined to procure attention for his work, and would probably not have liked to send copies of it to Maxwell without request. But he may have done, or a colleague may have done so for him.

Maxwell's instant perception of the quality of Gibbs was

not the least of his achievements. In 1874 he was very busy with the Cavendish Laboratory, which had just been designed, built and opened under his direction. In 1873 he had published his *Treatise on Electricity and Magnetism*. He succeeded, amidst all these activities, in detecting the merit of the work of an unknown young man in a distant country whose inhabitants at the time were making few contributions to theoretical physics.

The most extraordinary feature of Maxwell's prescience is that he drew the attention of English *chemists* to the importance of Gibbs' work. In a lecture to the Chemical Society of London, on the Dynamical Evidence of the Molecular Constitution of Bodies, delivered on February 18th, 1875, he said:

"The purely thermodynamical relations of the different states of matter do not belong to our subject, as they are independent of particular theories about molecules. I must not, however, omit to mention a most important American contribution to this part of thermodynamics by Prof. Willard Gibbs, of Yale College, U.S., who has given us a remarkably simple and thoroughly satisfactory method of representing the relations of the different states of matter by means of a model. By means of this model, problems which had long resisted the efforts of myself and others may be solved at once."

Maxwell also drew attention to Gibbs' researches in his articles on *Diffusion,* and *Diagrams,* in the *Encyclopaedia Britannica.* In the last paragraph of the latter article he describes the Indicator Diagram, and then concludes by mentioning that Gibbs has very completely illustrated the use of diagrams in thermodynamics, "but though his methods throw much light on the general theory of diagrams as a method of study, they belong rather to thermodynamics than to the present subject."

In spite of this recommendation the English chemists did not succeed in following Gibbs' work. They failed to appreciate his conceptions of chemical thermodynamics, which have provided the theory for the rational development of physical chemistry and chemical engineering. They missed the opportunity of exploiting the implications of his discoveries, and leading the creation of practical physical chemistry. The initiative passed to German, French and Dutch chemists who began to appreciate Gibbs' papers about ten years later, but were still in time to forestall the English. The body of chemical and physical research in the United States was not sufficiently developed to be able to take the first advantage of Gibbs' contributions. Gibbs' work was a product of the European rather than the American branch of the scientific activity of Atlantic civilization.

Maxwell died prematurely in 1879. He spent much time in his last years studying Gibbs' thermodynamic surfaces. He gave an exposition of their properties in his textbook on the *Theory of Heat,* and some practical details of how they might be constructed. He made a model of a surface with his own hands, and very shortly before he died, sent a plaster cast of it to Gibbs at New Haven. Gibbs received great pleasure from this distinguished gift, and highly valued the possession of it. The compliment to a young man on his first two papers, from the man whom many regard as the greatest physicist of the nineteenth century, was marvelous.

Maxwell's sympathy for Gibbs' work suggests that they had some similar methods of thought. Gibbs showed in his first papers that he could use geometrical illustrations to help the imagination without being tied to the obvious geometrical characteristics of bodies. The pioneers had put geometrical representations of pressure and volume directly onto paper. They tried to interpret phenomena by direct mechanical analogy. This method was pursued by Kelvin and others throughout their careers. They tried to explain all physical phenomena by analogy with simple machines, such as engines and springs and jellies, even when the analogy was not apt. This helps to explain why Kelvin had such a sense of failure at the end of his life. He had tried to explain the world in terms of simple machines, and the world was not,

in fact, like a simple machine, so the analogy had led him
into inextricable difficulties.

Gibbs and Maxwell were more subtle. They used geometrical and mechanical models when these had an analogy
to some *part* of their problems, but they did not try to force
the whole of their theories into forms of analogy to simple
machines. Maxwell discovered his electro-magnetic theory of
light with assistance from a model, which is described in his
first papers on the theory, but he dispensed with the model
when he had got what he wanted out of it. There is no
reference to the model in his *Treatise on Electricity and
Magnetism*.

The attitude of Maxwell and Gibbs, of using mechanical
and geometrical illustrations, without following them slav-
ishly, is consonant with that of contemporary physicists. The
behavior of atoms is investigated with the assistance of geometrical and mechanical analogies to parts of their behavior,
in so far as it resembles that of particles or waves, but the
attempt to invent a complete model of an atom, which would
operate according to the principles of simple machines, has
been abandoned. The belief that the behavior of atoms
should necessarily be strictly analogous with the simple
machines of common human experience is now seen to be
an egocentric delusion.

Gibbs and Maxwell were both sensitive to elegance in research. Gibbs' elegance was stately and architectonic, whereas
Maxwell's was brilliant and individual. Gibbs excelled Maxwell in rigor, but was inferior to him in striking practical
exposition. Maxwell's early death was unfortunate for the
prospects of Gibbs' work. He could present discoveries far
more persuasively to those who did not know how to appreciate them in their original form. As will be described presently,
Maxwell was equally swift in recognizing the merit of Gibbs'
next memoir. If he had lived, and had continued to act, as
it were, as Gibbs' intellectual publicity agent, the greatness
of Gibbs' discoveries might have been understood ten years
sooner, and physical chemistry and chemical industry today

might have been twenty years in advance of its present development.

Through his study of thermodynamic diagrams and surfaces, Gibbs discovered how to elucidate the physical and chemical behavior of mixtures of substances by thermodynamics. His models helped him to discover new aspects of systems, such as their thermodynamic potentials, and free energies, and to represent them by new mathematical functions. As thermodynamics is concerned only with the energy and entropy, the conclusions concerning any system, which may be drawn with its help, are of a general nature. They are independent of any particular assumptions concerning the constitution of the materials of the system, and of any physical or chemical changes which occur in the system. Thermodynamics is concerned, as it were, with the public life of systems, and ignores their private life. This is the source of its strength and limitations as a method of investigation. General rules of behavior may be defined by it, to which systems, whose private life may be of a complex and highly interesting character, must conform. The private peculiarities of such systems are often the most prominent and the first which engage the investigator's attention, but they are often also of baffling complexity, and impregnable to direct attack. It is often of great assistance to the investigator, whose chief interest may be in the private lives of systems, to be able to circumscribe those lives within public boundaries of some sort, even of the widest character. But it also often happens that a knowledge of the public boundaries is far too general to provide much insight into the private details of the system, which may be of chief practical interest, and in such cases, little can be accomplished through thermodynamics alone.

The science of thermodynamics was evolved out of the study of engines driven by steam. The first step towards generalization consisted of elucidating the principles of engines which were driven by any "working substance," or ideally perfect gas. Carnot, Mayer, Joule, Helmholtz, Clausius,

Kelvin and Rankine were naturally first interested in elucidating the laws for uniform, or homogeneous, substances. As the substances were uniform, the problem of the equilibria between their different portions did not arise. For example, the steam expanding inside the cylinder of a steam-engine is supposed to be in the same condition all through. It is not in one state at one end of the cylinder, and in another state at the other end. The founders of thermodynamics were inspired by the problem of the behavior of steam inside an engine cylinder. They were interested in the work they could get out of the steam, what work it would do in public. They were not interested in the private life of the steam, the internal relations between its different portions. They assumed the states were the same all through.

The problem before a chemist is quite different. He is interested primarily in the reactions inside a flask, not in the work which can be got out of steam inside a cylinder. His primary interest is in the relations, the equilibria, between the various substances in the flask. The chemist is interested in equilibria, while the physicist, inspired by the engineer, is interested in the production of work.

Owing to the source of their inspiration, physicists first applied the laws of thermodynamics to the problem of the behavior of uniform or homogeneous substances. They were not at first particularly interested in applying them to mixed, or heterogeneous systems, in which equilibrium between the parts is of primary importance. Consequently, they did not specially study, though they did not ignore, the application of the laws to the problems of equilibria. Horstmann was the first to investigate chemical equilibria with the assistance of the principle that when a system is in equilibrium, its entropy must be at a maximum. Gibbs began the publication of his vastly wider application of the same principle two months after the appearance of Horstmann's paper. He noted that little had been done "to develop the principle as a foundation for the general theory of thermodynamic equilibrium."

He set out to develop those aspects of thermodynamics

which are of interest to chemists, besides physicists and engineers. He put Clausius' famous statement of the two laws, "Die Energie der Welt ist constant. Die Entropie der Welt strebt einem Maximum zu" (The energy of the world is constant. The entropy of the world tends to a maximum), at the head of his memoir, and devised a mathematical apparatus by which they could be employed to elucidate the stability and equilibria of mixtures, or heterogeneous systems. He did this through the notion of the thermodynamical and chemical potentials of the components of a system, or mixture. Massieu had introduced the notion of thermodynamic potentials in 1869, but Gibbs rediscovered them, and exploited them with vastly greater power.

The chemical potentials of the components of a system are simple functions of the masses and energies of the various components. Through them, it is possible to introduce the masses of the components as the variables in the fundamental equation describing the behavior of the system. Heterogeneous equilibrium cannot be handled without using mass as a variable. The introduction and powerful use of mass as a variable constitutes Gibbs' greatest achievement.

He had succeeded in stating the problems of thermodynamic equilibria in convenient mathematical forms. He now started to deduce with extraordinary logical power numerous important conclusions from those forms. His arguments were mainly logical, and expressed in simple mathematics.

The conclusions had a wide application to the substances which occur in nature, for these consist of assortments of solids, liquids and gases approaching, or already in, equilibrium. The laws of thermodynamic equilibrium must be obeyed by the constituents of the primeval rocks which had solidified out of molten solutions in past geological times, the soil and the atmosphere, the substances in living bodies, liquids and the materials they hold in solution, solid solutions, which are of fundamental importance in metallurgy, and all systems which have non-uniform features.

L. J. Henderson, J. Loeb, Van Slyke and O. Warburg

have applied Gibbs' principles to the analysis of the equilibria of salts in the blood, and other living systems.

Irving Fisher applied Gibbs' theories and vector methods to the study of equilibria in economics. The principle of equilibrium in exchanges in chemical reactions is logically the same as in the exchanges of goods between persons, upon which the structure and stability of human society depends. In this instance, Gibbs' discoveries are seen to exert a direct effect on the conceptions of the mechanism of human society.

In the first part of his analysis, Gibbs considered the conditions of equilibrium in a system whose parts were different (heterogeneous), and in contact, but influenced by gravity, electricity, distortion of those masses which were solid, or by capillary forces. He explained that the choice of which substances are to be regarded as components of the system may be determined entirely by convenience. "For example, in considering the equilibrium in a vessel containing water and free hydrogen and oxygen, we should be obliged to recognize three components in the gaseous part. But in considering the equilibrium of dilute sulphuric acid with the vapor which it yields, we should have only two components to consider in the liquid mass, sulphuric acid . . . and . . . water."

The conditions relating to the possible formation of masses unlike any previously existing in the system are then explored. It will be seen that these conditions would apply to phenomena such as the appearance and growth of crystals in a solution hitherto clear, the formation of ice in a system of water and water-vapor, etc.

The importance of Gibbs' memoir *On the Equilibrium of Heterogeneous Substances* was immediately recognized by Clerk Maxwell. He even began to lecture on it before its publication was completed. He expounded Gibbs' theory of chemical potentials on a remarkable public occasion in 1876. The first international loan exhibition of scientific apparatus which had ever been organized was opened in that year at South Kensington, London, by Queen Victoria and the Empress of Germany. Historic apparatus was loaned from many countries, and many of the leading scientists of Europe attended, including Helmholtz, C. W. Siemens, Beilstein, Wöhler, Ewald-Herring, Andrews, Pictet, and von Ettinghausen, and conferences on many subjects were held for a fortnight. When Queen Victoria visited the exhibits, Clerk Maxwell himself demonstrated Otto von Guericke's original air-pump, and Magdeburg spheres, to her. On one day 11,969 persons visited the exhibits, and the *Times* devoted about twenty columns, spread over a few weeks, to the affairs of the exhibition. The Americans had not exhibited, as all of their material was at their Independence centenary exhibition. The *Times* dismissed Maxwell's lecture with the bare statement that he had spoken *On the Equilibrium of Heterogeneous Bodies*. One wonders whether Helmholtz, Pictet, Thomson, Andrews and the rest paid as little attention to his discourse. American interests had a poor showing on this occasion. No doubt the memories of 1776, and the duty of celebrating independence by the exhibition in the United States, prevented good Anglo-American coöperation over the London exhibition. In this way, political feelings may have balked adequate attention to Maxwell's recommendation of Gibbs' discoveries. If there had been a large contingent of Americans at South Kensington they might have taken special interest in the exposition of the work of one of their countrymen, and not have allowed it to be virtually ignored.

Maxwell published an abstract of virtually the same lecture in the *Proceedings of the Cambridge Philosophical Society* in 1876. This was two years before the publication of Gibbs' memoir had been completed. This abstract is included in Maxwell's *Collected Papers*, but there is an even more interesting one in the *American Journal of Science* for 1877. In the Cambridge abstract Maxwell wrote that Gibbs' methods in his memoir (he had read only the first part) "seem to me to throw a new light on Thermodynamics," and he wished "to point out to the Society," their value.

In the *American Journal*, he is reported as saying that Gibbs' methods "seem to me to be more likely than any others to enable us, without any lengthy calculations, to comprehend the relations between the different physical and chemical states of bodies, and it is to these that I now wish to direct your attention."

He explains that Gibbs "takes as his principal function the energy of the fluid, as depending on its volume and entropy together with the masses . . . of its . . . components."

"By differentiating the energy with respect to the volume, we obtain the pressure of the fluid with the sign reversed; by differentiating with respect to the entropy, we obtain the temperature on the thermodynamic scale; and by differentiating with respect to the mass of any one of the component substances, we obtain what Professor Gibbs calls the potential of that substance in the mass considered.

"As this conception of the potential of a substance in a given homogeneous mass is a new one, and likely to become very important in the theory of chemistry," he proceeds to expound Gibbs' definition of it. He explains that "the pressure is the intensity of the tendency of the body to expand, the temperature is the intensity of its tendency to part with heat; and the potential of any component substance is the intensity with which it tends to expel that substance from its mass."

The problem to be considered is: "Given a homogeneous mass in a certain phase, will it remain in that phase, or will the whole or part of it pass into some other phase?"

Maxwell quotes Gibbs' criterion of equilibrium, that for all possible variations of the state of the system, which do not alter its entropy, the variation of its energy shall either vanish or be positive, and then says that through this, "Professor Gibbs has made a most important contribution to science by giving us a mathematical expression for the stability of any given phase A of matter with respect to any other phase B."

In both abstracts there is an explanation of Guthrie's experiments, in which a solution of sodium chloride was solidified in three different ways by contact with three different substances, according to Gibbs' theory. In the Cambridge abstract the theory "was illustrated by Mr. Main's experiments on co-existent phases of mixtures of chloroform, alcohol and water."

Gibbs discussed the effect of a diaphragm which divides the system into two parts, and "is capable of supporting an excess of pressure on either side, and is permeable to some of the components and impermeable to others." This leads to the statement of the conditions of osmotic equilibrium. He deduced that the potentials of components which can permeate the membrane is the same on both sides, and that the pressure is not necessarily the same on both sides. He did not give any formula for the pressure differences, but he gave an expression for the potential of a solute as a function of the concentration, from which van't Hoff's law could be easily deduced. He did not make this deduction until 1897. Under the influence of van't Hoff, osmotic forces were regarded as the forces exerted by molecules of substances dissolved in liquids. Gibbs did not conceive them in this way, though it was commonly held for a long period. Gibbs conceived the osmotic pressure as merely the pressure which must be applied to ensure that the potentials of the diffusable substances are the same on both sides of the diaphragm.

F. G. Donnan has described himself as one of those who rediscovered some of Gibbs' arguments. Donnan derived his theory of membrane equilibrium in 1911 by applying Gibbs' method to a case which had not been thought of before. This is the case of a salt in which the membrane is permeable to one ion but not to the other. This particular problem could not have ocurred to Gibbs, because the existence of ions in solution had not been established at the time.

In order to clarify the conception of the constitution of mixtures, Gibbs introduces the term "phase." "In considering the different homogeneous bodies which can be formed out of any set of component substances, it will be convenient to have a term which shall refer solely to the composition and thermodynamic state of any body without regard to its quantity or form. We may call such bodies as differ in composition or state different *phases* of the matter considered, regarding all bodies which differ only in quantity and form as different examples of the same phase. Phases which can exist together, the dividing surfaces being plane, in an equilibrium which does not depend upon passive resistance to change, we shall call *coexistent.*"

He deduces, by means of his notion of chemical potentials, a rule governing the possible variations in a system of phases. "A system of r coexistent phases, each of which has the same n independently variable components is capable of n + 2 — r variations of phase."

Gibbs devoted four pages to the discovery and proof of this rule. He gave no concrete illustrations of it and proceeded to other problems.

Van der Waals was one of the first to study the phase rule. He explained it to a young Dutch chemist named Roozeboom, who was in difficulties with the equilibria of gaseous hydrates and double ammonium salts, and worked out a special case as an example for him, that he might find it of assistance in his researches. Roozeboom spent a large part of the rest of his life on applying it to mixtures of substances. Through it, he predicted the existence of new substances. In 1899 he used it to interpret the properties of steel as a system of carbon and iron. Iron may exist in several forms, which may be regarded as phases. Thus the phase rule indicates how many of these phases and the carbon will, under various conditions, appear together. Before Roozeboom's achievement, the theory of the composition of alloys was in a muddle, and had no adequate basis. His work was fundamental to the creation of modern alloy metallurgy, which is necessary for the production of aeroplanes, and innumerable machines which depend on the use of alloys with special properties. As Bancroft writes: "The variation of the engineering properties, such as tensile strength, torsional resistance, ductility, etc. with varying concentrations and varying heat treatment, is a subject which can only be worked out satisfactorily with the phase rule as guide."

The true constitution of Portland cement was worked out with the phase rule.

In ignorance of Gibbs' rule, van't Hoff had discovered some limited forms of it independently. One section of his later researches consisted of the application of the complete rule to the interpretation of the huge salt deposits at Stassfurt. These are the world's chief source of potash. The growth of chemistry and chemical industry in Germany has been conditioned by their existence. Without them, Germany would probably not have become a great power capable of challenging the world. The composition of the deposits was of high economic importance, for it enabled estimates to be made of the quantities of the various components available for industrial use. The deposits had been made by the evaporation of an inland sea in a past age, but when solutions of samples of salts were evaporated, they did not reproduce a mixture of the same composition as the original sample. Van't Hoff and his colleagues analysed the problem by treating it as an example of equilibria between sulphates and chlorides of sodium, potassium and calcium. They proved that the presence of the strange salts was due to the slow rate at which the evaporation had occurred in the past. They deduced from the order and solubilities of the salts in the deposits, the stages in the drying-up of the sea millions of years ago, and were able to determine how long the evaporation of the sea water had taken, and the temperature and pressure at which it had occurred.

It is said that the lives of the English explorers, Captain Scott and his party, were lost in the Antarctic, owing to the ignorance of the phase rule. When they started on their return from the South Pole, they found that the fuel oil can in one of their depots was empty. The solder of the can contained tin, which may exist in different phases. At low temperatures block tin may fall into powder, and cans soldered with it become unsealed. This appears to have happened to the cans upon which Scott depended for survival.

The equilibria of many systems have been investigated over wide ranges of temperature and pressure. Tammann discovered that water could exist in solid forms other than ordinary ice. Bridgman has investigated the equilibrium of the water system up to pressures of 20,000 atmospheres, and has shown that five different sorts of ice may exist.

Roozeboom discovered that some solutions have two boiling points. Under certain conditions the boiling point of a system may change suddenly from one temperature to the other, producing explosive boiling. A. L. Day and E. T. Allen have explained the volcanism of Mount Lassen in California as due to a change of this type in a system of silicates.

One of the most spectacular applications of the phase rule occurred in England during the last war. There was a sudden vast demand for ammonium nitrate, which is the chief intermediate product in the manufacture of explosives. As this salt is obtained from mixtures of other salts, efficient methods of manufacturing it cannot be devised rapidly without the application of the phase rule. If the English had not been able to engage F. A. Freeth, who had studied phase rule applications in the Dutch school, to supervise the rapid organization of the necessary processes, which he worked out graphically with the phase rule, they might have lost the war at an early stage, owing to shortage of explosives.

G. Tammann, who assumes the conventional view that the advance of technology is inspired by the prior advance of science, wrote that no abstract work has had such decisive influence on the development of basic industries as Gibbs' memoir on heterogeneous equilibria. He considered it improbable that Gibbs thought of the application of his laws to metallurgy, ore-dressing, the manufacture of refractory materials, or the equilibria between liquid slags and molten metals. This occurred through the quality which distinguishes a general theory, of growing beyond its creator, and being applied to realms outside his imagination. This is how, Tammann thought, the modern scientific technique of smelting has grown out of the abstract researches of a theorist with little experience of the world.

The phase rule will always be of great practical value in determining the general outline of many types of manufacturing processes. It indicates how many phases will be present when any reaction is finished and equilibrium has been reached at definite temperatures and pressure. It does not indicate the rate or nature of the reactions, nor the chemical constitution of the components taking part in them. Gibbs invented it incidentally as a minor clarifying aid in the development of his investigation of the general theory of the equilibrium of mixtures. For him it was an accessory fashioned in his attack on an immense intellectual problem. He dismissed it in four pages, but others created industries and saved countries with its help.

Gibbs invented the triangle diagram for representing three-phase equilibria graphically. It was reinvented by G. Stokes twenty years later, who had adapted Maxwell's color triangle diagram for the purpose.

He analysed the conditions which characterize the critical phases of substances, and what may happen when the conditions are altered. He attacked the thermodynamic problem of catalysis. In a section on the properties of solutions of gases, he virtually formulated van't Hoff's law of the osmotic pressure of dilute solutions. Van't Hoff inferred the law from the experimental observations of Pfeffer and others, whereas Gibbs had foreseen it deductively. In 1897, while solving one of Kelvin's difficulties, he showed that van't Hoff's law could be simply derived from his former work.

Mixtures contain components of different sorts. The surfaces, or interfaces, between the components are characteristic of mixtures, and have an essential rôle in their properties. Gibbs therefore analysed the theory of interfaces, and incidentally founded the thermodynamical theory of surface tension and capillarity, and hence of colloid chemistry. He gave an exact theory of the structure of the black spot in very thin soap films.

He investigated the theory of the forces at the surfaces of liquids and substances, which tend to concentrate molecules on the surface, and produce the phenomenon of "adsorption." When substances are dissolved in liquids they may become concentrated by adsorption on the liquid surface, and alter the magnitude of the tension of the surface. Gibbs gave an equation from which the size of this alteration could be calculated. It is fundamental in the theory of adsorption. The study and application of adsorption is now an important branch of chemical science. J. J. Thomson rediscovered Gibbs' adsorption equation ten years later, by a much less accurate method.

The ordinary electric battery or cell is one of the most interesting examples of a mixture or heterogeneous system. Gibbs applied thermodynamics to the elucidation of its mechanism, and showed that a theory of the battery proposed by Helmholtz was erroneous. In the course of his analysis of the cell, Gibbs derived an equation, which is the most important in the application of thermodynamics to chemistry, for calculating the free energy of a system. It was rediscovered by Helmholtz four years later, and is named the Gibbs-Helmholtz equation.

In 1887, nine years after he had published his correct theory of the cell, Gibbs was invited to comment on a symposium of the British Association on electrolysis, to which many of the leading physicists had made erroneous contributions. He repeated his correct theory, with additions, in two letters. He considered the relation between the electrical energy produced by the cell and the energy of the chemical reaction going on in it. Kelvin had suggested that these are equal. This was an incorrect application of the just law of thermodynamics because it assumed that no heat was absorbed or evolved in the cell itself. Probably no alternative was reasonable so long as there was nothing to indicate how much heat was so produced.

Gibbs identified the electrical energy with the change in the free energy, by showing that the cell when working in a state of balance is a perfect thermodynamical machine. Hence the heat produced in the cell is the difference between the energy of the reaction and the free energy of the reaction.

Other important laws which may be simply derived from Gibbs' theory are Konowalow's theorem of "indifferent points," Raoult's law, and Curie's theory of "crystal habit."

Gibbs outlined a complete theory of the thermodynamics of heterogeneous substances. These are mixtures, and therefore include the commonest natural objects. As Larmor wrote, "he made a clean sweep" of the science of chemical energetics. Boltzmann said that Gibbs' feat was the greatest synthetic achievement in science since Newton's construction of the theory of universal gravitation. Newton's achievement established the principles by which the mechanics of human life could be handled most efficiently. Gibbs' established the principles by which the materials of life and industry, which are mixtures, could be managed most efficiently.

V

The Use of Mathematics

GIBBS WAS THE VICE-PRESIDENT IN 1886 OF the American Association for the Advancement of Science. He delivered an address on Multiple Algebra, in which he expounded his view of the nature of mathematics. He quoted with approval the statement that "the human mind has never invented a labor-saving machine equal to algebra," and said that "it is but natural and proper that an age like our own, characterized by the multiplication of labor-saving machinery, should be distinguished by an unexampled development of this most refined and most beautiful of machines."

He considered that the most characteristic development in his own day was in multiple algebra. There was much interest in it, whereas, fifty years earlier, the work of the founders of the subject, Möbius, Hamilton, Grassmann, and Saint-Venant, had failed to secure recognition in any way commensurate with its importance. Reversing Gibbs' argument, it is permissible to conclude that the failure to appreciate Möbius, Hamilton, Grassmann and Saint-Venant was connected with the smaller development of labor-saving machinery in their day, and consequently less-developed conscious demand for labor-saving in all spheres of activity. The notion of economy in operations was not so strongly developed as in the age of Edison, and men had less conscious insight into the function of mathematics in civilization. The recognition that inventions apparently so different as multiple algebra, and, say, the sewing-machine (Gibbs mentions the sewing-machine and reaper as examples of labor-saving contrivances later in his address), both sprang from attempts to satisfy the same social motive; the saving of labor is fundamental for understanding the origin and rôle of mathematics in human society. Gibbs may have owed his insight into this matter partly to his American environment, where the social habit of invention was developed more noticeably than in Europe.

By classifying the invention of multiple algebra and of labor-saving machinery together, Gibbs implied that mathematical invention does not belong to a domain of human activity higher than that in which other labor-saving inventions are made. This was contrary to the traditional academic view, that the mental or spiritual quality of mathematics is higher than that of other human scientific activities. This view is still widespread, especially in popular writings on astronomy, in which the universe is represented as the materialization of abstract mathematical laws, if not the creation of a mathematician.

G. N. Lewis has quoted the story that Gibbs, during all the years of his membership in the Yale faculty, made one short speech only. After a prolonged discussion of the relative merits of studies in mathematics and in languages, as methods of education in culture, he arose and said merely, "Mathematics is a language." As this language was usually acquired late in life, it should not be used unnecessarily in place of the mother tongue, if an appearance of affectation was to be avoided.

Gibbs had a rationalistic and social conception of the nature of mathematics.

He quoted the history of the imaginary quantities of ordinary algebra, and pointed out that they were essentially a simple case of multiple algebra, in fact, double algebra. "This double algebra . . . was not sought for or invented (by mathematicians) . . . it forced itself, unbidden upon" their attention, "with its rules already formed." It arose out of the mathematics which had been devised for solving particular problems, such as those of trigonometry, which in turn had been invented in order to solve problems in practical affairs such as navigation.

Double algebra "with difficulty obtained recognition in the first third of" the nineteenth century. Mathematicians at first regarded imaginary quantities, as the name they gave to them implies, as useless and awkward things thrust on them by a perverse external world. Instead of trying to see what aspects of the world these quantities reflected, they regarded them as a blemish in the creation. Mathematicians have often assumed that their laws are superior to experience, and have forgotten that they are labor-saving devices for describing the behavior of the world. If they had examined the properties of imaginary quantities, or double algebra, without pre-conceived ideas of what mathematics and the external world ought to be like, they would have perceived, without so much unwillingness, that it could provide a more direct and economical method for solving many types of problems.

For instance, it may be desirable to analyse the behavior of a force acting in a plane. The force has size and direction. It may therefore be represented by a straight line, whose length represents the size, and whose direction represents the direction of the force. This directed line is one thing, and is named a *vector*, and may be represented by a single symbol. As this symbol contains in itself the simultaneous representation of two quantities, the system of calculating with it will be a double algebra, and the analysis of problems by the system is named vector analysis. The aim of multiple algebras or generalized vector analysis is to concentrate the representation of multiple properties into one symbol, and discover the laws governing the manipulation of this symbol. Gibbs said that the discussion of the forces, and movements of particles, discussed in mechanics, physics, crystallography, astronomy, etc., seems to demand treatment by multiple algebra or vector analysis because "position in space is essentially a multiple quantity and can only be represented by simple quantities in an arbitrary and cumbersome manner." Gibbs contended that the notions used in vector analysis are those which "he who reads between the lines will read on every paper of the greatest masters of analysis, or of those who have probed deepest the secrets of nature, the only difference being that the vector analyst, having regard for the weakness of the human intellect, does as the early painters, who wrote beneath their pictures 'This is a tree,' 'This is a horse.' "

He showed that Helmholtz's deduction of the motion of a fluid from its spin, which was regarded as a stroke of genius, could be solved by a beginner in vector analysis.

His vector methods have recently been applied to the design of electrical machinery, with important practical results. It is possible to reduce machinery design, with their aid, to the substitution of constants in general equations for any particular type of machine.

He aimed at the development of mathematical methods suited to the needs of physicists. He tried to look at physical phenomena without prejudice, and devise the algebras by which their properties could be most naturally and easily described. As Bumstead remarks, he had a "natural tendency toward elegance and conciseness of mathematical method." He was opposed to the indiscriminate application of old mathematical methods to new types of physical problems, merely because they happened to be at hand, and criticized the conservatism of mathematical astronomers, who failed to use vectorial methods in a subject which could be particularly amenable to them.

He explained that Lagrange and the greatest mathematical physicists unconsciously evolved new mathematical methods possessing some of the advantages of vector analysis. He wanted to see the search for improved methods in mathematical physics pursued consciously. The improvement of method is, in general, ultimately more fruitful than the solution of the most remarkable particular problems. According to Bumstead, Gibbs often remarked that he had more pleasure in the study of multiple algebra than in any other of his intellectual activities. This suggests that he was at heart a mathematician, which would help to explain his failure to expound effectively the practical significance of his deductive discoveries. But his account of his views of mathematics seems to show that he believed that the duty of mathematics was to assist the interpretation of physical phenomena. Pure mathematics was for him the most delightful of entertainments, but applied mathematics was of greater importance. He was a physical mathematician rather than a mathematical physicist.

Irving Fisher has written that Gibbs encountered the need of a new type of analysis through his attempts to represent physical relations, and the theory of electricity and magnetism, by geometrical methods. The old type of analysis with Cartesian coördinates required the writing and manipulation of three times as many equations as in vector analysis, and diverted attention away from the lines and surfaces which were of first interest to their projections on three arbitrary axes. Fisher considered Gibbs' most interesting lectures were on vector analysis. When he went to Berlin to continue his studies, he found that the German authorities did not care for vector analysis. Schwartz said "es ist zu willkürlich" (it is too arbitrary). They did not like a non-commutative algebra, such as vector analysis, in which a $\times$ b was not equal to b $\times$ a, but to $-$ b $\times$ a.

Fisher reported this to Gibbs, after his return to the United States. Gibbs' view was that if the object is to interpret physical phenomena, and it is found that this can be done more conveniently by using such a non-commutative algebra, then the criticism was irrelevant.

Gibbs' attitude was similar to that of Heisenberg and Dirac in their researches on quantum mechanics. They considered the physical data which required theoretical explanation, and then devised appropriate mathematical methods for analysing their relations.

Gibbs told Hastings that if he had met with any success in mathematical physics, it was largely because he had found ways of avoiding mathematical difficulties. He did not consider mathematical difficulty a merit. One of his main motives was simplification of method, and he considered the perfection of vector analysis was a useful contribution to that end. He approached mathematics as a mathematical physicist rather than a mathematician, but he was not insensitive to purely mathematical interests. He had studied under Weierstrass and appreciated the attraction of rigor in proofs. He discovered the convergence property of the Fourier series known as the Gibbs phenomenon of convergence. But he considered, as Wilson says, that the "union between reflective analytical thought and the world of fact" is of more importance to the mathematical physicist than rigor in mathematical proof; and believed that a superior training in pure mathematics was valuable because it assisted the study of the problems set by nature.

He regarded mathematics as a *language* for the discussion of nature. His views on the rôle of mathematics are similar to those expressed by Maxwell in 1871, in his inaugural lecture as first Cavendish Professor of Experimental Physics at Cambridge. He explains that knowledge which comes through the combined apprehension of its mathematical and its experimental aspects is "of a more solid, available and enduring kind than that possessed by the mere mathematician or the mere experimenter." New ideas can arise only by "wrenching the mind away from the symbols to the objects and from the objects back to the symbols. This is the price we have to pay." Maxwell writes that "there may be some mathematicians who pursue their studies entirely for their own sake. Most men, however, think that the chief use of mathematics is found in the interpretation of nature."

In spite of his realistic view of the use of mathematics, Gibbs is not known to have made a single experiment.

The difficulty of his writing is due to his aim of generality. He always attempted to give general solutions of problems, which did not depend, for example, on particular assumptions about the constitution of matter. He wished to discover laws which physical systems of any constitution must obey. The ordinary investigator prefers to attack narrower problems, which have close analogy with particular phenomena with which he is acquainted, so that his imagination may receive support from the ideas with which he is already familiar. Gibbs was opposed to this method. He often said that "the whole is simpler than its parts." This is true, when the mind is capable of handling the symbolism, perhaps vector analysis, which conveniently exhibits phenomena as a whole, but it is not true for the mind which cannot handle such a symbolism, and has to use a less powerful, but less exacting, symbolism. Gibbs' aphorism expresses the essence of his intellectual attitude, and the essence of the method of thermodynamics.

VI

His Personality

GIBBS HAD A DELICATE CONSTITUTION. HE was the descendant of a long series of educated ancestors. Perhaps he was frail because his ancestors had chosen mental rather than physical qualities in mating, and he was the result of a persistent selection for intelligence. This selection ended in the production of a mind of the finest genius in a body apparently too weak to reproduce itself. E. B. Wilson comments that his grandfather died at the age of forty-seven, and his great-grandfather at fifty. H. A. Bumstead writes that he was permanently weakened by an attack of scarlet fever in childhood. He had a slight figure and voice, and in his later years frequently suffered from minor illnesses, but careful attention to his health, and regular living, protected him from any grave illness until shortly before his death at the age of sixty-four. His work was never seriously interrupted through illness. He used to spend summer vacations in the mountains, especially at Intervale, N. H., and in the evening after the day's work he often walked for an airing in the streets in the neighborhood of the college.

He worked on his treatise on statistical mechanics in his last years. This may have sapped his strength, as Wilson suggests, for he could be seen working in his office on the second floor of the Old Sloane Laboratory in the morning, afternoon and evening; or he may have merely worked out his less than normal inborn supply of physical vigor, and died rather early. R. G. Van Name does not think that his death was quickened by overwork on the treatise, as he had recovered from that, when he was afflicted with an incurable intestinal obstruction. He told Wilson in 1902 that if he lived until he was as old as Methuselah, he would continue research for several hundred years. This shows that his zest and ideas were still vigorous. His head was impressive and he had an ingratiating smile. Former pupils report that he was unaffectedly modest, gentle, self-contained and dignified, and had no eccentricities. It should be noted, however, that his expression in the first portrait shown on plate VII, is not attractive. His mouth has a petulant, disagreeable curl. Perhaps he was highly strung, and exhibited that expression when he was irritated.

His friends believed that he never realized that he had quite exceptional mental power. He justly estimated the value of his own researches, but he appeared to believe that almost any other person, who had had the desire, could have made the same discoveries.

He had complete confidence in the accuracy of everything that he published. Ostwald remarked that so far not one mistake in Gibbs' calculations, nor in his conclusions, nor, where mistakes are most difficult to avoid, in his general assumptions, had been found. G. N. Lewis has since noted, however, that Gibbs' view that some processes are of infinite slowness is not supported by experimental evidence. His mind seemed to work without special effort at the highest levels. Owing to its natural power he did not need to sacrifice any minor duties in order to secure more time for research. He instantly laid aside without question any profound work when called to perform minor tasks. He never evaded the most trivial college duties, or withheld any of his valuable time from students who sought his instruction. Wilson writes, however, that it was not customary for Yale professors at that date to give time to students outside the lecture hours. He asked Gibbs why he did not give preparatory courses which would have enabled students to follow his lectures better, and Gibbs replied that he had never felt called upon to do it, though he would if desired.

As he never married, he lived in the family of his sister, who occupied a house that had been built by his father. Apart from a single visit to Europe he lived the whole of his life in New Haven, within a short distance of the school at which he had been educated, and the college where he had continued his education, and then taught. He had simple tastes and gave a full share of help in the common life of his sister's household.

He acted for many years as secretary and treasurer of the board of trustees of the Hopkins Grammar School, where he had been educated as a boy. He attended church regularly, but he took little part in social, religious and political affairs. He rarely attended the Graduates' Club frequented by many of his colleagues, but he rarely missed any meeting of the mathematical and scientific societies and colloquia. He followed the proceedings keenly, but was always considerate in criticism. He did not despise papers of a light or entertaining character, and on one occasion read a paper to the Yale Mathematics Club on the mathematics of the "Paces of a Horse."

Wilson states that there was no trace of austerity in his personality. An examination of his writings shows, however, that he had much intellectual firmness. In his controversy with Tait and others concerning the value and priority of Grassmann's methods over those of Hamilton's quaternions, his style and arguments were deadly. He was broad-minded and had a sensitive understanding. This is seen in the letter in which he replied to the request to write the obituary notice of Clausius.

New Haven June 10/89.
Professor J. P. Cooke
My dear Sir,

The task which you propose is in many respects a pleasant one to me, although I have not much facility at that kind of writing, or indeed, at any kind. Of course, I should not expect to do justice to the subject, but I might do something.

There are some drawbacks: of course it has not escaped your notice that it is a *very* delicate matter to write a notice of the work of Clausius. There are reputations to be respected, from Democritus downward, which may be hurt, if not of the distinguished men directly concerned, at least of their hot-headed partisans.

Altogether I feel as if I had to take my life in my hands.

Without making a positive engagement at this moment, as soon
as I can get a little relief from some pressing duties, I will look the
matter up and see what I can do, and will communicate with you
further.

Yours truly

J.W.G.

This letter shows profound knowledge and judgment, gen-
erosity, humor, sensibility and modesty. It was followed by
one of the most remarkable obituary notices in scientific literature, which contains the classical statement of the origin of
thermodynamics, and the extent of the contributions by the
various founders. It is not surprising to learn that he was be-
loved by those who succeeded in acquiring his friendship.

But he seemed to have some quality of deep isolation. Bumstead writes that he worked alone and apparently did not need
the stimulation of discussion with equals or inferiors. He rarely
told anyone what he was doing until his work was ready for
publication, and he was chary of publishing anything unless he
was convinced that it was a definitely original contribution to
knowledge. His reluctance to publish an account of his system
of vector analysis was due to this reason. He was not certain
that it was not more than an adaptation of the work of others,
rather than an original contribution.

As he did not discuss the progress of his researches with his
advanced students, they had little opportunity of acquiring
from him the mental attitude for research. They could not see
his mind at work, and see how discoveries were made. He
taught and explained his results admirably, but he did not reveal the processes by which he had discovered them.

This has a bearing on the great problem of Gibbs' career: his
failure to make an immediate commanding impression on the
contemporary scientific life of the United States. He had an
inhibited temperament. Perhaps this prevented him from discussing his thoughts easily with others. But Wilson writes that
he said in 1902 that during the thirty years of his professorship
he had had only about half a dozen really equipped to profit
by his courses. After he became professor in 1871, he lectured

only to graduate students, and usually had an audience of about six or eight. Like a German professor, he did not set examples to his pupils on the matter of his lectures.

Wilson writes that Gibbs promised to discuss themes for research after he returned from further study in Europe, but unfortunately this never occurred, as Gibbs died shortly afterwards.

Wilson observes that the classical type of collegiate education was still almost universal during the greater part of Gibbs' professoriate, and this may have helped to prevent him from receiving many adequately trained research students.

He did not attract graduate research students from other universities to Yale, in spite of his later international reputation.

As Wilson asks, it would have been interesting to have seen what would have happened at Johns Hopkins University if he had accepted the invitation to a chair there, which was offered him when the University was founded in 1884. Johns Hopkins was a graduate university designed primarily for research, and Gibbs might have created a school of mathematical physics in such an environment.

His isolation may have been due more to his psychological temperament than to the nature of the intellectual environment at Yale. Like some other great isolated workers, he wrote very little, and thought problems out in his head. The great Oxford mathematician, H. J. S. Smith, who created no school, wrote the whole of his life's researches in a few note-books. He used to think out problems in the theory of numbers while reclining on a sofa, and when, after hours of thought, he had found the solution, he wrote it straight down.

Joule wrote the descriptions of his researches almost straight out into four note-books. He also did not form a school.

After Gibbs' death, the papers he had left were found to be very meager. They consisted mostly of headings for lectures. There were nine lines of intended supplements to chapters in his thermodynamical researches, with a brief sketch of some of the first and fourth chapters. It appeared that he composed his works in his head and then wrote them down. Wilson writes that he composed his *Statistical Mechanics* in a year virtually without notes, but from ideas he had carried in his head for some years.

As he carried the substance of his lectures in his head and did not write it out previously, he sometimes failed to prove his demonstrations on the blackboard at the first attempt. Wilson relates that he attended a lecture at which Gibbs became confused in an exposition of the Carnot cycle. Gibbs came to the next lecture with the chief points in the argument written on a small piece of paper.

Bumstead has related that he once saw a young research student enthusiastically recounting the result of a laborious experimental investigation. Gibbs unaffectedly and naturally closed his eyes for a few moments, and then said: "Yes, that would be true." He could calculate in his head from general principles the result that the student had obtained empirically by a lengthy research.

The intensity of the mental effort of this method of working may increase tendencies to introversion, and damage the sociability of the thinker in the world of ideas. It would be interesting to know whether there is any relation between a mathematician's ability for leading a school of research and his methods of discovery. Does the man who writes much, and uses much paper in attempts to find solutions, have closer intellectual contact with his students than the man who tends to think everything out before writing?

Gibbs did not read exhaustively the literature of the subjects on which he worked. He often preferred to work out for himself results obtained by others, and said he found it easier than following another man's reasoning. It is significant in this connection that few succeeded in learning Gibbs' profound results from his own papers. Even Helmholtz and J. J. Thomson found it easier to rediscover his results than read his papers.

J. Willard Gibbs: Bibliography

The Collected Works of J. Willard Gibbs, Ph.D., LL.D. Formerly Professor of Mathematical Physics in Yale University. With a Biographical Sketch by H. A. Bumstead. 2 volumes. 1928.

Record of Celebration of the 200th Anniversary of Yale College. Edited by C. M. Lewis. 1902.

Four Years at Yale. By a Graduate of '69. 1871.

Memoirs of the Gibbs Family. Josiah Willard Gibbs. (A relative of the physicist.) 1879.

Modern Thermodynamics. E. A. Guggenheim. 1933.

Yale College: Needs of the University. Suggested by the Faculties to the Corporation & cont. 1871.

A Discourse Commemorative of the Life and Services of J. W. Gibbs Senior. George P. Fisher. 1861.

"J. W. Gibbs and His Relation to Modern Science." F. H. Garrison. *Popular Scientific Monthly.* 1909.

"The Influence of J. Willard Gibbs on the Science of Physical Chemistry." F. G. Donnan. *Journal of the Franklin Institute.* 1925.

A Commentary on the Scientific Writings of J. Willard Gibbs. Edited by F. G. Donnan and A. Haas. 2 volumes. 1936.

Thermodynamics. G. N. Lewis and Merle Randall. 1923.

"J. Willard Gibbs and the Extension of the Principles of Thermodynamics." F. W. Stevens. *Science.* Volume 66. 1927.

"J. Willard Gibbs." R. C. Cantelo. *Canadian Chemistry and Metallurgy.* 1924.

Thermodynamics and Chemistry. P. Duhem. 1902.

Theory of Heat. J. Clerk Maxwell. Fourth Edition. 1875. (Adapted for the Use of Artisans and Students in Public and Science Schools.)

J. Clerk Maxwell. *Collected Papers.* 2 volumes. 1890.

Regnault's Experiments on Steam. Macfarlane Gray. Proceedings of the Institution of Mechanical Engineers. 1889.

Metallography. C. H. Desh. 1922.

Gibbs Memorial Lectures. Proceedings of the American Mathematical Society. 1923, & cont.

American Journal of Science. Volume 13. Third Series. 1877.

Obituary Notice in *Nature* of J. Willard Gibbs. 1903.

Obituary Notice of J. Willard Gibbs in *Proceedings of the Royal Society of London.* Volume 75. 1905.

"Willard Gibbs: An Appreciation." John Johnston, *Scientific Monthly.* Volume 26. 1928.

"Reminiscences of Gibbs by a Student and Colleague." E. B. Wilson. *Scientific Monthly.* Volume 32. 1931.

Chemish Weekblad. Gibbs Memorial Number. July. 1926.

Encyclopædia Britannica. 11th Edition.

The Dictionary of American Biography. 1928 & cont.

Phase Rule Studies. J. A. Wynfield Rhodes. 1933.

The Phase Rule. A. C. D. Rivett. 1923.

The Phase Rule and Its Applications. A. Findlay. 1935.

Thomas Alva Edison
1847-1931

I
THE RELATION OF INVENTION TO SCIENCE

II
THE ORIGIN OF AMERICAN INVENTIVENESS

III
EDISON'S PERSONALITY

IV
HIS LIFE AND WORK

BIBLIOGRAPHY

I

The Relation of Invention to Science

THIS BOOK IS ABOUT CERTAIN AMERICAN MEN of Science. The first question which arises in connection with Edison is his status. He was undoubtedly an inventor. Is an inventor a man of science? Before this question may be answered, it is necessary to discuss whether "man of science" and "scientist" have the same meaning. The first term is broader than the second. "A man of science" means a man engaged in science, or making use of science, whereas the second is usually reserved to describe a person such as a research chemist, who discovers new facts and theories.

Edison was certainly a "man of science" because he worked with the facts of science, though he discovered very few new facts of the conventional scientific type. Nevertheless, he could claim to be a "scientist," even in the strictest sense, as he discovered the Edison Effect, a phenomenon of first-class importance.

It is permissible to contend that a man who creates new instruments, such as the carbon telephone transmitter, with the assistance of the theory of electricity, may be named a "scientist." A new instrument is a new fact in the world of natural existence. In this sense, its status is as good as any other newly-discovered fact of natural existence, such as a new chemical compound.

Sharp distinctions between "scientist," "man of science," and "inventor" are harmful, and to a high degree, artificial. Distinctions do exist, but they have been exaggerated, especially by scientists. The features that scientists have in common with inventors are far more important than their differences.

Scientists have tended to exaggerate their difference from inventors for reasons of social prestige. An inventor is engaged in making devices of use to man. He often makes things with his hands. He is closely connected with manual workers and business men. He tries to make devices which are profitable.

The scientist frequently claims that his researches are inspired by pure curiosity, and may have no practical value. He considers that he exercises his intellect solely to increase the dignity of the human mind, and not to serve any other human interests. He exaggerates these features in order to magnify the distinction between his aims and those of manual workers and business men. He wishes to become identified with the aristocratic leisure class, who receive salaries without duties, and are under no compulsion to do useful work. He desires to inherit the prestige of the magician, who could command nature without working.

All of these attributes are the traditional qualities of members of the governing class. Scientists claim them because they wish to be included in that class, and not in the working class. As inventors are evidently closely connected with the working class, scientists do not wish to be confused with them.

The orthodox conception of the scientist as distinguished from the inventor is permeated with the traditional ideas of the superiority of mind over matter, of theory over experiment, and other principles inherited from prehistoric magic, which have been rationalized, for instance, in Plato's philosophy.

The acceptance of this conception makes the history of science unintelligible. It is impossible to understand why particular scientific theories were studied at any particular time without considering their relations to contemporary inventions and technology. Theory and practice cannot be studied apart. The full importance of the discoveries of Faraday and Clerk Maxwell was not clear until inventors, such as Edison and Marconi, had proved that they were of profound value, and were far more than ingenious intellectual tricks. The separation of science and invention has obscured the origin and nature of science, and through this has retarded the growth of an adequate philosophy of history. If the rôle of science in history is not understood, then men will not know how properly to use science for the advance of civilization.

There is much evidence in the present condition of the world that man has not yet gained more than a rudimentary notion of the rôle of science in civilization. The failure to understand the ultimate inseparability of science and invention is an aspect of the wider failure to conceive an intelligible history of science.

Henry Ford's conception of the nature of scientists and inventors is more correct than the old view, evolved by scholars of the governing class in aristocratic, pre-mechanical civilizations. He writes (with Samuel Crowther):

In another age and time, each of Edison's inventions would have been considered either as unique scientific discoveries or as scientific toys. The older scientists made their discoveries as things of themselves and were so far away from the daily workaday world that they would have lost standing had they even suggested the possibility that their studies could have any commercial application. Then Edison came along—a greater scientist than any of them, but without being bound by the old scientific traditions. He was a scientist, but also he was a man of extraordinary common sense. It was a new combination.

Edison thought of science as an aid to mankind and, instead of being a specialist in any one branch, he reviewed every branch in order to assemble and select the best ways and means of accomplishing whatever he had in mind to do. He was not an inventor in the sense that he just thought up certain methods and devices. . . . He was a whole experimental laboratory in himself, and definitely ended the distinction between the theoretical man of science and the practical man of science, so that to-day we think of scientific discoveries in connection with their possible present or future application to the needs of man. He took the old rule-of-thumb methods out of industry and substituted exact scientific knowledge, while, on the other hand, he directed scientific research into useful channels.

The scientists of the old school have never considered Edison as one of themselves, because he did practical things instead of just making and recording experiments. The engineers have not considered him an engineer because he never worked on traditional engineering lines. In fact, he is both a scientist and an engineer, and he established the modern spirit in both science and engineering, which is to say that the engineers depend on the scientists and the scientists depend on the engineers.

Ford ascribes too much to Edison, because he credits him with introducing the modern conception of the industrial scientist. Many men before Edison contributed to the evolution of this conception, for it was brought into existence by the steam-age, and was implicit in the writings of Francis Bacon, and the aims of the founders of the Royal Society of London. But by the middle of the nineteenth century the social and utilitarian aims of the founders of post-Renaissance science had almost been forgotten. A new intellectual aristocracy had grown, and apparent uselessness tended to be regarded as a necessary qualification for admittance. The great scientists of the nineteenth century had immense social value, but they were often unconscious of its true nature, supposing that it lay in absence of evident connection with human interests. They considered that science was a disinterested search for pure knowledge, made in order to reveal the ways of Providence, and increase the intellectual dignity of man, or certain men.

Edison came into the current of nineteenth-century technology without having acquired the traditional view of science. He was able to express directly in his own career what society was expecting of science. He was in front of his contemporaries because he had escaped a tradition that was not in consonance with the most progressive social developments.

If Edison had lived at the time when the Royal Society of London was founded, he would have been elected a member before he was thirty years of age. In recent times, inventors such as J. W. Swan, D. E. Hughes and Charles Parsons were elected to the Royal Society. Edison was not elected a member of the National Academy of Sciences until he was eighty-one years old.

Scientists and inventors have more in common than in difference, so they need not be sharply separated. Their histories should be studied together. Edison discovered only one important scientific fact of the sort discovered by Faraday in

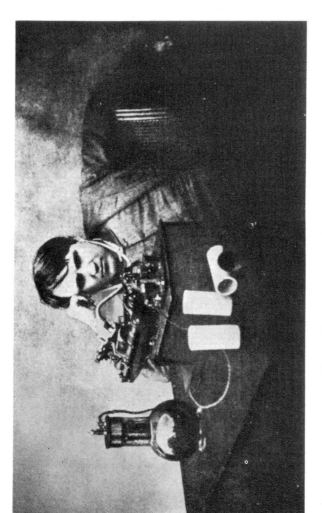

THE NAPOLEON OF INVENTION:

Edison had just completed five days and five nights of continuous work on the improvement of the phonograph, in 1888.

PLATE IX

scores. He found that electricity is emitted by hot filaments. The operation of the radio valve depends on this phenomenon. This difference between the work of Edison and Faraday would seem to show that they are of entirely different types. But the importance of Faraday's discoveries cannot be explained without reference to the work of Edison, and other inventors and engineers, so, in the last analysis, Faraday as a scientist and Edison as an inventor cannot be assessed separately. Both of them were great men of science, of different sorts. This is the explanation why Edison is truly a "man of science."

II

The Origin of American Inventiveness

EDISON IS ACCEPTED AS THE MOST TYPICAL example of an inventor. Why should he have appeared in the United States, rather than in any other country? The first part of the answer is that the United States has been the premier country of invention during the last hundred years. Edison was born in an environment fertile for invention. This circumstance enabled him to surpass equally talented inventors in less encouraging environments. As the majority of the Americans are relatively recent descendants of immigrants from Europe, their genetic constitution is very similar to that of Europeans. There is no evidence that they have some inborn inventive faculty of a sort not possessed by Europeans. The origin of American inventiveness is chiefly found in the circumstances of American history.

The first colonizers of America were the Spanish, and the second were the English. American inventiveness grew out of the second colonization, and is therefore connected with features which distinguish the second from the first. It might be attributed to lack of inborn inventiveness in Spaniards. But Spaniards have made remarkable inventions. At the present time de la Cierva has invented the auto-gyro, and Longoria a method of welding fine wires by exactly measured and controlled currents discharged from condensers. The significant feature of the careers of these Spanish inventors is that they have not developed their ideas in Spain, but in the industrialized countries of Europe and America.

There were fundamental differences between the social

structures of the Spanish and the English colonies. The former consisted of settled natives governed by a small class of rich conquerors, who did not introduce any new productive habits. Their aim was to govern, and take wealth from others by force, not to produce wealth themselves. Under these social conditions the governors had no incentive to invent, because they could live well without producing anything themselves, and the natives had no incentive because they had no rights.

The English colonizers came to America a century later, and from a country whose social and industrial system was developing rapidly. Their social philosophy was two or three centuries nearer than the Spanish to modern industrialism. Besides coming from an industrially more advanced country, the English came from different social strata. The New Englanders, whose philosophy ultimately had most influence on the evolution of American ideals, were mainly independent farmers, peasants, and skilled craftsmen, who came to America to acquire the freedom to live as they wished, without interference; to support themselves by their own work, and to secure to themselves all the profits thereof. They did not intend to exploit conquered natives. Self-help was fundamental in their philosophy. The New Englanders did not believe that manual labor was disreputable. This allowed them to think about the problems of doing things, and see how manual labor, with which they had intimate acquaintance, might be minimised. Slave-owners have little personal acquaintance with manual labor, and are under strong social influence to ignore the details of how it is done. Self-supporting manual workers can increase their profits only by working harder and more ingeniously, whereas slave-owners can increase profits by increasing oppression. Thus the New England colonists and the successors under the influence of the Yankee spirit had a personal interest in labor-saving and profit-increasing devices. They belonged to social classes who had lost the cowed spirit and fatalism of the European laborer. They brought the independence of the European middle classes to bear on the problems of laboring technique. The rise of American inventiveness has been deeply influenced by class-psychology and interests. Owing to the richness and emptiness of America these personal interests were stronger than those of their corresponding classes in Europe. The social order of European countries was fixed. England, France and Holland had populations of fairly stable size, as large as they could support. The incentive to middle- and lower-class production was limited by the privileges of the aristocracy, who could secure through their political power a part of all the new wealth created by other classes.

The social structure of North American society remained fluid for the first two centuries of its existence, owing to the steady extension of the frontier westwards. During this period the population never reached a stable number, as in the European countries. It increased rapidly, and moved continuously in tens of thousands across the continent. Under these continually changing conditions, the American crafts- man and independent worker never acquired a fixed concep- tion of his place in the social order. Vast supplies of land and resources were continually available to him for exploitation. His enterprise was not checked by the knowledge that he would inevitably have to share his profits with land-owners, and that success in collecting profits would not automatically qualify him for admittance to the governing class.

In these circumstances, it was worth while thinking out ways of increasing productivity and profits.

The social philosophy of the New England colonists was not that of slave-owning classes. In addition, there were no settled natives in the northern states. The land was very sparsely populated. As the intensive systems of farming and manufacture introduced by the Northern Europeans required a relatively dense population for successful operation, there was a large demand for labor, to extend the system in the unpopulated west. The shortage of labor stimulated the in- vention of labor-saving appliances.

There is a further factor. It is possible that there is some connection between inventiveness and independence of be- havior. The colonizers of America were naturally selected from the more independent members of the European populations, and may therefore have had slightly more than the average amount of inborn inventive ability found among Europeans.

All of these influences interacted from an early date to stimulate inventiveness in North Americans. As E. L. Bogart writes, "what had been an expedient now became a national habit." By the beginning of the nineteenth century, the habit of invention had become thoroughly established, and spread through a large and rapidly increasing population. The stimulating influences still existed and could work upon more human material. By the end of the first half of the nineteenth century, the stream of invention had been raised to a spate. For instance, American inventors revolutionized agricultural implements which had remained essentially unchanged since the days of the Roman Empire. The first important contribution towards the mechanization and modernization of domestic life was made in 1846 by the American invention of the sewing machine. In 1865 American apple-peelers, knife-cleaners, egg-beaters and clothes wringers astonished English observers. Morse introduced the recording electric telegraph in 1844.

American inventors were very prominent in the development of the steamboat. They developed the use of interchangeable parts early, and their exhibits at the London Exhibition of 1851 made a deep impression.

The American patent law had democratic characteristics. It allowed the protection of small improvements besides major inventions, so that small inventors, who would have been overawed by the patent law of other countries, were encouraged in America. On the other hand, the administration of American patent law had serious defects. Edison complained that it was far slower and far less competent than English patent law administration. In England cases had to be argued in front of the judges, and the essential points could be brought out quickly. The American judges could decide on written statements, in which the points were frequently lost. Edison said that it was easier to find first-class lawyers with a thorough grasp of scientific ideas in England than in America. The patent law of both countries was easily exploited to the advantage of rich clients. But the American protection of small improvements remained an incentive to the small inventor. It also helps to account for the enormous number of American patents. Edison himself was granted more than one thousand.

The rate of invention in America was much increased during the depression of 1837, and greatly increased during the Civil War after 1860 by the demands for economy and labor-saving.

Edison became mature when the American tradition of invention was a hundred years old, and had reached a period of very rapid growth and intense stimulation. He was the outstanding product of a flourishing tradition created by powerful historical forces, and his apparition in America at this particular date is not surprising.

III

Edison's Personality

THE AGE OF THIRTY-NINE DIVIDED EDISON'S life into two main periods. During the first, as Dyer and Martin observe, his work had the inconsequential freedom and crudeness of pioneer life. Ideas piled on him, and he rushed from one roughly finished invention to the next. In the second he was less brilliant. He married a second time, conducted his social life with more orthodoxy, and became an example of a successful man of the day, a model of the well-to-do American's ideal of a good citizen. His social philosophy was conventional and was adopted from his environment without question. But within the boundaries of these philosophical principles, his personal behavior was original. The respectability of the latter half of his life did not change his personal originality, and he did not try to imitate the imaginary figure of a cultured, dignified and benevolent gentleman, created by the media of publicity.

Edison was of medium height. His head was abnormally large. His eyes were gray or gray-blue, and in infancy his hair was fair. He had a good color and quick step. During the thirties he began to arrange his hair in a sweeping lock over the forehead, like Napoleon. His mouth had a rather surly twist, but this was less important in his expression than the power of his eyes. They were very bright when he was interested. Many men felt the domination of his personality from the first moments of contact with him. He employed and retained for decades able men who disagreed with him. He was known as *the Old Man* before he was thirty.

311

He led a rough but not poor or miserable life up to the age of twenty-three. He had little formal education, so he spoke the language of the masses. He never modified his accent. As he was auto-didactic, and could learn from his experience only, or from someone sharing his interests strongly, he would probably never have acquired a cultivated accent under any conditions. But he became deaf when a boy, which lessened any possibility that he would ever stop using the idiom of his youth. It is said that he could hear noises in which he was specially interested, such as background noises in phonograph records.

M. A. Rosanoff joined his staff in 1903, when Edison was fifty-six. He asked him what laboratory rules he should observe. Edison "spat in the middle of the floor and yelled out, 'Hell! there ain't no rules around here! We are tryin' to accomplish somep'n!'" Edison introduced himself to Rosanoff as "Don Quixote," and his assistant J. F. Ott, who had been with him thirty years, as "Santcho Pantcho." His colleagues were described as "muckers," and himself the "chief mucker."

He was an astute judge of character. His hold over others was partly due to his ability to expose their weak points. He utilized this insight to preserve the morale of his staff. Everyone was made to pretend that he was about to solve his problem, even if he was quite at sea. Everyone knew that Edison knew that he was in difficulties and was outwardly more cheerful than the situation justified. The inability to acknowledge this to Edison's face produced a state of guilt and fear that made them work harder than ever. Edison was a master of this auto-suggestive principle of tribal leadership.

He was not sensitive in the immediate handling of truth. He was slow to contradict erroneous exaggerations of his achievements. He said that "we always tell the truth. It may be deferred truth, but it is the truth!"

His early connection with journalists made him easy-going with the press. This helped the spreading of misleading accounts of his work, which angered many persons, especially academic scientists.

He was of Dutch descent, extremely pertinacious, and had enormous capacity for attention to details. His temperament was sanguine with some tendency to choler. He began work each day with the openmindedness of a child, and swiftly forgot failures. He could roar with laughter like an aborigine, and sometimes, when seriously vexed, his anger was terrifying. The skin in the center of his forehead used to be spasmodically rotated in these paroxysms. When thoughtful, he used to pull his right eyebrow.

He had no taste in art, music or literature, except in telling stories. The parts of his mind concerned with those subjects were arid. He strummed on an organ with one finger. He could not believe the report of one of his phonograph salesmen from Germany, that the Germans demanded records of classical music. He chose banal matter for the stories of the first commercial motion pictures.

The first words spoken by his immortal invention, the phonograph, were: "Mary had a little lamb."

Though without taste, he was lively and jolly. He liked and demanded cheerfulness and optimism. He organized singsongs among his staff, during long periods of work.

He was fond of stories, and showed skill in telling them. Many were based on personal experiences. The perfection of some of them seems to show that his inventive power was not restricted to mechanics.

Edison accepted the ethics of capitalist commerce. The trade secret of the composition of the wax for his phonograph records was stolen by a trade rival's spy. When Rosanoff, who had proved this by analysis, abused the methods of their rival, Edison was amused.

"What are you so excited about? Everybody steals in commerce and industry, I've stolen a lot myself. But I knew *how* to steal. They don't know *how* to steal—that's all that's the matter with them."

He adapted himself without difficulty to the bosses of Tammany Hall, when he required municipal permissions for constructing his electric light system in New York.

In his later years he was complacent about the financial methods of Jay Gould. This was probably a partial pose, as he had violently abused Gould when swindled by him in his early years. The pose was made in order to support the class-myth of the well-to-do American, that wealth is sacred, however obtained. Edison supported the myth in order to please the rich capitalist friends of his later years. He probably convinced himself that he believed in it. He did not support it in his personal behavior. He made no money at all out of his greatest inventions, the development of the electric light and power systems. He wished to be a great man, and leave an impression on history. He spent all the money that came to him on the achievement of new inventions to add to his monumental list.

His long hours of work were famous. He worked twenty hours a day for periods of months. When excited by some idea he could work continuously for days. On one occasion he worked continuously for five days and five nights.

He was able to sleep instantly at will, and to wake up instantly half an hour later, refreshed. He never dreamt. He drove his colleagues into working very long hours, which few of them could stand.

On one occasion, when his son felt sleepy, he recommended him to take a nap under the laboratory bench, from which position he was retrieved by his mother. Edison's resistance to sleep was abnormal, and he could work well with little sleep for long periods. But when he was not pressed, he would sleep nine hours.

In early life, he did not bother about choice of food. In middle age he dieted to keep his weight constant. He ate little meat, and was sparing with food. He smoked large numbers of strong cigars, chewed tobacco, drank much strong coffee, and took no exercise. He lived until he was eighty-four, which was rather shorter than many of his ancestors, so he probably suffered slightly from the effects of his mode of life. His intense intellectual work was not entirely harmless. Like many men who have worked with their hands he was fond of pastry. Manual work requires much energy, which is most easily obtained by eating large quantities of carbohydrates. The habit of pastry-eating often persists in men who have left manual work and enter sedentary professions. In members of the upper classes it is sometimes a mark of the self-made man.

Edison's extraordinary application may have been due to his physiological constitution, but it is possible that he also had psychological motives. His colleagues noted that he seemed to fear to be indolent, as if he had a New England conscience. He records that he had a deep feeling of guilt when a child because he failed to report the drowning of a playmate. Perhaps his efforts were partly an attempt at absolution. He sometimes showed masochistic tendencies, as when he copied out by hand a typewritten report of thirty pages needing only a few incidental corrections, which could perfectly well have been inserted in the typescript, and retyped by his secretary. He had a prodigious memory and an immense knowledge of miscellaneous scientific facts. His method of inventing was empirical, and consisted of trying combinations of these facts, whether or not they had any obvious connection. He said that all experiments were successful, because the knowledge of how a thing was not done was valuable as an aid to the discovery of how it might be done. His knowledge of scientific theory was slight. According to Rosanoff, he did not understand Avogadro's hypothesis. It follows from this that he could not have had a logical understanding of the elements of the atomic theory of chemistry.

He probably had an inferiority complex through his ignorance of academic science. He was particularly fond of telling stories against academically trained scientists, and jibing at those he employed. He was apt, when he did this, to exaggerate the simplicity of his manners. He defined genius as: "One per cent inspiration, and ninety-nine per cent perspiration."

His knowledge of science was superficial but very wide, and he was extremely inventive with what he knew. Persistent trying of combinations was probably the best way of exploiting his shallow oceans of scientific facts.

During the first part of his life he dressed carelessly. He appeared as dirty as any of his laborers. He was unkempt, and often not better dressed than a tramp. His assistants sometimes secretly daubed themselves with grime, in order to give an impression of intense activity, and recommend themselves to his prejudice.

Henry Ford admired Edison's power of driving other men. He echoed his philosophy of hard work and hustle. But his emulation of Edison has not been entirely happy. The strain of working in Ford's factories has broken some men, and prepared them for crime and gangsterism. Edison was not a solemn tyrant. His humor prevented overstrained colleagues from seeking revenge by attacks on society. He was not a doctrinaire, and not insensitive to the feelings of others. He created a new sort of sublimated gangsterism. He was the boss of a gang engaged in blackmailing nature. He oppressed the facts of science until he squeezed inventions out of them. He formed his gang out of men with compensating qualities. He imagined and thought out the experimental attacks. He was not particularly skilful with tools. He was primarily an imaginative thinker. He worked with sketches, and preferred giving instructions by sketch rather than verbally. Some of his assistants were brilliant mechanics and instrument-makers, some were brilliant fitters with exceptional steadiness of hand and patience, who could make provisionary models work. Some were mathematicians and theorists of the highest academic qualifications. These were employed to check the theoretical possibilities of his ideas. His assistants were often required to try things without being told why. This was a typical gangster-like procedure.

Edison could secure the intensest blind loyalty. His gang had confidence in his gifts and leadership. He muscled into invention, in Rosanoff's phrase, like a "happy hooligan."

IV

His Life and Work

I

THE CONSTITUTIONAL CONVENTION OF 1787 was dominated by the representatives of the two small but relatively rich classes of planters and traders. After a severe struggle the traders, under the leadership of Hamilton and Madison, persuaded the planters to accept a constitution based on principles favorable to the trading interests. The planters' ablest leader, Jefferson, was absent as American minister in Paris when the Convention began. It had reached a crisis in its proceedings by the date of his return. The opponents of the proposed constitution were still in a majority and Hamilton became desperate at his prospective failure to impose the principles of the traders onto the planters. Jefferson has described how, after his return, and before he had grasped the situation, Hamilton pleaded with him to persuade some of his planter colleagues to change from opposition to support of the adoption of the new constitution. Hamilton suggested that if the planters would accept the constitution, the traders would agree to the establishment of the Federal Government in Virginia, where, owing to geography, it would be under the planters' influence.

Jefferson agreed to this compromise, but soon perceived that he had been outwitted. He and his successors tried to retrieve their ascendancy. They swiftly gained political power, and steadily increased their strength during the next half-century.

Through their control of the Government they were able to minimize the operation of those features of the Constitution favorable to traders, but they never felt strong enough to seize economic power and rewrite the Constitution according to their own economic interests and principles. They failed to consolidate their power because of the economic strength of their opponents, and, among other reasons, the weakness of their own philosophy.

Jefferson is celebrated for the philosophical cast of his mind, yet the tragical mistake of his life was philosophical. He was outwitted by Hamilton because he had no clear theory of political economy and was unable at once to perceive the theoretical implications in Hamilton's proposals. The defects in his social philosophy arose from his attempts to base the idea of human liberty on the concept of private property; two ideas that cannot be combined together clearly and satisfactorily.

Jefferson had advanced views on nearly all social questions of secondary importance; for instance, it is said that he inspired the American patent law, which encouraged Edison and other inventors, but on the question of primary importance, the status of property, he was reactionary. This explains why he and his successors exhibited a combination of attractiveness and futility.

Madison and Hamilton plainly stated that they held private property sacred. Jefferson disliked this worship of private wealth, but he could not suggest any alternative basis for the social structure. He believed that private property in land was healthier than private property in banks and factories.

The struggle between the agricultural and trading classes continued through the first half of the nineteenth century. In that period both classes had grown in economic power and numbers, and the evolution had greatly altered the features of their struggle, though not its essence. By 1860 the traders felt strong enough to abolish the compromise of 1787. They were no longer willing to surrender the social prestige of political power for the substance of a constitution favorable to trade. They wanted both. The agriculturists, who had never had the courage to fight for a new constitution which suited them, now decided to fight for the retention of political privilege. The primarily agricultural states of the South seceded, with the intention of forming their own government and constitution. The primarily industrial states of the North wished to preserve and extend centralized banking, tariffs and unified distribution favorable to industrial development.

Both sides appealed to high principles of secondary importance when the conflict appeared inevitable. The South accused the North of cultural backwardness, which was partly true, owing to the exclusion of Northern representatives from political leadership. For several decades, the South monopolized the chief political appointments. The North accused the South of moral turpitude for practising slavery.

The result of the Civil War was as historically certain as that of the War of Independence. Franklin was confident of ultimate victory because the growth of population and economic power was in favor of the United States. The Northerners could have been equally confident because similar material forces were growing in their favor. Superiority in numbers and equipment finally gave them complete victory.

The circumstances of the War of Independence and the Civil War involved much consideration of the problem of human liberty. Many of the insurgents of 1776 were subsequently disillusioned when they saw that the Government of America had passed from a set of rich Englishmen to a set of rich Americans. Like many other revolutionaries they believed they were fighting for liberty and discovered they had achieved only a transference of power. But much of the illusion that the War of Independence was primarily concerned with human liberty has remained, and has haunted America since. Thinkers, such as Jefferson, believed that human liberty might be based on the institution of private property, and assented for that reason to its sanctification in the Constitution.

The implications of the combination of the sanctity of human liberty with the sanctity of private property in the Constitution were drawn out by the triumphant traders after the

Civil War. The military success of the North had demonstrated the superiority of its form of property. Property in land and slaves had to give precedence to property in money and industrial capital, in order that the god of property enshrined in the Constitution should, as it were, receive the due sacrifice. At the same time, the other god of human liberty was duly appeased by the liberation of the slaves.

After the Civil War, a governing class of industrial capitalists with little tradition, and believing in the incompatible principles of the sanctity of human liberty and the sanctity of private industrial capital, became free to exploit a rich continent for profit.

2

Thomas Alva Edison was born in 1847, when the social forces which motivated this historical development began to accelerate rapidly towards explosion. The beginning of his adolescence coincided with the outbreak of the Civil War, and he spent his most impressionable years in the midst of one of the greatest social battles in history. His ideas and intellectual conceptions of life, his ideology, were acquired during his adolescence, and are a product of the interaction between his inborn qualities and his historical environment.

Edison's ancestors were Dutch. They were members of a family of millers which had a considerable business by the Zuyder Zee. They emigrated to America in 1730, and settled on a bank of the Passaic River in New Jersey. By 1776, the date of the beginning of the War of Independence, the settlers had enjoyed some prosperity and grown into an energetic family of colonists. Different members of the family took opposite sides in the war. One Thomas Edison became an American patriot of some importance. He had been an official in a bank on Manhattan Island, and was appointed as a clerk in the office of the Secretary of the Continental Congress. He received authority to sign United States bills of credit, and his signature is found on Continental currency notes issued in

EDISON'S BIRTHPLACE

His parents were not poor

LINCOLN'S BIRTHPLACE

His parents were poor

PLATE X

1778. In spite of his eminence he was not clever in personal business affairs, and his debts increased as his status rose.

The traitor Benedict Arnold tried to exploit his situation, and bribe him to commit treason. Edison exposed this action to the Congress, which passed a resolution declaring that "Thomas Edison has by an essential service to the United States and singular proof of his fidelity to their interests, recommended himself to the attention and reward of Congress."

The members voted a sum of money for him. He spent much effort during his remaining years trying to collect this money, but without success. In 1783 a creditor had him jailed, but he, unfortunately, was unable to jail Congress for debt. He remarked that Congress was "void of all sense of honour or humanity," and if he had rendered assistance to savage tribes he would have experienced far better treatment.

He became dependent on private charity, but lived to the great age of one hundred and four years.

While Thomas Edison was giving important and loyal service to the American insurgents, his relative John Edison was fighting on the side of the British Crown. The biographers of Edison have supposed that John Edison was the son of Thomas Edison. Research by W. A. Simonds seems to show, however, that they were probably brothers or cousins.

When the war started, John Edison was a patroon, or possessor of estates held under Dutch forms of law, in Essex County. He had married one of the Ogden family and had several children. He was unable to prevent the people in his district from following the insurgents, and fled with his family to New York, which was in British hands. He enlisted in Lord Howe's troops and guided their pursuit of Washington through Jersey. He was presently captured by the Americans. He fortunately had to wait about a year in prison before being tried for high treason. If he had been tried immediately, when feeling was most intense, he would probably have been executed at once. Even after the delay, he was convicted and sentenced to death.

When his wife heard of the sentence, she increased her efforts to secure some mitigation. She was helped by several of her relatives who supported the Americans, and especially by Thomas Edison, the Congressional Clerk. Through their help, John Edison was released on parole. He returned to his family in New York.

When the War of Independence was ended, the colonists who refused to acknowledge the sovereignty of the United States were transported by the British to Nova Scotia. John Edison with his wife and seven children were among the thirty-five thousand persons who preferred to pioneer in the primeval forest rather than submit to the United States. In a former landlord this showed exceptional determination.

Besides migrating into the Nova Scotian wilderness, John Edison tried to obtain compensation for the loss of his American property by petitioning the British Government. Like his relative on the America side, he also failed to receive his due. His claim is extant in the Public Records Office in London. He asked for £388 in lieu of his seventy-five acres, house, black mare, fifteen sheep and three beehives.

John Edison remained in Nova Scotia for about twenty years. W. A. Simonds has shown that during this period John Edison's eldest son Samuel, who had accompanied him into exile at the age of sixteen, married Nancy Stimpson, and became the father of eight children. One of these was born in 1804, and was named Samuel Edison junior.

About 1811 the Edison family decided to migrate again, to some province more promising and fertile than Nova Scotia. As a British Loyalist John Edison was entitled to six hundred acres of virgin land in Canada. He took his family to New York to visit the Ogdens, and then traveled to the North past Niagara by ox wagon to a place near the present Port Burwell on Lake Huron. The family founded a village in the district and named it Vienna.

In 1812 the United States decided to go to war with the British again, in order to resist the British interference with American trade during the Napoleonic wars.

Regiments of militia were immediately recruited among the Canadians to resist American invasion. John Edison's eldest son Samuel raised a company of volunteers, of which he became captain. Samuel and his comrades successfully resisted the American expeditions, and in a few months returned to the Vienna settlement.

Under the influence and labor of John Edison and his sons Vienna was provided with land for streets, schools and a cemetery. The Edison house was always left with a meal laid on the table, so that strangers could find food if they called when the family was away.

John Edison probably died about 1814. His bold contests with the opposition of man and nature were aided by a fine physique. He and his sons were all more than six feet tall. They had similar features, and tended to suffer in childhood from a throat affliction.

Samuel Edison became the head of the family. His son Samuel junior, born in 1804, grew up into another strapping man. He was the local athletic champion, especially in running and jumping. He started an inn when he came of age. In 1828 he married an American girl, Nancy Elliot, who was the first schoolmistress to be appointed in Vienna.

She was seventeen years old, and was descended from a family which contained several preachers and a Quaker. She was a sensible woman, as she became popular in spite of being better educated than her neighbors. Nineteen years after her marriage she gave birth to Thomas Alva Edison.

Soon after her marriage, her father-in-law Samuel senior married again, near the age of sixty, and became the father of four more sons and a daughter. He died in Vienna in 1865, at the reputed age of one hundred and three, but was probably only ninety-six. Thomas Alva Edison when five years old was taken to see his old and formidable grandfather. He "viewed him from a distance, and could never get very close to him." He had "some large pipes, and especially a molasses jug, a trunk, and several other things that came from Holland." "He chewed tobacco incessantly, nodding to friends as they passed by." He walked with a very large cane, and resented assistance.

Long before Alva was born, his father Samuel junior was again exhibiting the political intransigeance of the Edisons. Great-grandfather John Edison had fought against the United States, and preferred the loss of a small estate and exile to submission. Samuel junior, the future father of Alva, now raised arms against the Canadian Government. In 1837 an insurgent named W. L. Mackenzie tried to organize a revolt in Canada on the ground of the old American principle of no taxation without representation. Samuel Edison sympathized with Mackenzie, and lent his inn at Vienna for conspiratorial meetings, and became captain of a band of rebels.

Mackenzie and his followers attempted to seize power in Toronto. While Samuel Edison and his men were marching to his support, they heard that Mackenzie had failed, and had fled.

It was evident that Samuel Edison would have to suffer exile to Bermuda or escape, so he chose to escape. He quickly returned to Vienna, said good-bye to his family, and ran through the woods for the United States. He covered about one hundred and eighty miles on foot before reaching the frontier, and eluded the pursuit of Indians and scores of Canadian militia. Old Samuel Edison and his second wife misled the searching parties sent to arrest him.

Samuel Edison presently arrived at Detroit and assisted in two more sallies against Canada. After these had failed he wandered round the shore of Lake Erie, seeking a new home. He decided to settle at Milan, a village on a canal connecting Lake Erie with the eastern cities. Before the Ohio railway system was built, as much as thirty-five thousand bushels of grain passed through Milan in one day. The village seemed to have the prospects of a Chicago.

Samuel Edison started a business in shingles. There was a large demand for them owing to the rapid building of houses. He called his family to Milan in 1839. He was soon able to establish them in a well-built brick house. Several more children were born and in 1847, his son Thomas Alva Edison.

Samuel Edison was now forty-three, with a prosperous business and many children. He might have been expected to continue in this happy condition for the rest of his life. Unfortunately, new railroads destroyed the use of the canal and Milan declined. He had acquired some wealth, and in 1854 moved to a large house in Port Huron, the southern end of Lake Huron. He became a dealer in grain and cattle-feed, and various other trades. There was a magnificent view of Lake Huron from his house, so he built an observation tower over one hundred feet high, from which the public could look out through a telescope, for a small charge.

Thomas Alva Edison spent his early childhood in this prosperous, changing, and beautiful environment.

The start of the Civil War provided Samuel Edison with another fine opportunity for opposing the majority. Though living in the far North, he publicly supported the South.

At the age of sixty, he easily could walk 63 miles from Port Huron to Detroit, and at nearly seventy he accomplished a jump approaching twenty feet from the side of a ship onto a quay. He died at about ninety years, and several of his sons, Thomas Alva Edison's brothers, lived over ninety years. His mother's grandfather was also reputed to have lived over a hundred years.

The inventor's paternal ancestors had exceptional physique and independent character, and his maternal ancestors were a professional family with more than the common education.

Endurance, obstinacy and sense could not be unexpected in a child of these strains.

3

Edison played around the canal, the warehouses and shipbuilding yards when he was an infant in Milan. He asked questions incessantly, and his demands for explanations of what seemed obvious to his elders created the belief that he was less than normally intelligent. As his head was abnormally large, it was thought that he might have a brain disease. He exhibited a good memory by learning the songs of the lumbermen and bargees before he was five years old. In old age he could remember having seen "prairie schooners," or covered wagons, at Milan when he was three or four years old, which had been prepared for the journey to the Californian gold fields.

A little later, he had an experience which may have left a strong psychological impression. He and another boy went to bathe in a creek. The other boy disappeared in the water. Edison waited for some time, and then went home, as darkness was falling. He did not say anything about the occurrence. Two hours later, the disappearance was discovered, and he was asked about what happened. As he described the circumstances, he had a feeling of guilt, as if he were responsible. It is possible that the intensity of his work in later life may have been due partly to a desire to expiate this feeling of guilt.

Edison's education was conducted by his capable mother. He had attended a school for three months, but made no progress. An inspector described him as addled. He has stated that under his mother's direction he had read Gibbon's *Decline and Fall of the Roman Empire*, Hume's *History of England*, Burton's *Anatomy of Melancholy* and the *Dictionary of Sciences* before he was twelve and together they had looked at Newton's *Principia*.

Edison's companions noticed that he showed surprising obedience when his mother called him in to take his lessons. At the age of ten or eleven he became interested in chemistry and experimenting. He had read a copy of Parker's *Natural and Experimental Philosophy*, a school textbook of physics and chemistry, or what would now be called "general science," at the age of nine, and presently tried many of the experiments described in it. He arranged a little laboratory in the cellar under the house. Like hundreds of other boys, he became deeply interested in the changes of matter, and the interactions of solids, liquids and gases. In his later years Edison said that this aspect of things remained his deepest interest, and he was more of a chemist than physicist or engineer.

He made the usual collection of bottles, and odds and ends, for his cellar laboratory. He had two hundred bottles containing chemicals bought from the local drug store. He labeled all of them "poison." This action was rather unusual. If he had been prompted by a purely scientific motive, he would have labeled as "poison" only those bottles containing poison.

He probably labeled all because he wished to frighten off other children who threatened to interfere with his things, and also to impress outsiders with the danger and mystery of his activities. This command of bluff was an important element in his character, and assisted his future success.

As Edison did not attend school, owing to his reputed dullness and the belief that his constitution was delicate, he could spare much time for playing in his laboratory. He was not without pocket money, which he spent on buying more chemicals, wire, copper and zinc, for making voltaic batteries, etc.

In a period of construction such as existed in the Great Lakes district at that time, bits of metal, wood, stone, etc., were always lying about. There was a general atmosphere of constructive initiative. Nearly everyone was making some new thing, and used his own hands if he could not obtain more skilled help. Edison's father tried a variety of trades with a lively and amusing energy, and with sufficient success to provide his family with plenty of the ordinary domestic goods. The rapid change, and relative ease of acquisition, engendered open-handed habits. This helped Edison to get the things he wanted. In the settled European countries it was more difficult for a youth to get unusual things because the routine of life was more definite. A city such as London might contain more inspiring resources and personalities than an American township, but this was discounted by inaccessibility due to social stratification. What was the use of knowing, perhaps, that Sir William Thomson lived round the corner, if it was not possible to make his acquaintance? The smaller amount of social exclusiveness in American life in the middle of the nineteenth century assisted initiative. It was less probable that persons with ideas would fail because no one had heard of them.

Edison spent as much time as possible playing with his chemicals. He increased his pocket money by doing odd jobs. At the age of eleven he drove a horse and wagon with vegetables from his father's market garden round the town, and sold $600 worth in a year. He also worked in the garden, but did not like it. He said afterwards that it was not surprising that humanity had invented city-life, after experiencing the toil of hoeing under a hot sun. He sought for some more attractive way of earning money. At that date, boys of twelve usually worked. Schooling was casual, and his father probably did not consider it important. He went to work partly because it was customary, and partly because he hoped to get more money to spend on chemicals and materials.

He fancied the task of selling newspapers and candy on the local railroads. He had much difficulty in persuading his mother to allow him to do this, but he received permission from her, and presently was at work on the trains between Port Huron and Detroit.

He was not sent to sell papers on trains, but started business as a newspaper salesman on his own initiative. He employed himself, and was virtually a member of the employing class from the age of twelve. Edison was not a poor boy who rose from the lowest social strata. He came from a family that had always produced leaders, and employed a modest number of workmen, and he exhibited their psychology while he was a boy.

Edison began to do business on the trains in 1859, just before the Civil War started. His establishment in earnest work before the development of this crisis was of first-class importance. Unlike an inexperienced schoolboy, he was in contact with the contemporary working life, and in a position where he could receive directly the impulses of the forces released by the vast struggle between different social and economic classes.

The train for Detroit left Port Huron at 7 A. M., and arrived back in the evening at 9.30. He continued to sell papers in Port Huron until 11 p. m. As a child of twelve years, he had acquired the habit of working very long hours, with little sleep. After he had been working on this train for a few months he opened two stores in Port Huron, one for periodicals and the other for vegetables, and fruit in season. He appointed two other boys to attend them, and gave them a share in the profits. Then he engaged a boy to sell papers on the new Detroit express.

The express had a little-used United States Mail, baggage and smoking car. He bought vegetables in Detroit markets, which were superior to those in Port Huron, and put them in this car. No one asked him to pay freight. He said that he could never explain why, though perhaps it was because he was so small and industrious, and "the nerve to appropriate a U. S. mail-car to do a free freight business was so monumental." Edison's success in obtaining free facilities was due also to the unfinished organization of the railroad system. Between 1850 and 1860 the length of the United States railroads was extended from 7,500 miles to 30,000. Empty cars and small newsboys were easily overlooked in this immense development.

He bought butter along the line, and a large quantity of fruit in season. He bought wholesale at a low price, and allowed the wives of engineers and trainmen to buy at a discount.

He employed a boy to sell bread, tobacco and candy on other trains. As the Civil War developed, he found the sales of daily newspapers became very profitable, so he closed down the vegetable store.

His businesses were relatively very profitable. He often made eight or ten dollars a day. He gave his mother one dollar a day for keep, and spent the rest on chemicals and apparatus.

The work on the train he served himself did not take all of his time, so he began to collect chemicals to play with on the way. The small smoking compartment was not used because it had no ventilation, so he turned it to his convenience.

He brought many of his bottles and chemicals from the cellar at home and arranged them as a little laboratory. At quiet times on the runs between the stations, and no doubt during the halt in Detroit, he experimented.

As his train arrived in Detroit about 10 A. M. and left about 7 P. M., he spent about nine hours a day in the larger town. He read technical literature in a library, bought chemicals from the drug stores, and spent much time in the Grand Trunk Railroad machine shops, and other interesting places. Expensive materials were bought on the instalment plan. With several dollars a day to spend, he could afford even rare substances.

He became acquainted with Pullman, who at that time had a small shop in Detroit, and was experimenting with his sleeping-car. Pullman made wooden chemical apparatus for him. Edison studied Fresenius' *Qualitative Analysis,* and tried the tests in his train-laboratory.

The stimulation of newspaper sales by the Civil War impressed Edison with the business possibilities of news. He decided to found his own paper. He bought a small press that had been used for printing hotel menus. This was kept at home, but on the train he had some supplies of type, so he could compose in spare moments. He named his paper the *Weekly Herald.* He sold it at three cents per copy, or eight cents per month to regular subscribers, and the sales of an issue sometimes exceeded four hundred copies.

The *Weekly Herald* was probably the first newspaper in the world to be published on a train. It was noticed by the London *Times,* and by Robert Stephenson when he inspected the Grand Trunk Railroad.

It contained boosts of friendly engine-drivers, or engineers, market prices, new train and road services, police and military news and advertisements of his own businesses. In one issue, there was an announcement under the "Birth" heading:

"At Detroit Junction G. T. R. Refreshment Rooms on the 29th inst, the wife of A. Little of a daughter."

Lower down the column, as a fill-up, he inserted:

"Reason, Justice and Equity, never had weight enough on the face of the earth, to govern the councils of men."

He recommended Mr. E. L. Northrop to the railroad direction as "being the most steady driver we have ever rode behind (and we consider ourselves some judge, haveing been Railway riding for over two years constantly)." Mr. Northrop was "always kind, and obligeing, and ever at his post. His Engine we understand does not cost one-fourth for repairs what the other Engines do." Perhaps Mr. Northrop was the engineer who sometimes allowed Edison to drive the train engine.

When he arrived by his train at Detroit one day in April, 1862, he found the newspaper offices surrounded by excited crowds reading bulletins of the battle of Shiloh. The Confederate armies had received several defeats in Kentucky and Tennessee, in the western area of the war.

Their commander, Johnston, received an indirect reprimand from his old friend Jefferson Davis, which prompted him to start an offensive campaign which might retrieve all that had been lost, and gain still more. The Northern forces of Sherman and Grant were situated near a log meeting-house called Shiloh, between two creeks running into the Tennessee River. A large part of the Northern troops were raw, and had learnt the elements of military drill only on the way to the front. Grant judged that learning some technique and discipline was more important than erecting fortifications. Johnston attempted to drive the Northern armies into the river and creeks. His troops attacked fiercely and many men on both sides soon retreated in panic. Grant saw four or five thousand panic-stricken Northern troops lying under the river bluff, who could have been shot without resistance. Similar disorder occurred at the rear of the Confederate army.

About five thousand soldiers were killed, and twenty thousand wounded in this battle.

Grant writes that until the battle of Shiloh, he and thousands of other citizens believed the secession movement would collapse after a decisive victory over any of its armies. But when after that battle, the Confederates were seen to be preparing yet another line and offensive, he no longer expected that the Union would be saved without complete conquest. Up to that time, the Northern armies had protected the property of citizens in invaded territory, irrespective of their sentiments, but afterwards Grant "regarded it as humane to both sides to protect the persons of those found at their homes, but to consume everything that could be used to support or supply armies."

The battle of Shiloh was the most ferocious fought in the West. The general conception of the Civil War changed after it, and became more profound and ruthless. Many soldiers and citizens had regarded the war largely as a sporting contest, in which men from the North and South fought duels in battalions, instead of pairs.

The first accounts of Shiloh which reached Detroit stated there had been 60,000 casualties. As the crowds, and Edison, stared at the newspaper bulletins, they acquired new insight into the seriousness of the war, and became more aware of the depth of the forces moving under the struggle.

Edison perceived that everyone would be anxious to read accounts of the battle, and there should be a large increase in the demand for newspapers.

"I then conceived the idea of telegraphing the news ahead, went to the operator in the depot, and by giving him *Harper's Weekly* and some other papers for three months, he agreed to telegraph to all the stations the matter on the bulletin-board."

He decided that he would need a thousand, instead of the usual hundred, copies of the Detroit newspaper. He had not enough money to purchase that number, so he determined in desperation to see the editor and get credit. He went into the editorial office and found two men in charge, one of whom, after the telegraphing scheme had been explained, said he could take the thousand copies. With the help of another boy, he lugged the papers to the train. The first stop was at Utica, where he usually sold two papers. He saw a crowd ahead at the station, and thought it some excursion, "but the moment I landed there was a rush for me; then I realized that the telegraph was a great invention."

The next stop was at Mount Clemens. Between the stations he decided to raise the price of the paper from five to ten cents, if there was a crowd. His expectation proved to be correct.

Edison used to jump off the train about a quarter of a mile outside Port Huron station. He had deposited some loads of sand at the place, in order to form a soft landing place. He was met here by a Dutch boy with a horse and wagon. On this occasion, the boys found a large crowd waiting for them as they entered the outskirts of the town.

"I then yelled: 'twenty-five cents apiece, gentlemen! I haven't enough to go round!' I sold all out, and made what to me then was an immense sum of money."

Some time afterwards his train laboratory was abolished through an accident. Some phosphorus was jolted onto the floor, and set fire to the car. The conductor put the fire out, but he turned Edison and his bottles and the printing type out of the train at the next station.

He continued printing his paper at home, but presently converted it into a gossip sheet, and changed its title to *Paul Pry*. Personal remarks in the paper provoked an enraged reader into throwing Edison into the St. Clair River.

If Edison had wished, he could have become a master of tabloid journalism.

Edison's experience of social types is illustrated by his account of an experience on his train in 1860, just before the Civil War started. Two fine-looking young men, with a colored servant, boarded the train one afternoon at Detroit for Port Huron. Edison presently came round to offer them evening papers. One of them said to him: "Boy, what have you got?" "I said: 'Papers.' 'All right.' He took them and threw them out of the window, and, turning to the colored man, said: 'Nicodemus, pay this boy.' I told Nicodemus the amount, and he opened a satchel and paid me. The passengers did not know what to make of the transaction. I returned with the illustrated papers and magazines. These were seized and thrown out of the window, and I was told to get my money of Nicodemus. I then returned with all the old magazines and novels I had not been able to sell, thinking perhaps this would be too much for them. I was small and thin, and the layer reached above my head, and was all I could possibly carry. I had prepared a list, and knew the amount in case they bit again. When I opened the door, all the passengers roared with laughter. I walked right up to the young men. I said: 'Magazines and novels.' He promptly threw them out of the window, and Nicodemus settled. Then I came in with cracked hickory nuts, then pop-corn balls, and, finally, molasses candy. All went out of the window. I felt like Alexander the Great!—I had no more chance! Finally I put a rope to my trunk, which was about the size of a carpenter's chest, and started to pull this from the baggage-car to the passenger-car. It was almost too much for my strength, but at last I got it in front of those men. I pulled off my coat, shoes, and hat, and laid them on the chest. Then he asked: 'What have you got, boy?' I said: 'Everything, sir, that I can spare that is for sale.' The passengers fairly jumped with laughter. Nicodemus paid me $27 for this last sale, and threw the whole out of the door in the rear of the car. These men were from the South, and I have always retained a soft spot in my heart for a Southern gentleman."

Perhaps the perfection of this story grew with the years, but it provides an artistic expression of differences in social class and ideals between the North and South.

Edison's father said that his son never had any boyhood of the usual sort. There was no period of adolescent irresponsibility.

Edison became deaf through an accident on the railroad. He said that he was waiting for some newspaper customers, when the train started. He ran after it, and had some difficulty in clambering on. A trainman reached down and grabbed him by the ears and hauled him into safety. Edison felt something crack in his ears, and afterwards he grew deaf. He said that

if the trainman had damaged his hearing, he had also saved
his life.

Edison has said that he became deeply interested in electricity while on the railroad, through his acquaintance with telegraphers and telegraph offices. He already knew something about the theory of the telegraph, as his textbook by Parker contained a short account of Morse's system. With his knowledge of chemistry and mechanics he constructed rough telegraphs, and learned the Morse signaling code. This was not remarkable, as hundreds of boys were playing with the telegraph at that time. The invention was still new. It appealed to the desire for power, and the ability to exert power at a distance. One reason why guns are fascinating is that they exert effects at a distance, and extend the feeling of human power. The telegraph allowed orders to be given almost instantaneously. It satisfied the primitive desire for superhuman power, or magic. This universal feeling had the first place in the motives of Edison's hundreds of young contemporary experimenters. But Edison had another motive. He had found by experience that "the telegraph was a great invention" because it had enabled him to make a relatively large sum of money. It was great because, in addition to its ingenuity, it had immense economic power. The recognition of this by a boy of fourteen, on the basis of personal test, was exceptional.

The first successful telegraph depending on electro-magnets was devised in America by Henry. Cooke and Wheatstone devised a telegraph, based on the results of Henry's researches, in England in 1837, and its practical value was first demonstrated through its assistance in detaining a murderer, who was escaping by train into London. It happened that the telegraph had been set up as a demonstration unit at the station where the murderer boarded the train. A description of the man was sent to London, and he was arrested as he got off the train. Before that event, the unit was regarded by the railway authorities and the public as an amusing toy.

A more convenient form of telegraph was invented by

S. F. B. Morse, an American painter. Morse went to Europe to improve his mastery of his art, and after four years' work, returned to America in 1832. He happened to meet on his ship fellow-passengers who were keenly interested in recent progress in the knowledge of electricity. During discussions with them, he conceived the possibility of communication by electricity, and he began to think how it might be accomplished. Like Leonardo he was able to apply skill in drawing to the design of mechanisms, and soon made some beautiful sketches. He gradually worked out a practical method, though he was not an engineer or scientist.

The creation of the practical electric telegraph by Cooke and Wheatstone, and Morse, was not done quickly. They worked persistently, under the pressure of social and economic importance of their aim. The railroads could not be developed extensively without swift communication for the control of traffic. Railroad and telegraph grew together. These methods of transport and communication were exceptionally important in America because distances were so great.

The extension of the railroad and telegraph between 1840 and 1860 vastly increased the unification of the United States. Before that period the states could without excessive friction enjoy "states' rights" because the communications between states were so bad. After 1840 the states were brought into much closer contact, and could not avoid taking detailed notice of the practices of their neighbors. For instance, it increased the difficulty of the problem of the restoration of escaped slaves. A negro slave in a Southern state was a piece of personal property. If he ran away, he had to be restored by his finder, like any other piece of lost property. Before the railroad was introduced an escaped slave could not usually go very far, owing to the cost and difficulty of transport, but afterwards he might travel thousands of miles by jumping on freight trains. The railroad increased the number of escaped slaves in the North, and set the problem of slavery with awkward concreteness in front of the Northern population. The introduction of the telegraph exacerbated the problem, be-

"Then I realized that the telegraph was a great invention."
Edison at the age of fourteen or fifteen.

PLATE XI

cause it could be used for helping to catch escaped slaves.

Improved communications made the United States much smaller, as they have since contracted the effective social size of the whole earth. They were brought forth by industrialism, fundamentally as means to increase trade. They grew much faster in the Northern states because they are more important to communities trading in manufactured goods, which need quicker transport than those trading in raw materials. Manufactured goods are far more valuable than raw materials, bulk for bulk. Northern traders enthusiastically pulled the whole of the United States together with rails and wires, in order to assist business, and presently discovered that the closer contact had exposed the incompatibility of the interests of the governing classes in the North and South. The former wanted the United States to be turned into an efficient organization, surrounded by a high tariff fence, for absorbing goods and producing profits, whereas the latter wanted security in slave property and free trade for increasing the export of raw materials. Neither class objected to slavery.

The power of the governing classes of the North and South was evenly balanced about 1850. After that date, the North became stronger, owing to the greater inherent possibilities of economic power in industrial capitalism, and to important changes in political circumstances, several of which were due to the railroad and telegraph.

Small farmers and tradesmen constituted a large part of the Northern population. In spite of their numbers, they had less influence than the rich on the direction of Northern growth and the formulation of Northern ideals. In the 1850's the Northern rich decided that the small farmers and traders might be engaged as allies in the fight against the Southern rich, through their fear of the extension of slavery. The small men found that the railroad and telegraph had brought slaves and the search for slaves into their own territories. They feared the introduction of slave competition, and they began to dislike the principle of slavery.

The Republican Party was formed to combine the Northern

capitalists and small men in the struggle against the Southern slave-owning planters. The aims of the two wings of the party were profoundly different. The capitalists were on the offensive and wished to control the South in their own interests. They did not object to slavery.

Morse, whose invention had done so much to assist the growth of industrialism, and to unify America in industrial interests, was an ardent supporter of slavery, which he justified by appeals to the Bible; and an equally ardent opponent of secession. His views agreed with those of New York bankers. He became the president of a Society for the Diffusion of Political Knowledge which was anti-war, pro-union, and pro-slavery; and was supported by a number of millionaires. Morse was extremely sincere and hated the hypocrisy of the slavery abolitionists. He based his arguments on what appeared to him as the highest religious truths. He believed abolition was "the logical progeny of Unitarianism and Infidelity." But his principles were in effect those of the Northern capitalists, who desired the preservation of the Union for the sake of efficiency, and no interference with slavery in order to preserve the sanctity of private property.

A purely capitalist policy was not possible, partly because of his own invention. The telegraph had helped to put the small men on the defensive, against the introduction of slavery which would undermine their personal positions.

They gained temporary political power through their defensive movement. The Northern capitalists were forced to compromise with them and form the new Republican Party, and accept their nominee, Abraham Lincoln, the former backwoodsman, as leader. The less subtle supporters of policies equivalent in practice with those of the pure capitalists, fiercely opposed Lincoln. At Lincoln's second candidature they nominated McClellan in opposition. McClellan was introduced at his biggest New York rally by Morse, who lent him his arm to lead him before the audience.

When Edison became acquainted with the telegraph it was the young nerve of the growing social giant of American industrialism. It attracted the courageous inventors and operators, who, today, would be interested in aeronautics and radio. It has been said that the telephone, which was the offspring of the telegraph, was "the little mother of the big trust." The servants of the early telegraph felt immense potentialities as they sent messages with triumphant instantaneity from state to state across a continent. Edison had already learned by experience that a corner in news could be arranged through the telegraph. He desired to become a professional telegrapher. This was not very easy, because the practice necessary for proficiency could not be obtained outside a telegraph office. Again he found his chance on the railroad. One day in August, 1862, his train was shunting at an intermediate station. He happened to see the infant son of the station agent playing on the line in front of a car which had just been shunted. He ran to the child and carried him out of the way of the approaching car. The grateful father was glad to reward Edison by teaching him train telegraphy.

Edison practised in the agent's office for several months, sometimes for eighteen hours a day. He made his own set of telegraph instruments in a gun-shop in Detroit. After he had acquired some proficiency, he attempted to start his own telegraph business. He erected a wire between the station and the village, which were about a mile apart, and hoped to make a living by sending messages over this short distance. He was disappointed, as no one wished to use a telegraph over a distance of one mile, so he was forced to seek employment as a company telegrapher. His attempt to start his own business before seeking employment by others was characteristic. He was assisted in finding a job by the Civil War. The telegrapher at Port Huron wished to enlist in the highly-paid United States Military Telegraph Corps, so he recommended Edison for his own job. Edison was fifteen years old. He used to work all day in the office, and then until 3 A. M., in order to practice the taking of press reports, which was the most difficult and highly-paid telegraphic work. Presently he obtained a post as night telegrapher on the Grand Trunk Railroad at Stratford in Canada. This was not far from the Edisons' old Canadian home.

Edison was not a very conscientious employee. He read scientific books and experimented with the instruments. He put on one side telegrams handed to him for dispatch, until he could conveniently interrupt his studies. He showed similar insensitiveness in borrowing other people's valuable tools. While at Stratford he heard of the existence of boxes of old batteries at another station. He asked the operator there whether he might have them, and was told that he could. The batteries consisted of eighty Grove cells, with electrodes which contained altogether several ounces of platinum. He was delighted with this acquisition, and still was using some of the platinum in his laboratory forty years later. He made his first invention at Stratford, when he was sixteen years old. Night operators were required to send hourly signals to show they were awake. He devised a clock which made the time signals automatically. This enabled him to sleep while on duty, and preserve his energy for his own interests during the daytime. He was presently found out and reprimanded. His automatic timing device was similar in principle to the apparatus introduced for calling district messengers from a central office.

Edison's job at Stratford ended through a misunderstanding over the signaling of two trains. They were allowed to run off towards each other on the same track, and a collision was averted only through the promptitude of the engine drivers, who could see each other's trains at a distance on the straight track. Edison was called to Toronto to explain the affair. His examination by the general manager was interrupted by two English visitors, and while he was waiting, he decided to run away. He returned to Michigan and got a job as operator on the railroad at Adrian. He was discharged owing to the misunderstanding between two superintendents who had given him contradictory orders. As they were friends, they laid the blame on him. He had no difficulty in obtaining another job, as the Civil War in this year, 1863, had fully developed. The Federal army had absorbed fifteen hundred operators, besides a few hundred who had enlisted as soldiers, so anyone with the roughest proficiency could secure a civilian job. Edison wandered over the central states from Detroit to New Orleans during the next five years. He became a member of the class of tramp operators which has a special place in American history. The shortage during the Civil War, and in the years of swift reconstruction and expansion afterwards, conferred a high degree of freedom on operators. If they disliked their superiors they could tell them what they thought of them, and often retain their jobs, or immediately get another elsewhere. Trade unionism was strong among them. They could travel free over the whole country, as the railroad men regarded them as colleagues, owing to the close connection between railroad and telegraph.

The operator's work, with the rough instruments of the time, required considerable skill, so the operators were brighter than the average man. Their contact with the news tended to keep them intellectually alert.

Such circumstances helped to maintain the high standard of freedom and intelligence among the operators, but others destroyed good habits. Many operators suffered from the strain of heavy telegraphing, and drank to relieve their nerves. As the rates of pay were high they could indulge in wild debaucheries, and as jobs were easy to get, sacking did not deter them. The drifting from place to place interfered with marriage.

Edison lived with such colleagues for five years, between the ages of sixteen and twenty-one, from 1863 to 1868. The living conditions during the war period were rough, and after the war, when the military telegraphers returned, were even wilder. The operators added handiness with guns to their other aberrations. They had lost much of even such routine as civilian operators possessed.

Edison obtained a post with the Western Union Telegraph Company in 1864 at Indianapolis. He left this post possibly owing to trouble over another invention. He had not yet learned to take press reports very quickly, so he devised an instrument which would take the messages as they came in, and then repeat them at a slower speed. He could write out the messages in beautiful copy with this assistance, without delay when the rate of business was normal, but at rush hours he was left behind. The newspaper offices complained of the slowness with which they received their copy. Edison's repeater consisted of a disc of paper which received the signal indentations along a volute spiral. He said later that this instrument helped him to conceive the phonograph while working on the development of the telephone.

Edison moved on to Cincinnati. A fellow telegrapher, M. F. Adams, has described Edison's appearance when he drifted in there for a job. He was badly dressed, and his manners were uncouth. He was thin, and his nose was prominent. He was unpopular, but had no superiors as an operator. He was always playing with the batteries and circuits, and trying to make telegraphy less irksome. He played jokes on his colleagues by making their instruments function abnormally, and arranged special circuits for electrocuting some of the rats which infested the offices.

Edison was in the Cincinnati office when the account of the assassination went through. The operator who took the press report was working so mechanically that he did not take in its sense. The telegraph office first learned the news from the newspaper office which had received their report.

Edison often went to the theater at Cincinnati. He was particularly fond of *Othello*. He increased his earnings by copying plays for the theater.

He was promoted into the most highly paid grade of operators, apparently, judging from his own account published by Dyer and Martin, through willingness to blackleg on other operators absent in connection with their union. At any rate, he seems to have been in the office when his unionist colleagues were out.

Soon afterwards he moved to Memphis in Tennessee, where the telegraph was still under military control just after the Civil War. Edison says that he devised a repeater which enabled him to connect New York and New Orleans for the

first time after the war. The superintendent was also working
on repeaters, and discharged him through jealousy. Edison
nearly starved in Alabama, and arrived in Louisville on an
icy day, wearing a linen duster suit.

Many of the operators who returned after the war found
civilian life too boring. Edison describes how colleagues used
to throw ink around the office, and pistol cartridges into the
fire.

"Everything at that time was 'wide open.' Disorganization
reigned supreme. There was no head or anything. At night
myself and a companion would go over to a gorgeously furnished faro-bank and get our midnight lunch. Everything was
free. There were over twenty keno-rooms running. One of
them that I visited was in a Baptist church, the man with the
wheel being in the pulpit, and the gamblers in the pews."

Edison describes how, while he was in Cincinnati during the
Civil War, he had to pass on an urgent cipher message from
the War Office in Washington to General Thomas at Nashville, who was threatened by the Confederate General Hood.
The connection to Nashville went through Louisville, so
Edison tried to call the Louisville office, but could not get any
reply. After much trouble a roundabout telegraph connection
was made through the Indianapolis-Louisville railroad. Inquiry showed that the silent Louisville office should have been
served by three operators, but one of them had fallen off his
horse and broken his leg, another had been knifed in a keno-
room, and the third had gone to Cynthiana to see a man
hanged and had missed the return train.

Edison stayed in Louisville for the long period of two
years. He had to serve a wire that passed through a badly
insulated cable under the River Ohio. This and other defects
rendered accurate reception difficult. He frequently had to
guess at unintelligible noises. He found he could not write
quickly enough to leave time for the working of his imagination, so he began to experiment with different scripts. He
evolved an efficient vertical style with simplified separate letters, of a sort which has since been much recommended by

educational psychologists to ease the learning of writing by schoolchildren. Edison's script was evolved in 1865, and is a beautiful example of functionalist design.

I think the most important line of 'investigation' is the production of Electricity direct from carbon.

Edison

Edison's Handwriting

The telegraph room at Louisville had lost one-third of the plaster from its ceiling. It was never cleaned. The switchboard was about thirty-four inches square. Its brass connections were corroded with age, and sparking from lightning flashes. According to Edison "it would strike on the wires with an explosion like a cannon-shot." The copper connecting wires were crystallized and rotten, and the fumes from the nitric acid battery had eaten away the woodwork in the battery room. One night a drunken operator came in and kicked the stove over, tore the switchboard off the wall, and then went to the battery room and knocked the batteries onto the floor. The escaping acid percolated through the floor and destroyed account books in the room underneath. Edison left the wreckage as it stood, for the manager's inspection. He rigged up a temporary set of instruments. When the manager came in, he asked Edison who had done it. "I told him that Billy L. had come in full of soda water and invented the ruin before him. He walked backward and forward, about a minute, then coming up to my table put his fist down, and said: 'If Billy L. ever does that again, I will discharge him.' "

Such was the influence of the shortage of labor at this time.

Edison wandered back to Detroit, and then to New Orleans with the intention of emigrating to South America with two companions. He was advised by an acquaintance in New Orleans not to go, so he presently returned to operating in Louisville and Cincinnati. He became acquainted with a brilliant operator named Ellsworth, who could imitate the transmitting styles of other operators. Ellsworth had fought with the Confederates, and had caused much confusion among the Federalists by tapping their wires and sending false messages over them. Ellsworth suggested that Edison should invent a method of sending dispatches which could not be intercepted, as he could obtain a high price for it from the Government. Edison said that he evolved the germ of his quadruplex system of telegraphy, by which four messages may be sent simultaneously over one wire, in his attempts to solve the problem Ellsworth had set him. Ellsworth presently disappeared, as he could not settle down after the war. He became a gunman in the Panhandle of Texas. After he had gone, Edison dropped the research.

Edison returned to his home at Port Huron in 1868. He soon became unhappy without work, so he wrote to his old operator friend M. F. Adams, who was at Boston, asking if he knew of a job. Adams showed a sample of his copy to the superintendent of the Western Union office, who was favorably impressed. Edison left for Boston, but his train was delayed by a blizzard, and arrived at Montreal several days late. An operator put him up there in the most cheerless boarding house he had ever seen. The food was inadequate, the bedclothes were short and thin, the temperature was 28 degrees below zero, and the water was frozen solid in the jug. "The usual livestock accompaniment of operators' boarding houses was absent," probably owing to the intense cold.

When he presented himself at the Boston office he looked raw, even as a pioneering American of 1868. His trousers were too small and light, his shoes were worn out, his butternut hat from the South was dilapidated, and he wore his hair in the cowlick style. His accent was uncultivated, as it remained through his life, he chewed tobacco, and spat copiously. The five years of wandering had assimilated his manners to the rougher part of the wild society in which he had lived. He had not acquired suavity by travel. But he had not been destroyed. He was not seduced from continual experimenting and reading by any environment. He fairly regularly sacrificed his employer's interests to his own. His successful self-control through these interesting but dangerous years was due mainly to the cast of his character, but was assisted by his deafness. This ailment made telegraph work harder, as a large part of reception at that time consisted of taking messages from a ticker by ear. There was also a benefit in deafness, as he was not distracted by the noise of instruments in other parts of the room. Perhaps the extra listening effort, which Edison had to make, increased self-control in other directions.

The deafness must have interfered with social life. It probably helped to separate him from dissolute companions, and fostered isolated studiousness, as it often does. His deafness increased his insensitivity to his surroundings, and allowed him to work and think in conditions which would have distracted many men. It strengthened the naturally strong individualistic, egoistic disposition he had inherited from his obstinate ancestors.

The Boston operators decided to "put a job on the jay from the woolly West." As his first assignment he was put onto one of the most difficult wires, and presently was told to take a special report for the Boston *Herald*. The Boston operators had arranged with New York to have it sent by one of their fastest senders. Edison sat down and began to take down the report, which came through slowly at first, and then with increasing speed. Through his special script he was able to write faster than any sender could send, so he kept up easily. On looking up, he noticed that the operators were watching him, and he guessed what they were doing. The sender began to slur words, abbreviate, and use other tricks, but Edison was accustomed to them. After a time, he took his own key, and "remarked, telegraphically, to my New York friend: 'Say, young man, change off and send with your other foot.' " The New York man dropped the joke after that, and turned the sending over to another man.

At Boston, as usual, Edison put his own interests first. He avoided the press telegraphy and chose the ordinary work because the free intervals between casual business could be used for reading and experimenting.

He was not the employer's ideal of a workman. If all American workmen had behaved with Edison's determined self-interestedness, the history of American industry would have been stormier.

He found and bought a set of Faraday's works in Boston. He said that he learned more from these books than from any others. He tried the experiments Faraday described, and he appreciated his simple, non-mathematical explanations. He considered Faraday the Master Experimenter. Edison said that not many of Faraday's works were sold in America at that time. Few people did anything in electricity, except telegraphers, and opticians who made simple apparatus for school science classes.

Edison became familiar with Charles Williams' factory in Boston for the manufacture of telegraph apparatus. Williams afterwards became the first manufacturer of telephones, in association with Bell. One of his men helped Edison with the construction of the model for his first patented invention. This was an apparatus for quickly recording votes in the House of Representatives. Electric buttons were to be placed on members' desks, so that votes could be registered without calling the roll of members' names, and walking into particular lobbies.

The idea and arrangement were simple. Edison thought the apparatus would be attractive because it would save much legislative time, but when he demonstrated it before the politicians in Washington, they explained that it would be unwelcome, because it would destroy the system of obstructing parliamentary business by calling for votes or divisions, each of which wasted time.

After this experience Edison decided to let the market set him his inventive work. He would not attempt inventions of value to humanity unless there was a definite market for them. This decision was historically important. Edison was the first great scientific inventor who clearly conceived invention as subordinate to commerce. He abandoned the traditional theory that inventions and discoveries are independent creations, having no necessary connection with other affairs. According to the traditional theory they are the products of pure thought. The moment at which they came into existence is supposed to depend only on the presence of a particular genius. It is assumed that if Isaac Newton had lived in China two thousand years ago, he would have presented the Chinese with the laws of gravitation. The traditional explanation of why the laws of gravitation were discovered in the seventeenth century is that Newton happened to be born then. As Pope wrote:

"God said: Let Newton be, and all was light."

According to this view, the light of gravitation would have been seen in b. c. 1665, instead of a. d. 1665, if God had chosen to let Newton be twenty-three years of age on the former date.

The old theory that inventions and discoveries are due solely to genius contains some truth, but more error. When stated boldly today it seems fantastically erroneous, as the contemporary mind has more sense of history than its predecessors. The notion that inventions come into existence through unaccountable acts of creation has become as unacceptable now as the Genesis story of the Creation, after Darwin had established the theory of evolution, in the nineteenth century.

It preserves its authority because it contains a fraction of truth, and because historians of science and invention have done so little towards working out a better theory. The sole generally known fact is that inventions and discoveries are produced by clever persons. The obvious connection between cleverness and invention has inspired the theory that invention is solely due to cleverness. But the clever person is only a small fraction of the phenomenon of invention. Important inventions are nearly always produced more or less simultaneously by several men, as the legal battles over patents prove. Cleverness probably does not contribute a twentieth part to any invention or discovery. The planet on which the inventor lives is one factor. The century and the country in which he lives, his social class and family, are other factors.

After these and others have been allowed for, the contribution of mere cleverness in invention does not appear overwhelming.

Edison's view that invention should be subordinate to commerce was an important advance in sociology. It made the way for the further advance to the conception of invention as a social product, with social responsibilities.

So long as invention was conceived as intellectual magic, it could not make an adequate contribution to human progress. After it had been made a servant of commerce, it could begin to evolve into a servant of humanity. It had to be made a servant of capitalism in order to acquire its correct position in future human societies.

Edison's career of invention has often been justified by fanciful estimates of the billions of dollars of wealth created through his work. These estimates have little meaning because it is impossible to disentangle Edison's part from those of others in the creation of this wealth. Some time ago it was estimated that Edison's inventions had brought into existence $10,300,000,000 of wealth in the United States alone. It would be more true to say that Edison's inventions had been brought into existence by $10,300,000,000. The potentiality of this wealth in the America of the nineteenth century created Edison far more than he created it.

When he decided to make inventions only for commercial demand, and not for the prestige of virtuosity, he admitted that that commercial demand, that potential $10,000,000,000, was the controller of his inspiration. He admitted the priority of commercial demand, so he renounced the priority of invention to wealth.

The traditional theory of invention is based on the notion of magic and superhuman power. In primitive society the clever man is supposed to have an element of divinity that places him above, and gives him rights over other men. The conscious aim of much scholarship, scientific research and invention is to qualify for this upper class of supermen, and enjoy its privileges and prestige. It is in the interest of members of this class to magnify the importance of cleverness in invention, because the amount of prestige is determined by the amount of magic. If the invention is very ingenious, the inventor is a great magician and entitled to great prestige. The more useless the invention, the greater its magic. Invention and discovery on the traditional theory are supposed to be merely pure acts of disinterested intelligence because such acts are the best qualification for entering the magical upper class, or leisure class, in Veblen's phrase.

Edison wrested invention from the magicians of the leisure class. He destroyed the illusion that inventors owe everything to their own cleverness.

The belief that innate qualities confer privileges is an essential part of the theory of aristocracy. When Edison undermined the prestige of the undirected inventive inspiration of the inventor who was merely clever, irrespective of the sociological value of his invention, he began to destroy the aristocratic elements in the traditional theory of invention. He began the advance towards a democratic theory in which invention would be cultivated in order to increase human happiness, rather than personal privileges. He did not suggest such a theory, but he abandoned the old theory, and thus made the approach possible.

At Boston Edison changed from a telegrapher interested in trying new arrangements with his apparatus, and studying science, into an inventor. He was twenty-one years old, and as he grew out of adolescence he immediately became a weightier personality.

After he patented his vote recorder, he invented a stock-ticker, for registering stock exchange quotations in any place by telegraph. The first stock-ticker had been introduced by Callahan in New York in 1867. It did not involve any major invention, but had to print stocks and prices in brokers' offices conveniently and reliably. A simplified form of printing tele-graph (first invented by D. E. Hughes in 1855) which could be installed in each broker's office, and operated from a central office in the stock exchange, was required.

Edison installed his stock-ticker in about thirty offices in Boston, but it was clear that New York, the chief center of speculation, was by far the best place for development. He visited New York in 1868, to attempt to sell his stock-ticker, but failed, and returned to Boston.

He had many occupations in Boston. He put up telegraph lines between private business offices, fitted with simple alpha-betical dial instruments, by which unskilled clerks could ex-change messages. Edison says they slung wires over the house tops without asking anyone's permission. Apparently they went to houses and stores which already had wires supported by the roofs, and told the occupants they were telegraph men and wanted to see the wires. They were always given permission to go up to them, and while there fastened up their own. This, apparently, is how it was possible for Edison, without capital, to put up his own small centralized telegraph system in the center of a city. He did not pay rent for wires slung over the property of others.

He also worked on duplex telegraphy in Boston, in 1868. This consists of sending two messages over one wire simul-taneously in opposite directions. The duplex apparatus which first achieved commercial success was worked out in the same year in Boston by J. B. Stearns. Edison demonstrated his ap-paratus at Rochester, but without success, owing, he says, to lack of competent assistance.

Edison was now absorbed in invention. He had accumulated large debts through borrowing money for experiment and construction. He decided to go to New York, as development and success seemed more possible in the great commercial city. He arrived there in 1869, nearly starving. He begged tea from a tea-taster whom he saw at work in a warehouse, and borrowed one dollar from an operator friend who was himself out of work. He considered carefully the best value that could be had in food, and chose apple dumplings and coffee for his first lunch.

He applied for a post as operator with the Western Union, and slept at night in the battery-room of the Gold Indicator Company. While waiting for instructions from the Western Union he studied the instruments of the Gold Indicator Company, who had their own system of tickers for telegraphing the variations in the price of gold to brokers and speculators. Edison had designed and introduced his own system in Boston. It was probably rougher and more amateurish than the New York system, and for those reasons had not been a commercial success. But Edison understood the principles thoroughly, so he could examine the New York equipment with professional interest. He mastered its details in a few days. This enabled him to profit from a development in the history of the United States, which became particularly prominent in 1869.

Hamilton and Madison, as the spokesmen of the rich, had conferred on the United States a constitution well adapted to their interests. The two chief features of the Constitution were the sanctity of human liberty and of private property. The Civil War was essentially an explicit struggle for power between two different classes of property owners, the Southern land and slave owners, and the Northern industrial capitalists. By winning the war the Northern money-owners established the precedence of their form of property. The Constitution was interpreted as sanctifying human liberty, and private property especially in industrial capital. The liberty of Americans was sacred, wealth was sacred, and rich Americans were therefore doubly sacred. In this climate of beliefs millionaires appeared to have a quality not possessed by other men, which made them seem slightly superhuman. The reaction against this view, and the social forces it expressed, had made some progress before the end of the century, when the awe of millionaires began to decline.

The growth of the ascendancy of the millionaire, and the evolution of a form of society in which he was dominant, was naturally easy in such a richly endowed country as the United States. Very rich men had appeared in the United States before the Civil War, but they appeared in far greater profusion after. The financing of the Civil War had stimulated the natural habits of Americans to think in millions. The Northern finances were managed by Jay Cooke, who raised the size of financial operations to a new degree. Vast quantities of paper money were created to meet war loans, and pay bonuses to soldiers. This became material for speculation by hundreds of thousands of persons who would not have dreamt of speculating before the war. Similar phenomena occurred after the war of 1914–1918.

As liberty and money were generally felt to be sacred, there appeared to be no way of controlling them. They were above the law. Millionaires, as free Americans and rich men, did as they liked, and the community could not see how they could be controlled. After the Civil War the circumstances enabled millionaires to speculate on a higher scale than ever before. They played with the wealth of America as they wished, except for such interferences as arose from collisions among themselves. The railroads formed a considerable fraction of the new wealth that had been created in America. They included not only their own expensive equipment of tracks and rolling stock, but enormous estates granted to them by the Federal Government. The millionaires who controlled railroad finance were among the richest and most powerful. Naturally they were prominent in the post-war financial campaigns.

The possibilities of the situation inspired some of them to new visions of financial power. In 1866 Drew, as treasurer of the Erie Railway Company, had devised a way of transferring a large part of the wealth belonging to the shareholders in the company from them to himself. The position as a servant of a company, appointed to advance the interests of the shareholders, had never been so successfully abused before. As C. F. Adams, Jr., in his classical account of this and the succeeding events, wrote: "Mr. Drew was looked upon as having effected a surprisingly clever operation, and he retired from the field hated, feared, wealthy, and admired."

Shortly afterwards, in 1868, Cornelius Vanderbilt, popularly known as the Commodore, conceived a far grander style of operation in railroad finance. He aimed at acquiring control of all the railroads serving New York, so that he would have dictatorial power over all the trade with that city, and a large part of the trade of the United States. C. F. Adams, Jr., observed in 1869 that by combining the power of the individual with the power of the financial corporation, he had introduced Cæsarism into corporate life. "He has, however, but pointed out the way which others will tread. The individual will hereafter be engrafted on the corporation,—democracy running its course, and resulting in imperialism; and Vanderbilt is but the precursor of a class of men who will wield within the state a power created by the state, but too great for its control. He is the founder of a dynasty."

By 1868 Vanderbilt had secured control of all the railroads serving New York, except the Erie, controlled by Drew. He now began a financial battle with Drew for the control of the Erie railroad.

"The cast of Drew's mind was sombre and bearish, Vanderbilt was gay and buoyant of temperament, little given to thoughts other than of this world, a lover of horses and of the good things of this life. The first affects prayer meetings, and the last is a devotee of whist. Drew, in Wall Street, is by temperament a bear, while Vanderbilt could hardly be other than a bull."

Vanderbilt was the ideal aggressive operator, and Drew the ideal defensive operator. They were ideal opponents.

Vanderbilt, "unconsciously to himself, working more wisely than he knew, . . . developed to its logical conclusion one potent element of modern civilization.

"Gravitation is the rule, and centralization the natural consequence, in society no less than in physics. Physically, morally, intellectually, in population, wealth, and intelligence, all things tend to consolidation. One singular illustration of this law is almost entirely the growth of this century. Formerly, either governments, or individuals, or, at most, small combinations of individuals, were the originators of all great works of public utility. Within the present century only has democracy found its way through the representative system into the combinations of capital, small shareholders combining to carry out the most extensive enterprises. And yet already our great corporations are fast emancipating themselves from the state, or rather subjecting the state to their own control, while individual capitalists, who long ago abandoned the attempt to compete with them, will next seek to control them. In this dangerous path of centralization Vanderbilt has taken the latest step in advance."

Drew was without constructive imagination. He could never have imagined such a scheme as Vanderbilt's. He had no initiative. But he was very astute in defending an inside position. He knew how to manipulate details with which he was familiar. Vanderbilt first attempted to capture him by maneuver. Drew outwitted him by chicanery of unequaled subtlety, and he became enraged at this affront before all Wall Street. He now attacked the Erie railroad "with the brute force of all his millions."

Both sides employed the judiciary against the other. They sought judges complacent to their desire, and obtained injunctions from them which handicapped the other side. Armed gangs of men besieged the garrisoned offices of the rival companies. Trains manned by armed partisans were charged into each other on single railroad tracks for which the parties were contending, and the respective crews engaged in hand-to-hand combat after the collision.

Drew's colleagues among the directors of the Erie company included Jay Gould, who was his equal in chicane, and superior in financial imagination; and Jim Fisk, a piratical blond who handled the organized violence on behalf of Erie.

This group proved too much even for Vanderbilt. He was forced to compromise with them and leave the Erie company entirely in their control.

During this contest the speculating public had grown accustomed to a new degree of wildness in the fluctuations of stock prices.

The old methods of registering price changes were unable to follow the new rates of fluctuation efficiently. There was a pressing demand for instantaneous distribution of stock prices to the rapidly increasing number of persons gambling on the large, swift changes in prices.

The unparalleled events of the Erie financial war were soon exceeded by the results of the attempts of the triumphant Erie directors to corner all the gold in the United States.

The inflation of the currency during the Civil War had greatly increased the price of gold, as the financiers clung to gold as a measure of value, as they still do today. The fluctuations in the price of gold governed the prices of all other commodities, so gold was the central material for speculation. A special office for buying and selling gold, and registering its price, was organized during the Civil War. The president of this office devised an indicator, like a scoring board. It had two faces, one of which could be seen from inside the office, and the other from the street. The figures on the indicator were controlled by an electrical mechanism operated by the registrar of gold prices.

The prices shown on the indicators were noted by messenger boys and carried to the various brokers' offices. The boys were often delayed, and made mistakes, so the automatic registration of prices in each broker's office, sent by the registrar from a master transmitter, was obviously desirable. Laws devised such a "Gold Reporting Telegraph," and introduced it in 1866. This primitive apparatus was evolved into a stock-ticker by Callahan.

It has been mentioned that when Edison arrived in New York in 1869, he slept in the battery room of Laws' Gold Indicator Company. On the third day after his arrival, while sitting in the transmitter room, the transmitter suddenly stopped with a crash. Within two minutes over three hundred boys besieged the office, yelling that the brokers' wires were out of order and must be fixed at once. The man in charge lost his wits in the pandemonium. Edison had learned how the apparatus worked, and after examining it, saw what was the matter; a contact spring had broken off, and jammed two gear wheels. As he went to the man in charge to explain what was the matter, Laws rushed in, "the most excited person I had seen. He demanded of the man the cause of the trouble, but the man was speechless. I ventured to say that I knew what the trouble was, and he said, 'Fix it! Fix it! Be quick!' "

In about two hours Edison had got the whole system working again. Laws asked him who he was, and after discussing his instruments, and hearing Edison's suggestions for improvements, he appointed him general manager of the system at $300 per month. This was far more than Edison had ever received before, and an enormous salary for a twenty-one-year-old young man who had been virtually starving seventy-two hours previously.

The tremendous burst of speculation created a sharp demand for stock-tickers. The capital of Callahan's company was increased in its first year to $1,000,000 and paid a dividend of ten per cent. Laws and Callahan presently amalgamated their companies, and Edison left Laws' employ.

The rising speculation in gold provided Edison with work and technical problems when he arrived in New York. It reached its extremest height a few months later in the autumn, when Gould and Fisk tried to complete the corner of gold. The Federal Government collected the duties on imports in gold. This helped to create a gold stringency, which the Government normally relieved by monthly sales of gold. The periodical shortages of gold became more acute in the fall or autumn, when farmers suddenly required money in exchange for crops.

In September, 1869, Gould and Fisk used the financial resources of the Erie railroad to acquire control of the relatively small amount of available gold. They obtained access to Grant, the President of the United States, by bribing his relatives. Grant was a remarkable soldier, who, after discharge from the army at the age of thirty-nine for drunkenness, rose from apparent failure, in the circumstances of the Civil War, to become commander-in-chief of the victorious army. On active service he exhibited outstanding military qualities, but in peace he showed less than the normal human capacity for the ordinary affairs of civil life.

Both his military success and his civil fecklessness appeared to be connected with his feeling of detachment from other men. He was the only American general who could conduct a battle without being perturbed by the number of casualties. Nearly all of the American generals were very political and their military judgment was warped by the consideration of the effect of casualties on public opinion, and their own political careers.

Grant had no political ambitions, interests or understanding. He shrank from any sort of strenuous social contact with other men, and was even prudish, as he once said that no one had ever seen him naked since childhood.

He was generous, amiable, and extraordinarily casual. He supposed that clever civilians were a superior human type, and was willing to give trusting admiration to the masters of the incomprehensible activities of civil life.

Like millions of others of the simpler Americans he admired the millionaires and their apparently miraculous financial exploits. They seemed to be the finest demonstration of the exercise of the American ideals of personal freedom, and the accumulation of private property.

Grant felt honored by invitations to the parties of Fisk. He was delighted to listen to any suggestions from such a great financier on how the Government finances might be conducted more efficiently.

Fisk and his friends convinced him that the sale of gold by the Government was bad for trade and agriculture, and persuaded him to suspend it. After Grant had given the order, he left for, or was got away to, an inaccessible part of the country. Gould and Fisk now increased the artificial shortage of gold by buying all that came into the market. Gold prices soon rose to extreme heights, as foreign trade could not be conducted without it. At the same time an attack on Vanderbilt's stocks was started. The price of gold on Tuesday, September 21st, rose to 138. On Wednesday the price of the stock of Vanderbilt's Central Railroad fell from 198 to 177.

"While Vanderbilt was hurrying back by special train from Albany, Director James Fisk, Jr., was manipulating gold in the manner peculiar to himself, offering great bets as to the point it would reach, proclaiming his intention and ability to break Vanderbilt down, and boasting of the power of his combination, in which he even dared openly to include the President of the United States himself."

All legitimate business was paralyzed, and "crowds of desperate men only left Broad Street to haunt the corridors of taverns, and to buy and sell and gamble, till the night was wellnigh worn away."

On Thursday the price of gold was driven still higher, in spite of opposition from the Government, which was now becoming thoroughly alarmed.

On Friday morning the streets, buildings and windows were filled with spectators who had come with fascination to watch their own ruin. The Fisk party knew that the Government was no longer passive, and that they could continue to force the price only by pure bluff. Fisk's brokers made quick successive offers without a taker, and ran the bidding up to 162. Suddenly a Government broker began to accept the bids, and the price collapsed to 134. "Meanwhile, across the street, Fisk was vapouring in his wild way, refusing offers of gold at 135, because he was buying at 160, proclaiming himself the 'Napoleon of Wall Street.' "

The Government sellers now demanded from Fisk the settlement of their margins. He agreed, and then disappeared through a back door.

During the day, "men forgot to act, and openly displayed

their inmost natures, . . . they seemed dazed or drunken; no one knew where he stood, or how he stood; but the mob of brokers and of lookers on surged to and fro, and in and out, some howling, yelling and gesticulating, others silent and confounded, and others again, almost crazy. Some, indeed, were quite crazy. . . ."

While Fisk had been brazening out the field, his colleague Gould had secretly withdrawn his money. By Friday evening, the clearing house found itself overwhelmed with an inextricable confusion of transactions totaling $500,000,000. The attempt to unravel the confusion was abandoned, and speculators cut their losses. Fisk was temporarily bankrupt, but Gould had deserted him, and escaped. They had engineered the attempted corner, and disorganized the commerce of America, on a liquid capital as small as $2,000,000.

As mechanical superintendent of the Gold Indicator System, Edison had to supervise the central transmitter of gold prices. It was difficult to make the machine work fast enough to keep up with the wild fluctuations in prices, but it was speeded up by putting a paper-weight on it. On the morning of "Black" Friday, the apparatus fell behind, but Edison had made it catch up with the current price by one o'clock.

He "sat on the top of the Western Union Telegraph booth (in the gold exchange office) to watch the surging, crazy crowd. One man came to the booth, grabbed a pencil, and attempted to write a message to Boston. The first stroke went clear off the blank; he was so excited that he had the operator write the message for him. Amid great excitement Speyer, the banker, went crazy and it took five men to hold him; and everybody lost his head. The Western Union operator came to me and said: 'Shake, Edison, we are O.K. We haven't got a cent.' I felt very happy because we were poor. These occasions are very enjoyable to a poor man, but they occur rarely."

Edison overheard messages which indicated there was some sort of conspiracy between the Government and Wall Street. He observed Fisk in "a velvet corduroy coat and a very peculiar vest. He was very chipper, and seemed to be lighthearted and happy. Sitting around the room were about a dozen fine-looking men. All had the complexion of cadavers. There was a basket of champagne."

Edison had witnessed through his presence in Wall Street on September 24th, 1868, and his connection with the gold price indicator, the power of telegraphic instruments in contemporary commerce. He had seen men go crazy after reading the indicator's figures. Six days after "Black" Friday he started a business with F. L. Pope, a talented operator friend, to design and operate public and private telegraphic and other electrical equipment. Early in 1869 the *Telegrapher* published the news that "T. A. Edison has resigned the situation in the Western Union office, Boston, and will devote his time to bringing out his inventions." This was the first occasion in history on which a man aged twenty-two, truly announced that he would make invention his profession.

In the announcement of the new firm in the *Telegrapher,* Pope, Edison & Co. described themselves as "electrical engineers." It is said that this was the first occasion when the term was used in the professional sense. It was an important contribution towards the conception of a new profession, the consulting electrical engineer.

Pope and Edison invented a stock-ticker which could be worked on one wire, and devised a system for importers and exchange brokers that was cheaper than the existing gold indicator service. This and other inventions interested the Gold and Stock Telegraph Company, which presently absorbed the Pope and Edison firm.

The president of this company, Marshall Lefferts, asked Edison to undertake the general improvement of the ticker apparatus. Edison rapidly secured a number of patents for improvements. In particular, he devised the "unison stop," by which all tickers could be brought back to a zero position by the operator in the central transmitting office. This saved the expense of sending mechanics to offices to synchronize tickers which had got out of step. Lefferts decided to buy the rights in Edison's early ticker inventions. When Edison received the request to go to his office, he had fixed in his mind a price of $5,000, and in any case, not less than $3,000. Lefferts asked him how much he wanted, but he suddenly lost his nerve, and dared not ask for $5,000, so he asked Lefferts to make an offer. Lefferts said: "How would $40,000 strike you." Edison nearly fainted, but managed to accept. At that time, he still measured the value of an invention by the time and trouble he had given to it, "and not by what the invention was worth to others."

Lefferts then handed a check for $40,000 to Edison, who had never received money in the form of a check before. When he presented the check it was handed back to him because it was not endorsed. Owing to his deafness he could not understand the clerk's explanation. He suspected that he had been swindled, and hurried back to Lefferts, who laughed at him, endorsed the check, and sent a young man with him back to the bank, to testify to his identity. The bank clerk then paid out the money in large packets of small bills, as a joke. Edison took the pile of bills home and stayed up with them all night, in fear of having them stolen. On the next morning he asked the amused Lefferts what he should do with them, and was advised to start a bank account.

Edison was now able, in 1870, at the age of twenty-three, to begin manufacturing electrical apparatus on a considerable scale. He employed fifty men in making large numbers of stock-tickers for Lefferts. He started double shifts as business increased, and worked on both of them as his own foreman. He did not sleep more than a few half-hours during each twenty-four hours. He drank strong coffee and smoked strong cigars without restraint. He drove his men on piece-work. They could earn high wages, and were treated with a rough cheerfulness as long as they fitted in with his methods, but they were discharged without consideration if they did not.

The staff of Edison's first shop included S. Bergmann and J. S. Schuckert, the founders of two immense German electrical engineering firms bearing their names, and J. Kruesi, who became the chief engineer of the General Electric Works at Schenectady. In later years, Edison engaged A. E. Kennelly, the eminent discoverer of the Kennelly-Heaviside layer, and E. G. Acheson, the inventor of carborundum. He had an aptitude for recognizing talented men.

Within a few years Edison acquired forty-six patents for improvements of stock-tickers. The American patent law permits the protection of many details not patentable under European law, but even after allowing for this difference, and that none of his stock-ticker patents was of the first degree of importance, and that he had already begun to exploit the assistance of talented colleagues, Edison's fertility was remarkable. His power of managing others was not less remarkable. Dyer and Martin have observed that he used men up in the achievement of his aims as ruthlessly as Napoleon or Grant.

At the age of twenty-three, in a works financed out of his own inventions, he had attracted and led such men as Bergmann and Schuckert. His choice of stock-tickers as a subject of inventive work showed he could recognize major social phenomena when they rose around him. He worked at tickers because they had obvious commercial and therefore social importance. He was without personal interest in speculation, and never speculated in his life, but he was willing to provide improved machines to make speculation easier. It was easy even for minor inventors to see that tickers were important in the New York of 1869.

By this time Edison must have become aware of the greatness of his inventive talent. He showed rare realistic talent in not spurning a field occupied by many other lesser talents, and in not succumbing to the vanity of risking his great talent on entirely new ideas beyond the range of the others. As he did not speculate in stocks, so he did not speculate in invention. He missed several first-class inventive scoops through his refusal to gamble in invention, but by his example he helped to remove the practice of invention from the sphere of gambling and magic. He helped to socialize invention, demonstrate its part in the development of human society, and establish it as a new profession.

He worked with extreme energy on many aspects of telegraphy in his first independent years. The development of automatic telegraphy required apparatus which would work at much higher speeds than hand-operated apparatus. It was found that the hand apparatus, which worked satisfactorily at the usual speeds, would not work properly at high speeds, owing to the effects of electrical inertia, or self-induction. The signals were drawn out, and lost definition.

Edison invented a method of preventing this. He exhibited it at the Centennial Exposition in 1876, and it was adjudicated a reward by Kelvin, who was then Sir William Thomson.

Kelvin reported that "the electromagnetic shunt with soft iron core, invented by Mr. Edison, utilizing Professor Henry's discovery of electro-magnetic induction in a single circuit to produce a momentary reversal of the live current at the instant when the battery is thrown off and so cut off the chemical marks sharply at the proper instant, is the electrical secret of the great speed he has achieved. . . . It deserves award as a very important step in land telegraphy."

Edison was sent to demonstrate the automatic system in England in 1873. He claimed his demonstrations were successful, but he was unable to persuade the British authorities to adopt his system. While in London he was asked if he would care to test his apparatus using a coiled cable 2,200 miles long as the telegraph wire.

Edison did not fully understand the theory of electrical self-induction, and did not foresee that the self-induction of the coiled cable would have an enormous value. He was astounded when a Morse dot normally one thirty-secondth of an inch long was extended into a line about thirty feet long. His ignorance of scientific theory raised criticism and opposition, especially among highly trained scientists and engineers without inventive talent. His insight into science was derived from intense practical experience of apparatuses involving scientific principles. When Kelvin invented an apparatus he embodied a scientific principle. Some of his electrometers look like a materialization of text-book diagrams on the theory of electrostatics. Edison's mental process worked in the reverse manner. His scientific ideas were abstractions drawn from apparatuses with which he had profound familiarity. His opinions on any subject of which he had experimental knowledge were always worth consideration, though his explanations were usually inaccurate and often wrong.

Edison introduced practical quadruplex telegraphy in 1874. This was his first major inventive achievement. It enables four messages, two in each direction, to be sent simultaneously over the same wire. The duplex, in which two messages are sent in opposite directions simultaneously on the same wire, had already been invented by Stearns. Edison devised a diplex system, in which two messages could be sent simultaneously in the same direction on one wire. He obtained the quadruplex by combining the duplex and diplex.

The functioning of the apparatus depends on two signaling currents. One current is made to transmit by altering its direction, and the other by varying its strength. The alterations in direction and in strength may be received independently by suitable relays at the other end of the wire. In this way, two messages may be sent simultaneously. Four messages may be sent by duplexing each of the signaling currents. This is done by arranging that the outgoing signal current shall operate the receiver at the distant station but not the receiver at the home station.

Suppose a dummy wire, whose electrical resistance and capacity are exactly equal to those of the main wire, is connected to the end of the main wire in the home station. If the signaling current is sent into the connected wires, one half will go through the main wire, and the other half through the dummy. Suppose, now, that the main wire and the dummy wire have each been wound an equal number of times, but in opposite directions, round the iron core of the home relay magnet. Then the signaling current from the home station will not operate the home receiver, because the two currents will cancel each other's magnetizing effect on the home receiver. But the current will not be split at the distant station, so it will operate the distant receiver.

Edison said the invention of the quadruplex system "required a peculiar effort of the mind, such as the imagining of eight different things moving simultaneously on a mental plane, without anything to demonstrate their efficiency."

It seems that he visualized the eight instruments simultaneously, and tried to foresee how they would react together. He did not try to analyse the properties of the instruments and circuits theoretically.

His concentration on these mental efforts affected the normal operation of his memory. On one occasion he had to attend the City Hall to pay taxes before a certain hour in order to avoid a surcharge. An official suddenly asked him his name. He could not remember it, and lost his place in the queue, which made him too late to avoid the surcharge.

He did not show more than the minimum necessary interest in money. As long as he had sufficient for his needs he was satisfied. He never applied his mind earnestly to money-making.

He combined lack of special interest in money with an original insistence on commercial practicality in invention. This shows that he was a social theorist. He believed a good invention must conform with the criterion of commercial success, yet he did not care whether or not he made money out of inventions. It is frequently supposed that Edison's insistence on the criterion of commercial success showed that he was mercenary, and wished to make invention a tool of acquisition. His behavior shows that he disinterestedly put invention at the service of what he conceived to be the proper social machinery, capitalist commerce. His view was far in advance of the old conception that the justification of invention is the enhancement of the dignity of human nature through exhibitions of cleverness, and that the practical application of invention is a vulgar activity of secondary importance.

He recognized that invention must have social justification. He assumed that the nineteenth-century American capitalists' criterion of justification was correct, and therefore judged invention by that criterion.

As he made relatively little money for himself out of his inventions he evidently did not apply the same criterion for judging his own private, personal success. His behavior shows that his public and private views of invention were not the same. He was casual with his private wealth.

He did not employ bookkeepers until the chaos of his finances prevented him from getting on with his work. He lost most of the royalties he should have received from his early patents through employing an unsatisfactory patent lawyer. A man of his ability would not have lost so much if he had been primarily interested in acquiring money.

The famous German theoretical and experimental chemist, Professor Nernst, invented an electric lamp, with a filament made of rare earths which conduct electricity and emit a bright light at high temperatures. The filament had to be heated by a surrounding platinum coil before it lighted up, so about fifteen seconds passed before it reached full brilliancy. The details of the lamp were complicated, and with the delay in reaching maximum illumination, prevented it from having more than a transitory commercial success. It gave way before the superior qualities of the carbon filament lamp, which was developed mainly by Edison.

When Edison met Nernst, he talked on his favorite topic on the need for inventions to be business-like and to invent what commerce required. He said that academic scientists generally failed to appreciate the commercial problems of invention, and did not offer inventions to industry in a practicable form.

Nernst listened to the strictures on the unpractical and unbusiness-like qualities of professors. He quietly asked Edison how much he had made out of the carbon filament lamp. Edison replied that he had made nothing out of it. Nernst then asked Edison if he knew what price he had secured for the rights in the rare earths lamp. Edison said he did not know. Nernst replied that the A.E.G. had paid $250,000 for them.

This story is usually related as a proof that academic scientists are not so impractical as hard-headed practical scientists, such as Edison, imagine.

It may also be interpreted as showing that Nernst's commercial sense was keener than Edison's, and that he was willing to receive a large sum of money for an invention whose commercial success was uncertain, and subsequently proved moderate.

Edison did not say that inventors should try to get more than an invention was worth. He said that they should make inventions which would be a commercial success. This did not even imply that the inventors should receive any money at all for them.

The attitude to invention of the graduate of the telegraphs of the Woolly West and of Wall Street was ethically superior to the attitude of the eminent graduate of German scholarship.

Edison's behavior shows that desire for private profit was not the spur to his inventiveness. His demand that inventions should be commercially successful did not imply that he should make a large private fortune out of them.

It is possible for an invention to be commercially successful without one man making more profit out of it than any other man. In fact, it may be commercially successful if every member of the community makes an equal profit out of it. It is often said that inventions would never be made if no one had any prospect of making large private profits out of them. Edison's conduct is in contradiction with this view, and his emphasis on the importance of the commercial success of inventions does not necessarily imply that there will be no invention unless inventors, or some other individuals, make large profits out of inventions.

Quadruplex telegraphy was very successful in the United States. It greatly increased the volume of business that could be transmitted over existing wires, and reduced the capital ex-

penditure on new lines. The effects of the very variable wind-
fall and drought on the resistance of the earth, and the insulation of the line, increased the difficulties of working the
system in England.

Edison's quadruplex and other telegraphic inventions were
used as pawns in financial operations by Jay Gould. The companies that owned his inventions were offered about $1,000,-
000 for them. Gould used the existence of this offer to depress
the value, and secure the control, of the Western Union stock.
He then repudiated the offer. The legal struggles over the re-
pudiation lasted thirty years. The reactionaries who controlled
the telegraph companies opposed the extension of automatic
telegraphy, and the development, which became extensive
before 1880, was allowed to die.

Edison had personal dealings with Gould in the early stages
of this affair. He took part in secret consultations with him, in
which the negotiators entered Gould's house through the
servant's entrance at night, to evade the observations of spies
from rival companies. Gould paid him $30,000 for his personal
interest in the quadruplex, but evaded paying him anything
for about three years' other work.

Dyer and Martin quote Edison as expressing contrary opinions on the treatment he received from Gould. On one occasion he said: "I never had any grudge against him, because he
was so able in his line, and as long as my part was successful,
the money with me was a secondary consideration." But in
1876 Edison had written bitter complaints that his relations
with Gould had been "a long, unbroken disappointment," and
that he "had to live."

Edison said that Gould had no sense of humor. He had a
peculiar expression, which seemed to indicate insanity. He
was extremely mean. He was very angry when the rent of his
stock-ticker was raised a few dollars. He had the machine removed, and preferred to do without it, in spite of the great
inconvenience, rather than pay. He worked very hard and
collected and thoroughly studied the statistics bearing on his
financial affairs. The extent of his relations with persons in

official life was surprising. He was entirely non-constructive, and was interested in money only. "His conscience seemed to be atrophied, but that may be due to the fact that he was contending with men who never had any." Gould did not care whether his companies were a success or a failure. When he secured control of the Western Union, Edison "knew no further progress in telegraphy was possible, and I went into other lines" of invention. Gould's colleague in the crippling of telegraphy in America was General Eckert, who had been Assistant Secretary of War to Stanton during the Civil War. The close connection between the victors of the war and the characteristic technological and financial post-war developments is significant. It provides one of the reasons why Americans were supine under the activities of such men as Vanderbilt and Gould. They did not fundamentally disapprove of them. Like Edison, they were prepared to admire their ability even when robbed by them of payment for years of work. Edison was not interested in money, but he could admire Gould who was interested in nothing else. This admiration of principles which one does not practise is a feature of the psychology of religion. The frenzies of the gold corner were manifestations of herd religious emotions. Men did not go crazy because they were ruined, as ruin was only a temporary condition for an American in 1869. He could not remain destitute long in such a rapidly developing country. The frenzies were due to excessive perturbations in the current religious worship of wealth. Everyone believed that owning wealth was of vital importance, and that loss of wealth meant damnation. The hysteria was induced by the fear of damnation by the god of wealth.

Within a few years of establishing his first shop Edison worked simultaneously on nearly fifty inventions. He assisted Scholes in the development of his invention of the typewriter, he invented the mimeograph, or stencil from which numerous copies of written matter may be pulled. The stencil was cut by a stylus, used as a pen, whose point was driven in and out rapidly by an electric or pneumatic motor, so that it left a line of five holes along the strokes of the writing.

He also invented paraffin paper now used for wrapping sweets and candy, and many other purposes.

The growth of the telegraph stimulated many attempts to invent multiplex systems, by which one wire could be used to transmit simultaneously a large number of messages. Several inventors were trying to devise multiplex systems in which the various simultaneous signal currents were picked out by tuning forks.

The transmission of sounds was incidental in these telegraphs to the transmission of ordinary dot-and-dash messages. The inventive workers on this sort of apparatus included A. Graham Bell, Edison, and Asa Gray. It was natural that one or two of them would begin to alter the perspective in which they were working, and consider the apparatuses as transmitters of sounds by electricity, instead of transmitters of multiple signals by electricity with the assistance of sounds. The conception of an electrical apparatus for transmitting human speech followed as an extension of this direction of thought.

Inventors had attacked the problem of the electrical transmission of human speech directly at an earlier date. The first electrical machine which could speak was devised by the German Professor Reis about 1860. He named it the "telephone." It depended on the starting and stopping of an electric current by a diaphragm made to vibrate by the sound waves of the human voice. Reis and the inventors who followed him could not make the machine repeat more than a few syllables before the make-and-break contact was thrown out of adjustment, so it was not a practical invention. A Reis instrument was explained to Bell by Joseph Henry, and Edison also had an account of it. No doubt Gray also knew it. Bell was the first to see how a practical telephone could be made. He was the son of A. M. Bell, a lecturer on elocution at University College, London, and an original worker on the analysis of speech. Graham Bell had grown up amidst studies of phonetics, vocal physiology, and original thought on the mechanism of speech. This background of knowledge probably increased his confidence in attempting to invent a practical telephone. Workers less familiar with the mechanism of the human voice may have given too much weight to the belief that sounds as complicated as human speech could not be transmitted without an equally complicated machine. Bell discovered that speech could be continuously transmitted by an exquisitely simple mechanism. He found that if an iron diaphragm was made to vibrate near a permanent magnet with a coil of wire wound round it, a current was induced in the coil. Suppose somebody speaks at the diaphragm. It will vibrate in unison with the sound waves started by the voice. The voice will be transformed into a varying current. If this current is sent through a wire to the coil on the permanent magnet of a similar instrument, it will attract its diaphragm back and forth, and reproduce the vibrations in the diaphragm of the first instrument. In reproducing the same sequence of vibrations it will reproduce the same sequence of sounds.

Bell's patent was registered on March 7th, 1876. A few hours later, on the same day, Gray made a claim for a similar patent. Edison had constructed in 1875 a resonator for analysing telegraph currents, which could reproduce human speech, but which had not been put to that use.

Bell's original telephone was a magnificent invention, but it had serious limitations. The transmitting current was produced by the unaided energy of the human voice, which had made the iron disc vibrate in a magnetic field and so produce the current. The energy of the sound waves from the human voice is very small, so the energy of the transmitting current was very small. The current was too faint to be effective beyond a short distance.

Edison now made two inventions which removed this limitation, and created the practical telephone which could communicate over long distances. He showed how to put virtually unlimited energy into the transmission. He placed a button of carbon or lamp-black against the disc. When the disc was made to vibrate by the waves from the voice, the pressure of the disc on the carbon varied. He found that the electrical resistance of the carbon varied with the variations in pressure. Thus the carbon button could be arranged to act as variable resistance in a circuit containing a current of any required strength. He placed the button in the primary circuit of an induction coil connected with a voltaic battery, and the distant receiver, of the Bell type, was put into the circuit of the secondary coil. This arrangement enabled the voice to be transmitted by high voltage currents which could overcome the resistance of long wires, and hence long distances.

At this time Edison was again working in connection with the Western Union. Their telephone department was managed by Twombly, Vanderbilt's son-in-law. The controllers of the Western Union started the customary financial warfare with the controllers of the company exploiting Bell's patent. The Western Union pirated Bell's receiver, and Bell's company pirated Edison's transmitter.

Edison now sought some payment for his carbon transmitter. He had privately decided that $25,000 would be a fair price, and then asked for an offer. He was promptly offered $100,-000. He said he would accept it on the condition that it was paid to him at the rate of $6,000 yearly for seventeen years, the life of the patent. He was glad to make this arrangement because he could not trust himself not to spend any available money on experiments, "as his ambition was about four times too large for his business capacity." It will be noticed that he might have invested the money, and have received $6,000 interest for seventeen years, and still have possessed the capital at the end of the period. He said that the arrangement protected him from worry for seventeen years.

At about this time Jay Gould renewed his stock exchange campaigns against the Western Union. He had bought Page's patent, which was believed to cover all forms of electromagnetic relay. The Western Union asked Edison if he could invent a method of moving a lever at the end of a wire, which did not involve a magnet. He immediately solved this problem by an application of a device he had patented in 1875.

He had discovered that moistened chalk became slippery

when a current was passed through it. Thus a lever held at rest by friction against the moistened chalk would be released when current was sent through the chalk. This invention was sufficient to check Gould's use of the Page patent against the Western Union.

Edison was again offered $100,000 for the rights, and again stipulated the payment of $6,000 for seventeen years. Thus he received $12,000 yearly for seventeen years for these two inventions.

The same invention was employed again in a patent contest in England. The Bell and Edison interests had started independent companies in England to exploit their patents. The Edison company found that they would not be able to pirate the Bell receiver under the British patent law, so they cabled Edison for instructions. He replied that he could soon relieve them from dependence on the Bell receiver. He invented a new receiver depending on the slippery chalk phenomenon. He mounted a cylinder of chalk on an axle which could be rotated steadily. One end of a small metal rod rested on the surface of the chalk, and the other end was attached to a mica diaphragm. The surface of the chalk cylinder was moistened with a solution of various salts. When the cylinder was rotated, it tended to drag the end of the rod, owing to the friction between the chalk surface and the rod. The drag on the rod, in turn, distorted the diaphragm at the other end. The receiving current from the telephone wire was now sent through the contact between the moistened chalk surface and the metal rod. It varied the degree of friction in proportion to its strength, owing to electrolysis on the chalk surface, and made the rod slip in step with the current variations. The slithering of one end of the rod made the mica diaphragm vibrate in unison. In this way, the mica diaphragm reproduced the sounds spoken into the distant transmitter. This new Edison receiver was a loud-speaker. The energy which worked it came from the rotation of the wheel, and could be far greater than the energy of the transmitting current. This receiver assured the freedom of Edison's English company from interference by the Bell company. The two companies then amalgamated to resist the pretensions of the British Post Office. Edison received £30,000, or $150,000 from the amalgamated company for his patent rights.

Edison's production of two first-class inventions, the nonmagnetic relay and the loud-speaking telephone receiver, in order to destroy the monopolies of other patents, is unparalleled. On nearly all other occasions in history, powerful inventions have not been produced to order at short notice. They have usually been produced after years of difficult struggle. Edison produced both of these inventions as weapons in stockexchange fights. The achievement exhibited invention in a new aspect. Hitherto it had been regarded as an uncontrollable activity, like the composition of poetry. Edison now showed that first-class invention could be done to order. This was an important contribution to sociology, as it helped to destroy the belief that invention depended on unpredictable inspiration. It strengthened the hope that humanity would learn how to reduce invention from a fortuitous into a controlled process of development of the machinery of civilization.

Edison's London staff, which had to demonstrate his telephones, included twenty carefully selected young American mechanics, G. Bernard Shaw, Samuel Insull, and other men who became well-known.

Shaw's experiences with Edison's London company had a formative influence on his ideas. He was about twenty-four years old, and was beginning to formulate his criticism of society in sociological novels. The first, written in 1879, was never published, and the second, *The Irrational Knot*, was written in 1880, after working for the Edison company. Shaw had to assist in the demonstrations of the loud-speaking telephone to prospective clients. He has given some interesting reminiscences of the American electricians in the preface which he wrote for the novel in 1905. They knew so little about the theory of electricity that he was able to hold his own with them, as he had read something, and even knew a relative of Bell. They were extremely energetic and profane, despised English class-distinctions, were proud of American ideals of liberty and cheerfully bore relentless bullying from American foremen. They attacked difficulties with courage and energy, but a large part of the energy was wasted through ignorance. They were rescued from false starts by English colleagues who often had better scientific qualifications, but less initiative.

Shaw's second novel, and first published work, exhibits an intense interest in class psychology. He wished to contrast the characteristics of members of the English leisure class with those of members of the skilled artisan or operator class, by depicting the intrusion of a talented artisan into the leisure class. The intruding hero is named Edward Conolly, an American mechanic and electrician, of Irish and Italian descent. He becomes assistant mechanic to Lord Carbury, an English nobleman with scientific hobbies. He invents an electric motor of great commercial promise. Carbury and his rich relatives, including one named Lind, finance a company for the exploitation of the invention. Conolly now has reputation and prospects of wealth. He is acquainted with Lind's daughter, a girl with natural charm, but without training, in virtue of her membership of the leisure class. Their marriage proves unhappy, as Conolly cannot adapt himself to the leisure class incompetence of his wife. She then elopes with a rich Etonian with an impressive figure and manners, and an Oxford literary education, in the belief that he has more feeling and sensitiveness than Conolly. She swiftly finds he is conceited and without creative ability. Presently she meets Conolly again. It has become clear that she will not be able to abandon the habits of the leisure class, so their reunion is impracticable. Conolly perceives that he has married beneath him in terms of ability.

The personality of the imaginary character Edward Conolly was very different from the personality of Edison, but probably it would never have been created if Edison had never existed. Conolly was represented as a very educable man. Edison was not educable, and remained uncultivated. Shaw could not

have idealized his American colleagues in London, because
they were extremely undisciplined, while Conolly had exceptional self-control. Shaw adopted from Edison and his American mechanics the elements of creative ability and independence of British upper-class manners. He needed a character
independent of the ideas and habits of the different English
social classes in order to criticize those ideas and habits. In
1880 the type of an American electrical inventor seemed to
him to be particularly suitable for that purpose. His choice
was an indication of the sociological interest of that type.

4

Edison's first wife was named Mary Stillwell, whom he
married in 1871. He had met her, while she was still a school-
girl, on the doorstep of his laboratory. She and her sister happened to stand there for shelter during a shower of rain.
Edison immediately liked her, and presently asked her to
marry him. Her parents said she was too young to be married
immediately. During the delay deemed necessary by her parents, Edison provided occupation for her in his laboratory.
She assisted in his experiments on the invention of paraffin
paper.

Their first child, a daughter, was born in 1873. At that
time Edison was still working in his Newark workshop. He
became dissatisfied with this in 1876. His wife was expecting
a second child at this time, which proved to be his first son.
Edison invited his father to search for a suitable site for a
new laboratory and home, and offered him the post of house-
manager or caretaker. Edison senior recommended a quiet
place named Menlo Park, about twenty-five miles from New
York. The place was not too accessible for casual visitors, and
allowed him to have his home and work close together.

A second son was born after he had been at Menlo Park two
years. He no doubt hoped that the country air would protect
the health of his family, but unfortunately Mrs. Edison was
delicate, and presently was infected with typhoid fever, of

which she died in 1884. Edison left Menlo Park soon afterwards.

His inventive fertility between 1876 and 1884, or the ages of twenty-nine and thirty-seven years, cannot be paralleled in history. It will be noticed that he had two children during the same period. His sexual power does not appear to have been seriously impaired by his extraordinary mental and physical exertions. During much of the period he worked on an average nearly twenty hours a day.

5

Edison designed the laboratory at Menlo Park according to his own wishes. Architecturally, it resembled a small Methodists' chapel. It was a plain rectangular building with two floors. He had not previously had the opportunity of working in a laboratory of his own design; he had had to work in such rooms as he could rent, or was provided with, by companies who financed some particular research.

Edison's Menlo Park laboratory was a new type of institution. It was the first institution designed for professional inventing. Hitherto, inventors had been amateurs who had means to work out their ideas, or had means provided for them by some company which employed them on its own premises. The inventor had an idea. He took this idea to a capitalist. The capitalist helped him to put this one idea into a practical form. He might supply him with money and workshops for this purpose. Edison's aim at Menlo Park was fundamentally different. His laboratory was not designed for the perfection of one invention, but of all inventions. He intended it to be a place where persons who needed inventions of any sort could have their needs satisfied. He aimed at inventing anything. Edison wished to change from invention by inspiration to invention by request. He wished to escape from the usual concentration on one line accidentally chosen, to work on all required lines. He wished to generalize and professionalize invention.

His first major work at Menlo Park was concerned with the carbon telephone transmitter. He was attempting to invent a transmitter better than Bell's at the request of companies to which he was attached. He remembered that when he was working on multiple telegraphs, some years before, he had devised various forms of resistance to represent the dummy line, whose part in duplex and quadruplex telegraphy has already been explained. He had found that resistance could be conveniently made out of loose carbon pressed together. The size of the resistance could be varied by varying the pressure. He invented the carbon telephone transmitter by arranging for the pressure on carbon to be varied by the impulse of sound-waves from the human voice.

In an earlier research he had assisted Scholes in the development of the typewriter. He undertook this work in the interest of the telegraph companies, as it was thought that typewriters might be of use to telegraph operators. The replacement of general handwriting by machinery was not the primary aim of Edison's work on typewriters, but the assistance of telegraphy.

Edison's powers and limitations were illustrated by his experiments on what he named "etheric force" in 1875. He believed he had discovered that when a telegraphic battery circuit was broken, it might under certain conditions produce sparks in unconnected circuits. It appeared that some "etheric force" was capable of producing electrical effects at a distance. The nature of the circuits used seemed to show that the effects were not due to ordinary electromagnetic induction. Edison wrote detailed accounts of numerous experiments on this supposed new force.

It has naturally been assumed that Edison had discovered some effects due to radio waves. But a careful study of the descriptions of his experimental arrangements seems to show that the energy used in his circuits would have been insufficient to produce electromagnetic waves capable of making sparks observable with his equipment. The sparks were probably due to some spurious effect. Edison saw that if his results were genuine, they implied the possibility of electrical communication without wires.

He explained that "the cumbersome appliances of transmitting ordinary electricity, such as telegraph poles, insulating knobs, cable sheathings and so on, may be left out of the problem of quick and cheap telegraphic transmission; and a great saving of time and labor accomplished."

He did not persevere with his experiments, so any chance that he might have invented communication by radio-waves vanished.

Edison applied for a patent in 1885 for wireless communication by electrostatic induction. He erected two high masts separated by a distance. A metal surface was fixed at the top of each mast. The metal surface on the top of the sending mast was connected with one of his loud-speaking telephones near its base. Transmission was accomplished by discharging the induction coil through the aerial into the metal surface at the top of the mast. The electrostatic charge on the metal at the top of the sending mast induced a charge on the metal at the top of the distant receiving mast, which sent a current down the aerial, and produced a click in the telephone. When radio-telegraphy was invented, it could not be developed without Edison's system of aerials, though it employed electromagnetic waves instead of electrostatic induction for the transmission of energy across space. Rivals of the Marconi Company wished to secure his aerial patent in order to obtain a share of control over the development of the Marconi system. Edison refused their offers and sold his rights to the Marconi Company in 1903.

Edison invented the phonograph or gramophone at Menlo Park in 1877. It was his most original invention. When his application for a patent was submitted to the Patents Office, no previous reference could be found in its records to any suggestion for a machine for permanently recording the human voice in a form which enabled it to be reproduced. Bell's telephone invention had drawn attention to the problems of the reproduction of speech. Edison had joined in the extensive efforts to improve the telephone, and had introduced his carbon transmitter. He had become familiar with the elastic properties of discs, which enabled them to vibrate in tune with the vibrations of the voice. Though the familiarity with this property was essential to his discovery, he did not approach voice recording from this aspect. Some time before, he had invented an automatic recording telegraph. This consisted of a disc of paper, which could be rotated round a vertical axis, as in an ordinary gramophone. The paper disc was set in rotation, and the dots and dashes of the incoming message were embossed on it along a volute spiral. Thus several of the features of the record of the telegraphic message were similar to those of the present gramophone record. When the disc telegraphic record was removed from the receiving machine and put into a similar transmitting machine, and rotated, the embossed marks lifted a contact lever up and down, and thus sent the message on to the next station. The apparatus could transmit Morse messages at the rate of several hundred words per minute. It was noticed that if the disc record was rotated very quickly, the rattling of the lever was raised to a musical note. Edison now reasoned that if the disc could produce a musical note it might be made to produce sounds like human speech. He knew from telephone experience that diaphragms would vibrate in tune with the vibrations of a human voice, and that these vibrations were of a considerable size and could be made to do mechanical work. He had devised a toy to illustrate this. He concluded that if he could record the movements of the diaphragm on some sort of disc or strip, and then use the marks on the record to set another diaphragm in motion, the second diaphragm would reproduce the sounds which had fallen on the first diaphragm.

He designed a grooved cylinder which could be rotated around a horizontal axis. The cylinder was to be covered with tin foil. A diaphragm with a needle was fixed over the foil-covered cylinder so that when words were spoken near it, the vibrations started in the diaphragm were embossed by the needle on the soft tinfoil. A sketch of the machine was prepared, and marked $18. Edison's mechanics worked on a minimum wage and piece-work system. If the job cost more than the estimate the mechanic received the minimum wage, if it cost less, he received in addition to his wage the difference saved. The phonograph sketch was given to John Kruesi. When the machine was nearly finished Kruesi asked what it was for. Edison told him it was to record talking. Kruesi thought the idea absurd. When the machine was finished, Edison shouted at the diaphragm: "Mary had a little lamb," etc. He then adjusted the reproducing diaphragm and rotated the cylinder. "The machine reproduced it perfectly. I was never so taken aback in my life. Everybody was astonished. I was always afraid of things that worked the first time. Long experience proved that there were great drawbacks found generally before they could be got commercial; but here was something there was no doubt of."

Edison's power of imagining the scope of invention is illustrated by his summary of the possibilities of the phonograph in 1878. He wrote:

"Among the many uses to which the phonograph will be applied are the following:

"1. Letter writing and all kinds of dictation without the aid of a stenographer.

"2. Phonographic books, which will speak to blind people without effort on their part.

"3. The teaching of elocution.

"4. Reproduction of music.

"5. The 'Family Record'—a registry of sayings, reminiscences, etc., by members of a family in their own voices, and of the last words of dying persons.

"6. Music-boxes and toys.

"7. Clocks that should announce in articulate speech the time for going home, going to meals, etc.

"8. The preservation of languages by exact reproduction of the manner of pronouncing.

"9. Educational purposes; such as preserving the explanations made by a teacher, so that the pupil can refer to them at any moment, and spelling or other lessons placed upon the phonograph for convenience in committing to memory.

"10. Connection with the telephone, so as to make that instrument an auxiliary in the transmission of permanent and invaluable records, instead of being the recipient of momentary and fleeting communication."

The early development of the phonograph was indifferently successful. As the machine was too crude to satisfy artistic feeling, it could not immediately succeed as a musical instrument. It was exploited as an astonishing toy. Its possibilities as a mechanical stenographer were the first to receive serious commercial attention, but the attempts failed, as ordinary clerical staffs found the operation of the machine too difficult. Edison neglected the phonograph for the next ten years. In 1888, after he had launched his incandescent electric light system, he returned to the phonograph, and rapidly improved it by intensive work. On one occasion he worked continuously on the machine for five consecutive days and nights.

Edison's performances with sound-reproducing machines such as the telephone and the phonograph are exceptionally remarkable because of his deafness. He had to depend in a large degree on the hearing of his assistants in the researches on the improvement in the quality of the mechanical articulation. His sister-in-law has written that he often suffered from severe earache at Menlo Park. His deafness may be contrasted with the previous acoustical interests and trained hearing of Bell, and of the musician D. E. Hughes, who invented the microphone and the printing telegraph. Edison's work on the invention of acoustical apparatus did not receive any impulse from long-cultivated special interests such as elocution or music. His deafness may have given him an unconscious interest in acoustical appliances, and he may have had some hope that he could invent a mechanical aid for his affliction. But it seems more probable that deafness would have created a distaste for acoustics. If that was so, Edison's mastery of his revulsion, followed by great acoustical invention, becomes psychologically still more remarkable. The eminent British electrical engineer, J. A. Fleming, whose association with Edison will be mentioned presently, invented the first radio-valve by the application of an electrical discovery made by Edison. As a component of electrical apparatus for sound amplification, the valve is perhaps the most important contribution to recent acoustical invention. Fleming, like Edison, suffered from deafness.

After the excitement of the invention of the phonograph, Edison looked for another suitable subject for inventive research. His friend, Professor Barker, suggested he should consider the problem of the sub-division of the electric light. By 1878 the electric arc-lamp had become commercially established, and was being rapidly developed. It was efficient, but could be made with commercial success only in large candle-powers. Its light was glaringly brilliant, and liable to flicker. These properties did not impair its use for lighting streets and railway yards, but prevented its use for the illumination of offices and living rooms. It was unable to compete with the gas-light jets, which could be turned down to any desired candle-power.

A practical small, steady, mild electric light would have evident advantages. It would not blind or worry the eyes, like arc-lights, nor pour the hot and often disagreeably odorous products of burnt gas into room atmospheres providing air for the respiration of human occupants. Many inventors were familiar with these considerations, and had attempted, at least as early as 1841, to make small electric lamps whose light was produced by a platinum wire raised to white heat by an electric current. These attempts failed owing to the relatively low melting point of platinum. The platinum wire gave little light except near its melting point, so any slight excess of current over the strength needed to give light immediately fused the wire. It was not possible in practice to evade such slight current fluctuations. Some inventors tried to find less easily melted materials which also conducted electricity. Carbon was an obvious material for experiment, though its fragility and combustibility in air at high temperatures were very serious defects. A carbon incandescent electric lamp was made in 1860 by J. W. Swan, a pharmaceutical chemist of Newcastle-on-Tyne, England. It was not of practical value, as the carbon rapidly burned up. Swan was unable to exhaust enough air from the bulb to prevent combustion of the carbon, owing to the lack of a sufficiently good vacuum pump.

The cost of electric current was another serious limitation at that time, as all current was obtained from expensive voltaic batteries. Until cheaper sources of current were created, the electric lamp could not compete with gas. For these reasons, Swan dropped his work on carbon electric lamps. But the situation changed during the next seventeen years. The progress of science and technology was being delayed in many directions through the lack of high-vacuum pumps. The general need brought forth the required instrument, when Sprengel invented his mercury pump in 1865. This invention was essential for the creation of modern physics, as it enabled physicists to make improved vacuum tubes which led to the discovery of the cathode rays and the electron.

The development of the railroads in the 1860's stimulated the demand for illuminated railway yards for night working. Serious fires in theaters emphasized the unsuitability of gas for theater-illumination. These and other influences had increased the demand for arc-lamps, which in turn increased the demand for improved dynamos giving cheaper current. The self-exciting dynamo was invented about 1867, and Gramme re-discovered in 1870 the ring armature, giving steady currents, which had been invented some years previously by Pacinotti.

Swan returned to experiments on carbon electric lamps in 1877, with the assistance of C. H. Stearn, who was familiar with the latest advances in vacuum technique. He constructed and exhibited in 1878 a vacuum lamp with a carbon rod as the light-emitter. In 1880 he patented the process of heating the carbon filament during the exhaustion of the bulb, in order to drive occluded gases out of the carbon. This was the patent which prevented the development of the incandescent lamp in England without Swan's collaboration.

Edison's researches on electric lamps, started in the fall of 1878, led to the completion of a practical lamp in 1879. He found that he could not evade Swan's patent in England, so he wisely made terms with him. The carbon electric lamp was known in England as the "Ediswan" lamp. Edison's compromise with Swan proves that the incandescent carbon lamp is not exclusively his invention. The invention of the carbon incandescent lamp is often ascribed exclusively to Edison. This is inaccurate, and creates a false view of the history of science and technology, and even of Edison's greatness.

Swan produced a workable, though not commercially practicable, lamp. If Edison had never lived, Swan's lamp would probably have been gradually improved, and introduced commercially within the next thirty years. Edison made his lamp commercially successful, and so of practical use to humanity, within three years. This sociological achievement was more distinguished than his large share in the invention of the lamp. By inaccurately ascribing the invention wholly to him, his fame has been made to rest more in a priority he did not wholly possess, than in his unique practical inspiration. His invention of a complete direct current system was more important than the invention of the lamp. Edison's successes and failures in the development of the electric light present a balanced story far more impressive than the myth which ascribes the development entirely to him. His mistakes are even more inspiring than his achievements, because they reveal his common humanity, and destroy the illusion of omnipotence, created by misguided admirers, which is so discouraging to aspiring followers.

Edison worked on the improvement of the platinum lamp before he invented the phonograph. He tried to devise automatic controls which prevented the wire from being fused. He also tried to make incandescent sources consisting of particles of refractory substances, such as boron and chromium, set between conducting points. These were raised to a white heat by sending current through them. He dropped these experiments during the work on the phonograph, and did not return to the electric lamp until after his conversation with Barker. He now attacked the problem thoroughly. In his usual manner, he made a comprehensive collection of data of the scientific, technical and economic aspects of illumination. He bought the back numbers of gas journals, and collected statistics of gas installations. He estimated the quantity of capital sunk in the world gas industry in 1879 at $1,-500,000,000, drew graphs of the prices of iron and copper, of seasonal gas consumption, and so on. The price of coal at that time was about seventy-five cents, or three shillings a ton. This was one of the factors which enabled electric current to be made from steam power at a competitive price. These figures revealed the technical and economic position of the gas industry, with which a successful electric lamp industry would have to compete. They assisted him to calculate the minimum efficiency necessary in an electric lamp system for successful competition with gas.

He saw that the electric lamp should use as little volume of current as possible. If it used much current, the conductors for supplying the lamp system would have to be thick, and this would involve an excessive capital expenditure on the expensive metal, copper. Thus high voltage and low amperage lamps were desirable. But the voltage should not be too high, because high voltages are dangerous. This was particularly important at the beginning of domestic electrification. An excessive number of accidents then would have prejudiced the public against electricity. Edison and his assistants made detailed calculations and experiments on many of these points, and also on the precise structure of the filament and lamp. They systematically investigated the relations between electrical resistance, shape, and heat-radiation of filaments, and studied the specific heats of materials.

The effect of increasing the ration of the resistance to the radiating surface of a wire, by coiling it closely so that the coils obstructed each other's radiation, was examined by calculation, and experiment. This work is particularly interesting in relation to the recent introduction of the "coiled coil" lamp, and shows Edison's grasp of the same principles of design nearly sixty years ago.

The reduction of the diameter of the filament by one-half increased the resistance four times, and reduced the surface to one-half. Thus the ratio of resistance to surface was increased eight times. A filament one sixty-fourth of an inch in diameter became incandescent with eight times less current than a filament one thirty-secondth of an inch in diameter. As a simple implication of the arithmetical relations between the resistance, radiating surface, and temperature of filaments, it followed that a reduction of the diameter of the lamp filament by one-half reduced the volume of current, and hence the amount of copper conductors, and the capital investment on copper conductors in an electric lighting system, by a factor of eight.

The quantitative approach of Edison's work on the electric lamp was of outstanding merit. Swan and others made carbon lamps which worked, but their researches, compared with Edison's, were qualitative. Their lamps worked irrespective of cost, while the costs of his were measured at every point.

Edison now energetically attacked the problem of making thin carbon filaments. He was very familiar with the properties of carbon owing to his researches on the carbon telephone transmitter. He succeeded first with a filament made from cotton sewing thread, which remained incandescent for forty hours in an exhausted bulb. He tried thousands of carbon-containing materials from tar to cheese. He experimented with six thousand different sorts of vegetable fibers, collected from all parts of the world. He found that bamboo gave the most durable filaments.

Sawyer and Man invented a method of treating the carbon filaments by heating them in coal gas. The carbon released by the decomposition of the gas by the heat settled on the filament and strengthened it, especially in the thinnest and therefore hottest places. This treatment simplified the manufacture of filaments uniform in shape and electrical properties, and helped to create the possibility of applying mass-production methods. After 1883, the process of making filaments by squirting a solution of cellulose, or cotton wool, through holes, began to supersede the bamboo process. The cellulose threads, resembling artificial silk, were carbonized in a closed box in a furnace, and then finished by the Sawyer and Man process.

The cost of Edison's researches up to the construction of his cotton-thread filament lamp had been about $40,000.

His experiments with lamps led to a first-class discovery in 1883. It had been noticed that the inside of bulbs containing carbon filaments gradually became blackened by a deposit of carbon. The blackening was not uniform, as a less blackened line was often left on the glass, in the plane of the carbon filament loop. This indicated that atoms of carbon were being shot off the filament, and that some parts of the filament obstructed the flight of atoms from other parts, so that all of the atoms did not directly reach the glass surface. Edison placed a small metal plate, held on a wire sealed through the bulb wall, between the legs of the carbon filament. The filament was then made incandescent by switching the lamp on in the usual way. He found that if the positive leg of the filament was connected through a galvanometer to the plate, a small current was registered, whereas no current was registered when the negative leg was connected to the plate. This experiment showed that an incandescent lamp could act as a valve which permitted negative, but not positive, electricity to pass. The phenomenon is known as the Edison Effect. He patented it, but did not investigate it further himself.

J. A. Fleming, who at the time, in 1883, was a scientific adviser to the Edison companies in London, began a long series of researches on the effect. With the discovery of the electron in 1896, the nature of the effect became much clearer. It was due to streams of electrons shot off from the hot carbon filament. By 1904, Fleming had recognized the possibility that the hot-filament lamp might be used as a valve or rectifier for obtaining direct currents from oscillatory currents of the type started by radio waves in radio receivers, and had constructed his thermionic valve for detecting radio waves. The addition of the third electrode, or grid, to the Fleming valve, by Lee de Forest, completed the invention of the modern radio valve.

The history of the Edison Effect and the radio valve shows how the demand for electric light, stimulated by the search for new directions for the investment of the swiftly increasing surplus capital produced by the exploitation of America, incidentally revealed information which assisted the invention of new directions for the investment of surplus capital in the twentieth century. As H. S. Hatfield has explained, surplus capital is more attracted to the exploitation of new inventions, rather than the efficient exploitation of old inventions. It is easier to find capital for the exploitation of the spectacular, than of other commodities equally profitable and often more useful. Hatfield considers that the progress of invention is not inevitable, and argues that the tendency to favor the exploitation of spectacular inventions may be a sign of the gradual cessation of invention in contemporary civilization. The relation of invention to the evolution of history is very imperfectly understood.

The incandescent electric lamp with bamboo filaments had commercial promise, so Edison now had to solve the complicated problem of designing and manufacturing a complete system of electric lighting. This involved the invention of practicable forms of glass bulbs, the manufacture of glass bulbs, vacuum-tight joints, interchangeable lamp sockets, cables and protected wiring, electric light brackets, and all the details of domestic wiring. He had to design a current meter for measuring the quantity of current used by each consumer, and fuses for protection against excess currents.

It was necessary to invent and design central electrical power stations. The incandescent electric lamp system required a combination of voltage and current characteristics of which there was little previous experience. Efficient new types of dynamo for supplying such currents had to be designed. It was necessary to work out the most economical networks of wires for distribution. Edison and J. Hopkinson devised almost simultaneously the three-wire system, which led to the saving of large quantities of copper, and therefore of capital. At this time the theory of electrical networks was primitive. Many electricians were not sure whether electric lamps could be worked in parallel. The eminent electrician of the British Post Office, W. H. Preece, believed for some time that the subdivision of an electric current among many lamps was theoretically impossible. It was believed that the balance of currents in the network would be upset when lights were switched in and out. Most of these errors were due to ignorance of electrical theory, but up to that time, practical men had not needed much electrical theory, and electrical theorists had not come into contact with many practical problems except in telegraphy and arc lighting. The dynamos for delivering varying loads of current at constant voltages required original design. There was a fallacious belief that the internal resistance of a dynamo should be equal to that of its external circuit. This reduced its working efficiency to less than fifty per cent. Edison correctly decided to build big dynamos with very low internal resistance. He introduced mica laminated armatures, and mica insulated commutators, and invented insulating tape.

On the other hand, he made elementary mistakes in design. He believed the magnetic field could be prevented from leaking from the magnets by encasing them in zinc. It is true that zinc is diamagnetic and is less permeable than air by lines of magnetic force, but the quantitative difference between the permeabilities of air and zinc are negligible, so no practical advantage is gained by zinc jackets for magnets. He erroneously believed, too, that multiple legs on the magnets, each separately wound with copper wires, were more efficient than single legs wound with one coil.

The state of dynamo and electric motor engineering about this time is illustrated by the accidental discovery at a Viennese exhibition in 1873, that it was possible to drive a dynamo as an electric motor with current from a similar dynamo. Someone happened to connect a stationary Gramme dynamo to another Gramme dynamo driven by an engine, and found that the second dynamo began to drive the first as a motor. Before then, electricians had not reached the conception, which is the basis of the modern theory of electrical machinery, that the dynamo is a reversible engine.

The mistakes of principle in the design of the Edison dynamos were removed by J. Hopkinson, a British engineer with a thorough theoretical training. He worked out the theory of the magnetic circuit by calculation and experiment.

Edison was probably influenced in his adoption of direct current by his familiarity with it in telegraphy. He knew many of its properties from much experience and it was easier to solve the numerous new problems of electrical engineering for direct current, than for the more complicated alternating current. He foresaw, for example, that there would be a demand for current to drive electric motors, charge storage batteries, and run arc-lamps. At that time, alternating current could not be used for these purposes, so the demand for it would be less than for direct current. His choice securely launched the development of electrical current engineering. Alternating current has theoretical advantages over direct current, but is more difficult to handle. If Edison had tried to use alternating current in the first central electric supply systems, he might have experienced disasters which would have delayed the development of electrical current engineering for many years. He chose the safer way and succeeded with direct current. After success had been achieved with direct current, engineers could attack with greater confidence the problems of alternating current engineering, which are inherently more difficult.

The successful invention of central electrical power stations introduced electricity as a new commodity to the market. Edison's companies sold electricity to the consumer in units measured by an electrolytic meter. They retailed electricity.

Many new electrical manufacturing industries were required to meet the demands for lamps, dynamos, cables, and fittings. Edison personally supervised the production side of the original factories supplying materials for his electric light systems. His business manager was Samuel Insull. When the factories had grown to employ several thousand men, Edison sold his interests to a syndicate organized by Henry Villard, which consolidated the factories as the Edison General Company.

Jay Gould and the financiers of the first period of exploitation of electricity, in the form of telegraphs, were succeeded by a different type in the second period of electrical exploitation, in which electricity became a commodity. The telegraphs of a country are analogous to the nerves of an organism, whereas electric power supply is analogous to the muscles. The telegraphs do not require massive and correspondingly expensive equipment, but their possession gives instant control over the life of the country. A relatively small amount of capital invested in telegraphs may give immense power. This is one of the explanations of the peculiar wildness of telegraph finance. Ownership of the capital of electricity supply companies also confers great influence on the life of a country, but as it involves far more capital than ownership of telegraphy, it is more stolid. The large quantities of fixed capital tend to produce more conservative conduct. This helps to explain why the growth of electricity supply has been accompanied by the evolution of a new type of financier in the electrical industries. Jay Gould and the leaders of telegraph finance have been succeeded by Owen Young and the leaders of electrical supply finance. A transitional type is seen in Samuel Insull. He became Edison's secretary in 1881 at the age of twenty-one, and learned the technique of finance when the Gould tradition was still the strongest. He had operated the first telephone exchange in London. He grew up with the new electricity supply industry and acquired the more cautious technique suitable to manipulators of a more stolid form of capital. As long as American business expanded without serious checks, he was very successful, but when the first profound crisis occurred, his position did not remain secure. The United States Government conducted an inquiry into his affairs and requested him to attend an examination. He did not voluntarily comply with this request, and ultimately was extradited from the Balkans to the United States, for public examination.

The leaders evolved in the later stage of the electricity supply industry, such as Young, have passed through the crisis with less difficulty, owing to their more stolid methods.

The growth of the electrical industry also provided more scope for engineers. Henry Ford was employed by one of the Edison power companies, and was introduced to Edison as a young man who had made an automobile. Ford states that the first understanding and encouragement he received in his development of the automobile came from Edison.

An indirect effect of Edison's development of the electrical engineering industry is seen in journalism. The demand for copper increased, and provided Hearst with a vast income from his copper mine. He was able to use his profits from copper in the development of his newspaper system, which, it is said, has not been profitable. The profits on copper pay for the losses on journalism.

To some degree, commodities choose the sort of inventors needed to develop them, and the sort of financiers needed to exploit them.

Edison developed new methods in manufacturing. He estimated the effective economic price of an article, and then aimed at manufacturing it in relation to that price. He had calculated that lamp sales should be successful at the price of 40 cents, so he offered to supply lamps to the electric light companies at 40 cents each, if they would contract to pay that price during the life of the lamp patents. This offer was accepted. The manufacture of his early lamps cost $1.25 each. In the first year he lost 70 cents on each of twenty thousand lamps. In the second year, he lost 30 cents on each lamp, and in the third, the loss had been brought down to 10 cents, by improved processes and machinery. In the fourth year, the cost had been reduced to 37 cents, leaving a profit of 3 cents. The total profit in that year was sufficient to cover the total previous loss. Presently he reduced the manufacturing cost of the lamps, sold in millions at 40 cents, to 22 cents. He then sold the lamp factory to a Wall Street syndicate.

This method of selling at a fixed low price and then forcing the costs down by production in large quantities has been followed with particular success by Henry Ford in the manufacture of automobiles.

Edison states that the introduction of labor-replacing machinery contributed largely to the cheapening of production.

"When we started, one of the important processes had to be done by experts. This was the sealing-on of the part carrying the filament into the globe, which was rather a delicate operation in those days, and required several months of training before anyone could seal in a fair number of parts in a day. The men on this work considered themselves essential to the plant and became surly. They formed a union and made demands.

"I started in to see if it were not possible to do that operation by machinery. After feeling around for some days, I got a clue how to do it. I then put men on it I could trust, and made the preliminary machinery. That seemed to work pretty well. I then made another machine which did the work nicely. I then made a third machine. Then the union went out. It has been out ever since."

This is an example of the use of invention as a social weapon. Edison's description implies that the machine was invented in order to break strikes, and the reduction of the cost of lamp manufacture was incidental. The invention of the sealing-on machine was directly inspired by struggles between employer and employed, and reveals the limitations of the theory that invention is due to pure inventiveness, by analogy to the fallacious theory that discovery is due to pure curiosity.

Edison left Menlo Park about 1884, and built a large laboratory and house at West Orange, to which he moved in 1886, when he was thirty-nine years old. The change marked a profound alteration in many aspects of his life. His first wife had died in 1884, and he married a second time in 1886. His second wife was Mina Miller. She was twenty years old, and had been well-educated. He began to live in a different social stratum. Large quantities of money passed through his hands. He spent most of it on experiments, but he also lived as comfortably as he wished. He became a public figure of world-reputation. The inventive brilliance of his Menlo Park years passed as he approached forty years of age. The system of organized invention that he had created at Menlo Park was gradually transformed into more ortho-dox management of production factories. Edison's invention became less brilliant but the weight of organization and re-sources became much greater. The return in invention on effort and expenditure became much less. The new electricity cor-porations began to construct research laboratories as part of their equipment. This innovation was largely inspired by the example of Edison's inventions research laboratory, but it had an essential difference. Edison's laboratory was for general research on inventions. Its aims were not subordinated to the needs of any particular industry. The research in the new corporation laboratories was subordinated to the corporations' industrial interests. The results of research in corporation laboratories were disappointing for several decades, but have recently become more satisfactory, due partly to the increas-ing importance of large-scale experiments. Powerful apparatus is now necessary in many branches of research. Million-volt transformers and high-tension rectifiers cannot be made with-out the wealth and manufacturing resources of large electrical factories. Brains and the skill of a few mechanics are no longer sufficient. The corporation laboratory has definite advantages under certain conditions. When these conditions arise, it nat-urally achieves results beyond the scope of the cleverest in-vestigator dependent on his own resources.

Edison made many important inventions after 1886, but most of them experienced peculiar failures besides great suc-cesses. He made the first commercial motion-pictures in 1891.

The history of the cinema is complicated and Edison's part
has often been exaggerated, but it was noteworthy. He saw
that Eastman's invention of the flexible film made the manufacture of motion-pictures practicable. The flexible film could
be produced in long narrow ribbons bearing a sufficient number of pictures to create a sustained illusion of motion. Edison
devised a camera for photographing moving subjects with
continuous films. He made pairs of holes near the edges of
the film to accommodate the teeth of wheels which moved the
film forward. The width of the film and the size and distance
of the holes were fixed by him, and remained the standard
in the film industry for fifty years. He organized the first
film studio. This consisted of a hut built on a pivot so that
it could be turned to the sun, in order to facilitate photography.
Short scenes of exchanges between boxers, and so on, were
photographed. The pictures were not projected onto a screen
by a projection apparatus. They were run through a machine
inside a box with a peep-hole. The machine was started by
putting a small coin in a slot. The spectator applied his eye
to the peep-hole, and saw the subjects in motion. These boxes
or kinetoscopes were erected in fair-grounds, and similar
places. Motion-pictures were commercially exploited for the
first time with these machines. But they did not show motion
pictures to audiences of unlimited size, and they were also
very short. Edison treated his early motion-picture work as if
it were trivial. He did not bother to patent his kinetoscope
in England. He chose the lower grades of popular interests
as subjects for his films. He aimed at inventing and manufacturing motion-pictures which could be sold to the fair-
ground public. Edison must receive some of the credit for
creating the tradition of motion-pictures as a popular entertainment meeting the demands of the masses; the quality
which makes the cinema, in Lenin's view, the most important
form of art. He must also bear some of the blame for the
vulgarity of the cinema tradition, which has aimed so much
at the worst instead of the best aspects of popular taste.

Edison's extended researches on the separation of iron ore

by magnetic methods illustrate another combination of achievement and lack of foresight in his later period. He worked with enormous application for nine years on the separation of iron ore from rocks. He designed large crushers which ground the rock to powder. The iron ore was separated from the powder by systems of magnets. He developed the automatic conveyor system of handling the materials to a new degree. Henry Ford states that it was the most complete which had been designed up to that date. Edison's contribution to the development of manufacturing processes is again evident here. His iron-ore separation works was successful until the discovery of the very rich ores of the Missabe Range. His vision of a process which would control the world steel industry disappeared, and his works had to be closed. He lost the whole of his savings, about $2,000,000, in this failure. It is possible that magnetic separation will again be commercially valuable, when the very rich iron ore deposits have been exhausted. But Edison's insight into the geological aspects of the steel industry in his own time proved faulty.

When the iron-ore works failed, he considered to what new object he might apply his knowledge of handling minerals. The rapid growth of the building industry suggested that the cement industry might provide suitable scope. He started cement manufacturing. His processes were not particularly original. His rational courage in turning immediately from iron ore to cement after a huge loss was the most remarkable feature of these activities. His interest in cement prompted him to devise methods of making houses by pouring cement into a suitable mould. He hoped that it would be possible to produce concrete houses in large numbers at a low price. He devised moulds made of unit sections which could be assembled in a variety of forms, so that the houses would be of many designs. His architectural conceptions were in consonance with some principles of modern functionalism.

During the first decade of the twentieth century he worked on the development of steel alkaline storage batteries. He gradually worked out an effective design, mainly by persistence. The alkaline battery had many ingenious features, but as a product of a mountain of labor and resource, it was not outstanding. Forms of alkaline battery are much used in electric traction, and in submarines. They store more energy per unit weight than lead batteries, and will safely discharge and charge far more rapidly, and will stand more rough usage, but give current at a much lower voltage.

Persistence had always been exceptionally prominent in his method of working, but as he became older, the subtler qualities of imagination and foresight declined first. This left the impression that his persistence became even more marked, and with age grew into obstinacy.

Like many great men who lived to a great age, he became a semi-mythical figure in his last years. He was continually consulted on all sorts of problems, and often gave advice of value below the magnitude of his reputation. This was natural, because the powers of his youth had declined, and the ideas and methods which had been so brilliantly successful fifty years before were no longer entirely suitable to modern circumstances.

Edison was granted over one thousand patents. About two hundred of these were concerned with telegraphy and telephones, and included duplex, quadruplex and sextuplex systems, automatic and printing telegraphs.

Several hundred patents were granted to him for inventions connected with the incandescent electric lamp, and the central electric power systems. These included dozens of patents concerning the design and manufacture of carbon filament lamps, of dynamos for supplying power stations, of systems of wiring, and the innumerable details of a complete electrical power supply system.

He was granted scores of patents for the design and manufacture of phonographs or gramophones, and all their parts, especially gramophone records.

Other large groups of patents were granted for the magnetic separation of iron ore, and the manufacture of Portland cement.

He was granted dozens of patents in connection with his development of the alkaline accumulator battery.

Besides these whole classes of patents, he had others of a key nature. He had a patent for aerials, which was essential for the development of radio and was purchased by Marconi. He held key American patents in connection with the projection of motion-pictures.

He invented the dictaphone, the mimeograph, gummed paper for fastening parcels, and many other individual contrivances.

Most of these patents depended on an intimate acquaintance with the facts of science, especially in electricity and acoustics. They entitle their author to the claim of being a scientific inventor.

By virtue of the importance and variety of his work, including the absolutely original invention of the gramophone, which was the chief contribution towards the democratization of culture since the introduction of printing, he is the greatest inventor recorded in history.

T. A. Edison: Bibliography

Edison: His Life and Inventions. F. L. Dyer, T. C. Martin and W. H. Meadowcroft. 2 volumes. 1929.

Edison: His Life, His Work, His Genius. W. A. Simonds. 1935.

"Edison in His Laboratory." M. A. Rosanoff. *Harper's Magazine.* Volume 165. September. 1932.

Fifty Years of Electricity. J. A. Fleming. 1921.

Edison: Obituary Notices. *Science.* January 15th. 1932.

My Friend Mr. Edison. Henry Ford, with Samuel Crowther. 1930.

The Irrational Knot. Bernard Shaw. 1905.

History of Telegraphy. J. J. Fahie. 1837.

A Popular History of American Inventions. W. B. Kaempffert. 2 volumes. 1924.

Edison: The Man and His Work. G. S. Bryan. 1926.

Memoirs of a Scientific Life. J. A. Fleming. 1934.

A History of the Wireless Telegraph, 1838–1899. J. J. Fahie.

Imminent Dangers to Free Institutions of the United States. S. F. B. Morse. 1835.

Letters and Journals of S. F. B. Morse. E. L. Morse. 2 volumes. 1914.

The Inventor and His World. H. Stafford Hatfield. 1933.

Personal Memoirs of U. S. Grant. 2 volumes. 1885.

A Chapter of Erie. C. F. Adams, Jr., 1869.

401

Index

Index

405